NATO

Recent Titles in
Contemporary Military, Strategic, and Security Issues

International Crime and Punishment: A Guide to the Issues
James Larry Taulbee

Serving America's Veterans: A Reference Handbook
Lawrence J. Korb, Sean E. Duggan, Peter M. Juul, and Max A. Bergmann

Military Doctrine: A Reference Handbook
Bert Chapman

Energy Security Challenges for the 21st Century: A Reference Handbook
Gal Luft and Anne Korin, editors

An Introduction to Military Ethics: A Reference Handbook
Bill Rhodes

War and Children: A Reference Handbook
Kendra E. Dupuy and Krijn Peters

Military Justice: A Guide to the Issues
Lawrence J. Morris

Military Space Power: A Guide to the Issues
Wilson W. S. Wong and James Fergusson

American Missile Defense: A Guide to the Issues
Victoria Samson

Private Armed Forces and Global Security: A Guide to the Issues
Carlos Ortiz

Women in the United States Armed Forces: A Guide to the Issues
Darlene M. Iskra

War Crimes, Genocide, and the Law: A Guide to the Issues
Arnold Krammer

NATO

A Guide to the Issues

Brian J. Collins

Contemporary Military, Strategic, and Security Issues

PRAEGER

AN IMPRINT OF ABC-CLIO, LLC
Santa Barbara, California • Denver, Colorado • Oxford, England

Library of Congress Cataloging-in-Publication Data

Collins, Brian J.
  NATO : a guide to the issues / Brian J. Collins.
    p. cm. — (Contemporary military, strategic, and security issues)
  Includes bibliographical references and index.
  ISBN 978-0-313-35491-5 (hard copy : alk. paper) — ISBN 978-0-313-35492-2
(ebook) 1. North Atlantic Treaty Organization. I. Title. II. Title: North Atlantic
Treaty Organization.
  UA646.3.C593 2011
  355'.031091821—dc22   2010047140

ISBN: 978-0-313-35491-5
EISBN: 978-0-313-35492-2

15 14 13 12 11   1 2 3 4 5

This book is also available on the World Wide Web as an eBook.
Visit www.abc-clio.com for details.

Praeger
An Imprint of ABC-CLIO, LLC

ABC-CLIO, LLC
130 Cremona Drive, P.O. Box 1911
Santa Barbara, California 93116-1911

This book is printed on acid-free paper ∞

Manufactured in the United States of America

Contents

Preface

I found writing this book a daunting task. NATO has over 60 years of history that span quite significant events such as the Cold War, the growth of the European Union, wars in the Balkans, and military and civil operations in Afghanistan. There are already many books, articles, and publications dealing with NATO and its past, present, and future. Many of these publications are available on the Internet, as is an ever-increasing amount of primary source material such as meeting reports that NATO has declassified and made public.

Consequently, one of my assumptions is that the reader can easily go to NATO's Web site; NATO Allies', Partners', and potential adversaries' Web sites; as well as the Web sites of a host of other organizations, such as the United Nations (UN), European Union (EU), Western European Union (WEU), or the Organization for Security and Cooperation in Europe (OSCE). In addition, readers can simply Google terms, consult Wikipedia, or use any of a number of similar tools to get definitions and different perspectives, or to further research ideas that occur to them as they read this book. This book then aims to provide an overview touching on a variety of issues, some in detail, others less so, but with enough key terms and concepts included to arm the reader for further exploration.

My intent is to provide a high-level introduction and understanding of NATO, its history, current issues that the Allies are struggling with, and some questions about its future. The book is designed to be textbook-like, and I have purposefully eschewed footnotes and endnotes, indicating the source of quotes in the text itself. I also attempt to explain processes and concepts to provide the reader with an introduction to practical as well as theoretical aspects of NATO. I have also tried to avoid needless detail. The exact titles of specific NATO commands, staff divisions, and routine documents change over time, but the basic functionalities tend to remain, so I have tried to focus on the functionalities.

Since the story of NATO is a complex story with lots of interlocking parts, I initially tried to organize the presentation along a *who, what, when, where, why, how* framework for simplicity. However, I found it difficult to keep the *when* in proportion to the rest of the chapters. I looked at different ways to break the history of NATO into manageable pieces, and finally decided to use the story told by NATO's consecutive strategic concepts to address the *when* (the time periods of each strategic concept), the *why* (the threat), and the *how* (the planned response). I have tried to minimize duplication, but still show the chronology and the interrelationships between the chapters. There is some duplication, however, because I have tried to write this book so that it can be read in two different ways. Some readers may want to use the traditional approach of reading from front to back, whereas others may want to pick and choose chapters based on their content. Consequently, I have made the chapters readable as freestanding pieces, each focusing on specific aspects of the NATO story.

I capitalize the word *Ally* to signify a member of NATO, the word *Partner* to signify a country that is a member of NATO's Partnership for Peace (PfP) program, and the phrase *the Alliance* to signify NATO. I also call the provided Timelines (Appendix I) and Acronyms to the reader's attention. I must also remind American readers that the United States is a member of NATO, and that after reading this book, you will see that it is inappropriate to speak of NATO as a foreign entity in which the United States has no say.

In each chapter, I provide "Questions for Considerations." Apart from the text itself, no answers are provided for these questions. The questions are designed to stimulate the reader's thinking. They may encourage the reader to take a step back from the text to try to see the bigger picture of what was or is going on, to think critically about the ideas presented and the assumptions behind them, and at times, to spur further investigation of the issues raised.

Finally, I am grateful to E, S, and T for taking the time to thoroughly read and comment on earlier drafts, and as always to M.

Acronyms

ACCHAN	Allied Command Channel
ACE	Allied Command Europe
ACLANT	Allied Command Atlantic
ACO	Allied Command Operations
ACT	Allied Command Transformation
AEW	airborne early warning
AMF	ACE Mobile Force
ARRC	ACE Rapid Reaction Corps
ASW	antisubmarine warfare
AU	African Union
AWACS	Airborne Warning and Control System
CFE	Conventional Armed Forces in Europe (Treaty)
C4ISR	command, control, communications, computers, intelligence, surveillance, and reconnaissance
CFSP	(EU) Common Foreign and Security Policy
CHODS	Chief of Defense Staff
CINCHAN	Commander-in-Chief Channel (1952–1994)
CJTF	combined joint task force
CPG	comprehensive political guidance
CSCE	Conference on Security and Cooperation in Europe (became OSCE)
CSDP	(EU) Common Security and Defense Policy
DC	Defense Committee

DCA	dual-capable aircraft
DPC	Defense Planning Committee
EAPC	Euro-Atlantic Partnership Council
EC	European Community (forerunner of EU)
ECSC	European Coal and Steel Community
EDC	European Defense Community
ESDI	(NATO) European Security and Defense Identity
ESDP	(EU) European Security and Defense Policy
ETA	Basque Homeland and Freedom (Basque nationalist [terrorist] organization)
EU	European Union
FRG	Federal Republic of Germany
FYROM	Former Yugoslav Republic of Macedonia
GDP	gross domestic product
GDR	German Democratic Republic
GLCM	ground-launched cruise missile
ICBM	intercontinental ballistic missile
ICI	Istanbul Cooperation Initiative
IFOR	Implementation Force (became SFOR)
IMS	International Military Staff
INF	Intermediate-Range Nuclear Forces (Treaty)
IPP	Individual Partnership Program
IRA	Irish Republican Army (Irish nationalist [terrorist] organization)
IRBM	intermediate-range ballistic missile
IRF	Immediate Reaction Forces
IS	International Staff
ISAF	International Security Assistance Force
ISMERLO	International Submarine Escape and Rescue Liaison Office
KFOR	Kosovo Force
MAD	mutually assured destruction
MAP	Membership Action Plan
MBFR	Mutual Balanced Force Reductions

MC	Military Committee
MD	Mediterranean Dialogue
MDF	Main Defense Forces
MFA	Ministry of Foreign Affairs
MilRep	Military Representative (to the Military Committee)
MNC	Major NATO Command/Commander
MOD	Ministry of Defense
MOU	memorandum of understanding
MSC	Major Subordinate Command/Commander
NAA	North Atlantic Assembly
NAC	North Atlantic Council
NAEWF	NATO Airborne Early Warning Force
NATO	North Atlantic Treaty Organization
NBC	nuclear, biological, and chemical (weapons)
NGC	NATO-Georgia Commission
NGO	nongovernmental organization
NMA	NATO Military Authorities
NPG	NATO Planning Group
NPT	Treaty on the Non-Proliferation of Nuclear Weapons
NRC	NATO-Russia Council (successor of the PJC)
NRF	NATO Response Force
NSIP	NATO Security Investment Program
NUC	NATO-Ukraine Commission
OEF	Operation Enduring Freedom
OIF	Operation Iraqi Freedom
OPEC	Organization of Petroleum Exporting Countries
OSCE	Organization for Security and Cooperation in Europe (successor to the CSCE)
OTAN	Organisation du Traité de l'Atlantique Nord
PARP	Partnership for Peace Planning and Review Process
PC	Political Committee
PermRep	Permanent Representative (to the NAC)
PfP	Partnership for Peace

PJC	(NATO–Russia) Permanent Joint Council (became NRC)
PSO	Peace Support Operations
RAF	Red Army Faction (terrorist organization, primarily operated in West Germany)
RRF	Rapid Reaction Force
SACEUR	Supreme Allied Commander Europe
SACLANT	Supreme Allied Commander Atlantic
SACT	Supreme Allied Commander Transformation
SALT	Strategic Arms Limitation Treaty
SERWG	Submarine Escape and Rescue Working Group
SFOR	Stabilization Force (successor to IFOR)
SG	Standing Group (of the Military Committee)
SHAPE	Supreme Headquarters Allied Powers Europe
SLBM	submarine-launched ballistic missile
SLCM	sea-launched cruise missile
SOF	Special Operations Forces
SOFA	Status of Forces Agreement
STANAG	(NATO) Standardization Agreement
STANAVFORMED	Standing Naval Force Mediterranean
START	Strategic Arms Reduction Treaty
U.K.	United Kingdom
UN	United Nations
UNSC	United Nations Security Council
U.S.	United States
USSR	Union of Soviet Socialist Republics
WEU	Western European Union
WMD	weapons of mass destruction
WP	Warsaw Pact

CHAPTER 1

What Is NATO?

The question *what* is NATO should not be confused with the question *who* is NATO. The second question looks more to which countries comprise NATO and give it its identity. This question is examined in the book's last chapter, whereas the first question, *what* is NATO, deals more with describing what the organization does. Several concepts come to mind. Some might describe NATO as a collective defense organization, others as an alliance of democracies; still others might label it a security community, and to some it is a European security organization. One can find all three descriptions in common use. This chapter looks at the shortcomings of each and examines some of the implications or byproducts of the answers to the question of what NATO is, before concluding with a brief look at what NATO is not.

Questions for Consideration

- How would you describe what NATO is, based on your current knowledge?
- What does the term *collective defense* mean to you?
- How would you institute a collective defense pact with two or three other countries?

  - Would the pact be unlimited, or would you have to set conditions, and define what or who you were defending against?
  - How could you be sure that the other countries in the pact would come to your assistance if you were threatened or attacked by a different state?
  - Would your nation really help one of your allies if that ally was threatened by a state that also had allies?
  - What would you do if two of your allies became antagonistic towards each other?

- What does the term *alliance of democracies* mean to you?
  - If a country became less democratic, would it have to leave the alliance?
  - If a country became democratic, would it get to join the alliance?
- What does the term *European security organization* mean to you?
  - How would you define *Europe*?
  - Is *European* a state of mind, based on a shared historical, cultural, and institutional development, or a geographic term?
- What is the difference between NATO and the European Union (EU)?

The concept of collective defense is a good starting point since it is mentioned in the preamble to the Washington, or NATO, Treaty of 1949. At its simplest, collective defense implies that two or more states or groups have agreed to work together in some manner for the benefit of all parties so inclined, and this cooperation is in the field of defense, which usually suggests military operations. One can go as far back as Thucydides's *History of the Peloponnesian War* to read about military alliances, wars and negotiations between alliances, intra-alliance discussions on whether a particular event requires alliance action and what each ally should feel committed to do, as well as domestic political discussions in a state's capital about that particular state's interests and its relationship to alliance commitments. Weaker actors may enter into a collective security agreement in an attempt to deter a stronger state from taking military action against them individually, through the expectation that, like the musketeers, an attack on one is an attack on all. The Brussels Treaty, which will be discussed in the next chapter, was such an agreement by several Western European nations after World War II to protect themselves from a potentially resurgent Germany. If there are two major powers, weaker powers are likely to want to ally with a guarantor, and the two major powers may engage in an *ally race*, as each tries to secure more allies to gain advantage over the other. The major powers may also court allies in order to cover all the squares on the board. Over the long run, this would theoretically eliminate further competition of this sort; however, in the short run, it increases the risk of crises on the periphery that could lead to instability and war, and that instability and war could blowback to the central area. This describes the Cold War. In a multipolar world, one sees examples of various alliance motivations and possibly more shifting of alliances as states try to balance or gain power. The shifting alliance structures among the European powers in the late 19th and early 20th centuries prior to World War I provide an example of this.

In all these examples, one can see how concepts such as security dilemma, deterrence, free riders, and chain gangs come into play. These concepts identify typical byproducts of alliances, and the last two concepts, that of free riders and chain gangs, arise out of inter-ally relations. *Security dilemma* refers to the phenomenon that as an actor, whether an individual, group, state, or alliance, increases its military capability in order to build up its own sense of security, at some point, the increased military capability makes other actors in the system feel more insecure. If the other actors felt that a balance had existed, they perceive the other side must now be seeking military advantage. This can lead to an arms race as each side reacts to the other's actions. Under certain conditions, simply creating an alliance can create this effect since it changes the relative balance of power within the perceived system. Consequently, one might make the argument that the presence of the Soviet Army in Eastern Europe after World War II led the West European governments to band together in a collective defense in order to increase their collective feeling of security, but that the creation of NATO in turn led the Soviet Union to feel insecure, and that it then created the Warsaw Pact in order to balance NATO and return to its prior perceived level of security.

Deterrence is achieved within the alliance through the idea that by banding together, the actors in the alliance will have enough military power to dissuade an opponent from attacking since the alliance's military power would prevent the opponent from achieving his aims, or by making it so costly that an attack would not be worth it. In order to be effective, the opponent must perceive that the alliance both has the military capability and the political will, or credibility, to carry out the threat. In the simplest case, the threatened reprisal is tied to the action to be deterred. For example, a strong conventional defense would repel a conventional attack. However, the issues of deterrence become more confusing when the threatened reprisal is disconnected from the action to be deterred. For example, one might threaten to respond to a conventional attack with long-range delivery systems (aircraft, missiles, or hijacked aircraft) carrying either conventional weapons or weapons of mass destruction (WMD—nuclear, chemical, biological, and radiological weapons) deep into the opponent's heartland. One might also threaten to respond to an attack from an apparent minor ally of the major opponent power by striking the major opponent. However, in these cases credibility suffers because of the disproportionality of the threatened retaliation. Credibility also becomes an issue if the major opponent has similar capabilities. For example, the United States was unable to effectively use its nuclear power as a deterrent against the Soviet-backed communist Chinese in 1949 or against the North Koreans, Beijing, or Moscow during the Korean War.

Although countries join together to achieve military capabilities sufficient to deter opponents, an alliance's deterrent threat is also grounded in the alliance's credibility, that is, in its perceived degree of cohesion. Each alliance member's individual security rests not only on his own, but also on his allies' military capabilities as well as the opponent's belief that all alliance members will act in unison. In order to keep the presumed benefits of the alliance's security, an acknowledged degree of interdependence may at times lead individual members to take actions that are not completely in their self-interest in order to support the alliance and to keep it functioning. At the same time, individual members want to be sure that all of their allies are pulling a fair share of the load, not just free riding and getting maximum security at little or no cost. However, there is tension in interdependence and it has limits. For one thing, alliance members do not want to be drawn into a war provoked by an ally that was relying on the alliance to automatically back its venture. This phenomenon has been labeled chain ganging, with the vision that all the allies are chained together, and if one suddenly gets it in his head to run and jump off a cliff, the rest will be pulled along. At some point, an actor's self-interest might so outweigh the benefits to be gained from the alliance, or the presumed benefits may turn into such heavy liabilities that the ally leaves. If all of the members are not firmly committed to their planned course of action, the alliance might collapse under its own weight, or an opponent may be able to successfully attack the alliance and break it apart.

Another issue, however, is what to do when the adversary is beaten. Many would argue that collective security arrangements tend to work best when there is a specific threat. Without a specific threat, it is often difficult to determine what actions need to be taken and whether all the allies are pulling their fair share. If a new threat or opponent cannot be found quickly and substituted in place of the old one, the alliance can lose its sense of purpose and eventually collapse. For example, the Quadruple Alliance between Austria, Britain, Prussia, and Russia, created to defeat Napoleon and then revised to enforce the peace settlement, began to fray once it was clear that Napoleon was finally contained. Russia, Prussia, and Austria argued that liberalism was the new threat in Europe, but Britain did not agree. Consequently, Europe shifted to the concert system of ad hoc great power conferences to defuse political crises, with France quickly returning to great power status.

In balance of power theories, if one alliance collapses in a bipolar model, the members of the remaining alliance should redistribute and seek balance within, tying in former members of the old opposing alliance as needed as the system seeks new stability. At first glance, one might be tempted to draw the conclusion that the NATO's emphasis on the development of the European pillar within NATO in the post–Cold War decade is evidence of an attempt to balance the presumed American pillar. However, the Alliance began trying to strengthen European contributions during the Cold War in order to better distribute the burden sharing among all the Allies and to be more balanced internally. In any event, using balance of power models requires a determination of who is in and who is out of the system, and this can become problematic as the system changes. For example, most people considered Afghanistan beyond the bounds of the Euro-Atlantic security system prior to 9/11. It is interesting to note, however, that international relations theories of constructivism, and more particularly liberalism, offer competing models to realism's balance of power paradigm.

Rather than limiting themselves to the simple status of a military alliance for collective defense against a particular bully, the NATO founders articulated what they were for. The NATO Treaty preamble stated that the NATO Allies were "determined to safeguard the freedom, common heritage and civilization of their peoples, founded on the principles of democracy, individual liberty and the rule of law." This statement leads to the characterization of NATO as an alliance of democracies; however, *freedom* appeared to be defined as anticommunism, and the *principles of democracy* were left undefined.

Of the original NATO founding members, Portugal was clearly not democratic, and did not become so until the mid-1970s, although it did have the trappings of democracy in the form of elections. However, it owned the Azores and had let the United Kingdom and United States use them during World War II. The mid-Atlantic island bases provided a refueling point for aircraft transiting the Atlantic and also served as a base for maritime patrol aircraft controlling the North Atlantic. In the case of the other Allies, democratic traditions and governments at home did not translate into democratically administered colonies. The initial NATO enlargement consisted of Turkey and Greece, which were included for geo-strategic reasons, after the West had supported the Greek government's successful anticommunist counterinsurgency and Turkey's stand against Soviet pressure for military bases. Both governments were democratic in form, but both underwent military coups and later increased democratization while remaining members of NATO. However, other NATO Allies pressured the military governments to reinstitute democratic governments. Spain under Franco was certainly anticommunist, but was not extended an invitation to join NATO until the 1980s, that is, after Franco's death and Spain's return to democratic governance. However, the United States had negotiated the use of air and naval facilities with the Franco government in the 1950s. Since anticommunism was no longer an issue, NATO made democratic governments and clear evidence of the rule of law prerequisites for membership consideration in the post–Cold War enlargement waves. On balance, it is clear that NATO in its current form is an alliance of democracies.

Another way to characterize NATO's metamorphosis is that it has moved from an organization for collective defense to an organization with an integrated defense, then deepened to integrated security, and is now the prototypical security community. *Integrated defense* captures NATO's defense planning process in which all members share detailed data on their forces and the planning calls for the integrated use of those forces. Instead of simple coop-eration, using perhaps geographic boundaries to separate the national forces' areas of responsibility, by using common doctrine and standards, the forces can be mixed, to an extent, in exercises and operations. For example, Dutch reconnaissance units can be attached to a German tank unit, and Spanish fighter aircraft could provide close air support to both. NATO's standing naval forces are also made up of ships from different Allied nations working together under NATO's integrated command. *Integrated security* captures the Allied nations' historically expanding use of NATO forums for consultations on a variety of security-related issues that go beyond purely military opera-tions. Examples include the discussion of out-of-area national operations, discussions on U.S. negotiating positions with respect to Russia on nuclear reductions, the training of civilian police forces in Bosnia, and discussions on cooperation with respect to international terrorism, international crime, or cyberspace protection.

The concept of the *security community* is that the members of the com-munity, through a combination of shared values and institutions, gradually arrive at the point where war between the members is unthinkable. Since NATO's shared values include such democratic values as individual liberty, the rule of law, and civilian control over the military, the argument can also be made that the NATO members are also evidence of the democratic peace theories that democratic governments are less likely to go to war against each other. Some would take this even further and argue that membership in an organization like NATO has a similar effect, even if some of the coun-tries do not meet the shared values in practice. The Turkish invasion of Cyprus in 1974 in response to a Greek-sponsored coup on the island makes an interesting case study in this respect. Even though Greece was ruled by a military junta and even though the Turkish military was involved in domes-tic politics as a result of the 1971 coup, the Greek and Turkish governments' machinations concerning Cyprus did not spread to a larger war between Greece and Turkey. Both remained in NATO and later returned to demo-cratic governance, although the Cyprus issue remains unresolved to this day. Similarly, NATO's institutions of transparency in defense budgets and de-fense planning, consultations, and consensus decision making are credited with playing a major role in Germany's transition from adversary to Ally. There is no fear of a Franco-German war in the traditions of the wars of 1870, 1914, and 1939.

Of course, Germany's transition from adversary to Ally is also the re-sult of the increasing integration among the EU members, in their evolu-tion from the European Community, which had once been the European Economic Community, which had originally been the European Coal and Steel Community. NATO provided a foundation of trust and a secure

European environment for these economic and political events to occur. NATO not only provided security, it economically provided that security. The integrated defense allowed nations to have security without spending as much as they would have had to as a group of independent, potentially adversarial nations. As the EU has evolved, NATO has also provided the capability for the EU members to double-hat their forces and to use them for NATO or EU operations, provided that these Allies consult with their NATO Allies first.

In addition, the NATO's Partnership for Peace, the NATO–Russia, and NATO–Ukraine councils demonstrate NATO's role in spreading its democratic values, traditions, and institutions with non-members in its belief that these and other confidence- and security-building measures between NATO and Partners and among Partners will increase the collective sense of security within Europe and on its periphery. Finally, while NATO does try to spread these values and has always stressed the importance of healthy economies to its members' long-term security, NATO's military or security backbone has served as an anchor that keeps the Alliance somewhat focused and prevents a drift into chaos or a continual growth in missions. It also limits the overlap in missions between NATO, the EU, and other European or security-type institutions.

What NATO Is Not

Sometimes, when trying to describe or define what something is, it is helpful to describe what it is not. Given the plethora of potential complementary or overlapping competencies between NATO and several well-known international organizations and regimes, it seems pertinent to draw distinctions here. Several international regimes and organizations are presented here in chronological order of their appearance.

First of all, NATO is not an alliance in the sense of the World War I–era alliances. The Washington Treaty does not contain secret clauses, NATO does not have territorial ambitions, and the Alliance is defensive in nature. NATO does not have the intent to preemptively attack or wage preventative war. Which nations are members of NATO is public knowledge, and NATO has expanded its membership in the past based on the potential members' fit with NATO's evolving paradigm of values. Over time, NATO's integrated military command structure and defense planning has led to unparalleled openness with respect to military capabilities between the Allies. Finally, the NATO treaty is not iron-clad with respect to Allies' responsibilities. Article 5 of the NATO Treaty states that if one Ally is attacked, each member "will assist the Party or Parties so attacked by taking forthwith . . . such action as it deems necessary." The treaty does not contain an automatic, specifically required response, and although some of NATO's military contingency plans may have been designed for rapid, almost automatic execution, there is room for flexibility in Article 5. A crisis need not provoke an automatic response that would lead to war.

NATO also differs from the World War II alliances. First of all, the NATO Treaty was purposefully created in peacetime, and it has endured. The NATO Alliance is not based on expediency or a common enemy as its primary justification, but based on shared values that have gradually deepened and created a security community with long-standing inter-Alliance cooperation. The NATO Treaty does not mention specific potential adversaries; it is geographically limited in its applicability; and its members are real countries with existing governments and territories.

NATO also differs from the United Nations (UN) Organization in several respects. First, the NATO Treaty essentially subordinates itself to the UN Charter in its various references to the UN Charter, its articles, the duty to report armed attacks on NATO members and NATO's actions to the UN Security Council, and NATO's obligation under Article 5 of the treaty to terminate its actions once the Security Council "has taken the measures necessary to restore and maintain international peace and security." In addition, the NATO Treaty states clearly that it does not affect the Security Council's primary responsibility "for the maintenance of international peace and security." NATO's focus is also geographically limited by the NATO Treaty to the North Atlantic Area. In addition, NATO is different in its internal structures. NATO does not have an organizational equivalent to the UN Security Council, which grants special powers to the World War II victory powers. All NATO members are equal with respect to the Alliance's decision making process. NATO also does not have an equivalent to the General Assembly, and NATO decisions are reached through the consensus of all members, not through voting in any manner.

NATO also differs from the now-defunct Warsaw Pact. NATO does not have any puppet governments. Although the United States has historically owned, controlled, and planned the use of its strategic and tactical nuclear weapons, the United States does not have special powers. In fact, the British and French control their own nuclear weapons, and all the Allies are afforded some degree of consultation with respect to the nuclear weapons issues. The United States does not run NATO (all decision making is done by consensus), and the United States does not oversee NATO Allies' militaries or governments.

NATO's transatlantic link and security emphasis are two key distinctions between it and the EU. The *transatlantic link* is frequently used to describe the membership of Canada and the United States in NATO, but it and the term the *North Atlantic Area* both highlight the importance of the Atlantic lines of communication, and perhaps hint at the importance of Iceland and Norway. Although 21 nations are members of both NATO and the EU, the memberships are not inclusive. The NATO Allies Canada, the United States, Iceland, Norway, Albania, Croatia, and Turkey are not EU members, and the EU members Ireland, Sweden, Finland, Austria, Cyprus, and Malta are not NATO Allies. Although the NATO Alliance does extend beyond purely military issues into foreign policy and some budget issues and hosts intra-Ally consultations on a variety of issues, NATO does not comprise an internal market, and NATO's decision making through consensus is different from the EU's evolving governing infrastructure with the supranational EU Commission as well as a parliament, judiciary, and central bank. The potential overlap as the EU develops its Common Foreign and Security Policy and capability for military action independent of NATO through the European Security and Defence Policy has been minimized through NATO-EU coordination and consultation. The nations that are members of both organizations have finite numbers of military forces, and they can only be in one place at a time. Consequently, the transfer of command of the NATO–led Stabilization Force (SFOR) in Bosnia to the EU Military Force (EUFOR) in December 2004 was easily accomplished since most of the troops did not depart; they simply changed their patches and chain of command from NATO to the EU. However, the units of NATO Allies in EUFOR were no longer available for duty with NATO.

In comparison to the Organization for Security and Cooperation in Europe (OSCE), NATO is smaller in terms of membership and geography, and has a different focus, although both are described as security organizations. The OSCE began as the Conference on Security and Cooperation in Europe (CSCE) as an outgrowth of détente in the 1970s, forming an umbrella organization to provide a basis for East–West meetings, discussions, and negotiations, primarily between NATO and Warsaw Pact members. After the Cold War ended, the CSCE became the OSCE, with a new mandate for conflict prevention, crisis management, and post-conflict rehabilitation from Vancouver to Vladivostok and the 56 countries in-between. NATO has also assumed a crisis management role, but NATO's security focus, actual military capability under an integrated command structure with defense planning, provides a quite different capability than the OSCE's. In addition to politico-military dimensions of security, the OSCE also looks at the economic, environmental, and human dimensions of security issues.

Readers looking for a concise one- or two-sentence definition of NATO here may be disappointed to discover that no right answer is provided here. NATO is a complex international organization, and the answer to the question what is NATO depends on both the context of the question and your understanding of NATO. This chapter has laid the foundation to the answer by examining some concepts typically used to describe NATO. It has also pointed out some differences between NATO and other alliance structures and international organizations. The next chapter begins with a pithy, frequently quoted definition of NATO, but that definition only makes sense in the particular context in which it was made.

CHAPTER 2

The Founding of NATO

NATO's purpose is to keep the Russians out, the Americans in, and the Germans down.
— Attributed to Lord Ismay, NATO's first Secretary General

Questions for Consideration

- What do you think about the statement above?

  - What stereotypes are behind it? Are they valid?
  - What does it mean to keep the Americans *in*?

- Were all communists simply marionettes controlled from Moscow?

  - Were there political benefits to conservative politicians in France or Italy portraying communists this way?
  - Which political parties had fought or resisted the German occupations more, and could this have been a factor in postwar elections?
  - Was Tito in Yugoslavia a communist or a nationalist?

- Why was China a victory power in World War II?
- What does the term *isolationist* mean to you?

  - Can the United States really be isolationist?

- What is the meaning and what are the political implications of the U.S. Constitution's provision that the U.S. president "shall have Power, by and with the Advice and Consent of the Senate, to make Treaties, provided two thirds of the Senators present concur"?
- Are there disadvantages to worst-case planning?

  - What is the effect on further planning and analysis if what you thought was a worst case actually turns out to be too optimistic?

World War II changed the international political landscape in ways almost unimaginable to contemporary Europeans and Americans. Germany was destroyed; Britain, France, and the Soviet Union were the European victors. However, it was not clear that the wartime alliance had been anything more

than a marriage of convenience. Democratic Britain and France, with their colonial empires, were unlikely to have long-term interests compatible with those
of the rising, anti-imperialist, communist Soviet Union. The division of labor
between the wartime allies had been very unequal. The Soviet Union had suffered the most during the war and was intent on dominating eastern Europe in
order to prevent another devastating invasion from the west. Its inherited Russian empire was not overseas, but contiguous, and so was its primary focus. The
general European situation was further complicated by the issue of communism
and the relationship of communist parties to Moscow. The French communists,
for example, followed Moscow's lead but also had played such a large role in
the resistance to the German occupation that they were a major political party
in liberated France. The situation was similar in Italy, and in Yugoslavia, Tito's
communists were very popular because they were largely responsible for the
liberation of the country. Consequently, they provided the foundation of the
postwar government. In Greece, communists were battling the government for
control of the country. Furthermore, the Soviets were installing communist regimes in occupied East Europe. The tendency in the West was to view all communist movements as controlled from Moscow and to minimize differences
between and among the national movements. Underlying all of this was the
memory of Germany's military resurrection under Hitler within a generation
of World War I despite the punishing Versailles Treaty. An important question
was how to best prevent the reoccurrence of a resurgent Germany.

France and Britain, though victory powers (along with the United States,
the Soviet Union, and China), were very weak. The Soviet Union had become the dominant continental power, and U.S. intentions were not clear.
The United States had provided the decisive manpower and materiel for victory in western Europe in World War II. The United States had also played
key roles in establishing institutions designed to push wars to the distant periphery of international behavior with the League of Nations after World War
I and with the United Nations after the victory in the European theater in
World War II. After World War I, however, the United States did not join the
League because the U.S. Senate did not ratify the treaty. The United States
had turned its focus inward. Would the United States turn isolationist again,
or would it remain involved in international politics? As the only nation with
the capacity to project military and economic power throughout the world,
the United States's answer to this question was of considerable importance.

In hindsight, it was clear that the United States was not going to retreat
into isolationism. The U.S. Senate passed a resolution in November 1943
supporting the general concept of a United Nations–type organization, and
the democratic Roosevelt administration included republican Senator Vandenberg, a recently converted internationalist, in the U.S. delegation to the
San Francisco Conference, where the United Nations Charter was drafted.

The United States was firmly tied to the initiative and to international engagement in the postwar world.

The U.S. decision to remain engaged meant that the United States had to establish policies towards its wartime allies and foes. With respect to the Soviet Union, George Kennan's *Long Telegram* from Moscow in February 1946 was one of the key early documents laying the foundation for what became known as the *containment* strategy. On March 12, 1947, President Truman spoke before a joint session of Congress to ask for financial and material assistance to Greece and Turkey "to support free peoples who are resisting attempted subjugation by armed minorities or by outside pressures." The Soviet Union was supporting the armed minorities in Greece and applying pressure on Turkey, but the speech was the articulation of the Truman Doctrine—the United States would extend support to all "free peoples" in the same situation as Greece and Turkey. Truman also explicitly mentioned that this aid was necessary because Great Britain was no longer in a position to provide it. Congress approved the funding for Greece and Turkey in May 1947, and on June 5, 1947, Secretary of State George Marshall laid out the European Recovery Program, better known as the Marshall Plan, at the Harvard University commencement. The rationale and the principles behind the evolving U.S. containment strategy were laid out publicly in July 1947 in Kennan's "X" article, "The Sources of Soviet Conduct," in *Foreign Affairs*.

Unlike the case of Greece and Turkey, where assistance was simply to be given, Marshall's proposal required European governments to come to agreement on the exact requirements for a program that would lead to European economic recovery as well as what the Europeans themselves were willing to contribute to the program. In return, as Marshall stated at Harvard, the United States would assist "in the drafting of a European program and of later support of such a program so far as it may be practical for us to do so. The program should be a joint one, agreed to by a number, if not all, European nations." The United States was interested in establishing a long-term program in which it would help the Europeans help themselves. The United States chose to force Europeans to work together to foster a spirit of cooperation in order to make the program more efficient and easier to administer, but also to overcome nationalist sentiment in the various European countries. Americans generally considered nationalism a causal factor in both world wars, and the United States was particularly interested in finding a way to reintegrate a nonthreatening Germany into the European economy.

Britain and France took the lead in coordinating a response to Marshall's proposal. In the end, they did not invite fascist Spain, and the Soviet Union, along with Albania, Bulgaria, Czechoslovakia, Finland, Hungary, Poland, Romania, and Yugoslavia, declined to participate. Britain and France, as well as Austria, Belgium, Denmark, France, Greece, Iceland, Ireland, Italy, Luxembourg, the Netherlands, Norway, Portugal, Sweden, Switzerland, and Turkey negotiated a combined program during the summer and fall of 1947. In September 1947, the Soviet Union created the Communist Information Bureau (Cominform) with the other eight declining East European nations. President Truman submitted his Marshall Plan budget draft to Congress in December 1947. The financing was hotly debated for several months, but the Communist Party coup in Czechoslovakia in February 1948 was one outside event that contributed to the decision to fund the Marshall Plan. President Truman signed the bill in April 1948.

Another outside event of importance during the U.S. congressional debates on the Marshall Plan funding was that the foreign ministers of Britain, France, Belgium, Luxembourg, and the Netherlands began negotiating what was to become the Brussels Treaty of Economic, Social and Cultural Collaboration and Collective Self-Defence, which was signed on March 17, 1948. The Brussels Treaty played to the Truman Doctrine and to the Marshall Plan in that it gave further evidence of a group of European states working together and making their own contribution to their economic and security betterment.

The Brussels Treaty is often cited as the first concrete step along the road leading to the signing of the North Atlantic Treaty in Washington DC on April 4, 1949. The inclusion of the Brussels Treaty in the NATO founding mythos is particularly interesting because the Brussels Treaty's emphasis on economic, social, and cultural cooperation differed radically from the NATO Treaty. In fact, the Brussels Treaty's standing Consultative Council was established to deal with two specific, yet quite different threats: "with regard to the attitude to be adopted and the steps to be taken in case of a renewal by Germany of an aggressive policy; or with regard to any situation constituting a danger to economic stability." The Europeans wanted to keep Germany down, and to have economic stability.

There is some discussion as to whether the explicit references to Germany were a red herring that was purposely designed by the treaty governments to secure the acceptance of the basic gist of the treaty among their populations while lulling the Soviets into believing that the treaty was not aimed at them. Whether a disingenuous plan or not, the specific mention of the threat of a resurgent Germany in the Brussels Treaty, the popular acceptance of its inclusion in the treaty, and the linking of the Brussels and Washington treaties gave credence to the supposition that NATO initially was directed at Germany as well as the Soviet Union. At the time, Germany was still under Allied occupation; its final status had yet to be resolved, but the expectation was that the final resolution would be a united Germany. (See the Timeline of European Security Cooperation in Appendix I.)

The NATO Treaty was limited to the issue of collective defense, but there were similarities between the NATO and Brussels treaties with respect to defense. Both treaties referred to the then relatively new Charter of the United Nations (UN) in the first sentence; both specifically cited Article 51 of the UN Charter with its provision for collective defense; and each established a council, made up of representatives from each member state, that could meet quickly at any time. However, the treaties differed importantly with respect to the responsibility to assist a treaty partner that was the object of armed attack and with respect to the threat of a resurgent Germany. The Brussels Treaty required the treaty members to "afford the party so attacked all the military and other aid and assistance in their power."

Although the Brussels Treaty was positively regarded in the United States, it was not clear initially that the United States would be willing to give up George Washington's long-standing advice to avoid entangling alliances. In addition, the United States, located at a distance from Europe and populated by large numbers of German immigrants and their descendents, had fought "the Nazis," or "Nazi Germany" during World War II and maintained a distinction between "Nazis" and "Germans" more than its allies had. Consequently, a treaty explicitly aimed at a resurgent Germany would be difficult to sell in the United States.

Perhaps more important, the U.S. Senate was unlikely to agree to a treaty that potentially took away Congress's power to declare war. After all, the Brussels Treaty could be interpreted to require an automatic rendering of military assistance. In fact, the Senate alluded to this point in the Vandenberg Resolution, which it passed on June 11, 1948, just three months after the signing of the Brussels Treaty and two months after the Truman's signing of the Marshall Plan. It was also two weeks prior to the beginning of the Soviet blockade of Berlin. After making clear that it would not forfeit constitutional process in such a treaty, the Senate explicitly endorsed the United States joining regional collective self-defense treaties: "Association of the United States, by constitutional process, with such regional and other collective arrangements as are based on continuous and effective self-help and mutual aid, and as affect its national security" ("Vandenberg Resolution," 1948). Since the Vandenberg Resolution was passed by 64 votes to 4, the Senate was believed to be willing to ratify a treaty with some degree of alliance entanglement.

The U.S. and Canadian governments entered into discussions with the signatories of the Brussels Treaty in the summer of 1948 concerning the drafting of a regional collective defense treaty for the North Atlantic area. By the fall of 1948, it was clear within the U.S. government that, as laid out in National Security Council (NSC) 20/4 of November 23, 1948, "the gravest threat to the security of the United States within the foreseeable future stems from the hostile designs and formidable power of the USSR, and from the nature of the Soviet system." There was no threat of a resurgent Germany. The "iron curtain" was drawn along the Lübeck–Trieste line, and western Germany was in the west. The Soviet Union and the United States were locked in a political struggle for power that could turn into military conflict "at any time." In fact, according to NSC 20/4, if the Soviet Union were so inclined, Soviet armed forces could overrun continental Europe, the Near East to Cairo, and important continental points in the Far East within about six months. The Soviets could also attack Great Britain with aircraft and missiles. By 1955, NSC 20/4 estimated that the Soviets would be able to launch air attacks against the United States with atomic, chemical, and biological weapons; seize advance bases through airborne operations; and attack the United States with submarine-launched short-range missiles. NSC 20/4 argued that even if the United States maintained an effective military, the Soviets would likely retain the capability to overrun Europe, the Middle East, and parts of the Far East through 1958.

However, these worst-case intelligence estimates of Soviet capabilities were not an immutable fate. First of all, it was not clear that the Soviets would actually resort to war. In addition, NSC 20/4 offered several offsets that the United States and the Western democracies could do that would change the underlying assumptions of the scenario: If the Marshall Plan was successful; if the United States supported the development and operation of a Western Union; or if the United States, United Kingdom, and other nations increased their military effectiveness, then the situation would change significantly. In addition, if internal dissention developed within the Soviet Union and between the Soviet Union and its satellites, the basis of the estimates would also be altered. In order to be successful in the struggle with the Soviet Union, NSC 20/4 stated that the United States must "help such of those nations as are able and willing to make an important contribution to U.S. security, to increase their economic and political stability and their military capability." This was an expansion of the Truman Doctrine, and the U.S. Senate and executive branch were in general agreement on the benefits to be gained with some sort of Western union.

In the meantime, the Brussels Treaty signatories established a committee to study the economic aspects of their joint defense plans. As with the Marshall Plan, the United States had indicated that before any economic aid could be discussed, the signatory nations should first establish their requirements as well as inventory their own capabilities to meet their national and mutual requirements. The United States was interested in helping those who were helping themselves and their allies. The signatory nations selected Field Marshall Viscount Montgomery as the chairman of the permanent common military organization, and agreements were reached on financing armaments and the common military staff as well as on the initial troop contributions to the common pool of forces.

Although their was general consensus for some sort of Western union and the Brussels Treaty members were moving ahead with their plans, it was clear that the Brussels Treaty was not the answer for the United States. Consequently, the objective in the NATO Treaty negotiations was to find acceptable wording for the U.S., Canadian, and other potential future members' governments. The United States pushed to broaden the circle of nations involved beyond the Brussels Treaty signatories, and in March 1949, Denmark, Iceland, Italy, Norway, and Portugal were invited to participate. In the negotiations between the United States, Canada, and the Brussels Treaty signatories, the economic, social, and cultural aspects of the Brussels Treaty were quickly pared away, although a generic paragraph (Article 2) promoting "free institutions" and encouraging economic cooperation remained in the NATO Treaty, also known as the Washington Treaty. The Brussels Treaty's specific references to the threats of a resurgent Germany and economic instability were also dropped. In fact, no threats were specified in the NATO Treaty. The drafting of the treaty as a collective self-defense against an armed attack from any quarter gave the Washington Treaty a degree of adaptability.

The final wording of the NATO Treaty's Article 5 was acceptable to all. It remedied the Brussels Treaty's objectionable automatic military assistance clause:

> The Parties agree that an armed attack against one or more of them in Europe or North America shall be considered an attack against them all and consequently they agree that, if such an armed attack occurs, each of them, in exercise of the right of individual or collective self-defence recognised by Article 51 of the Charter of the United Nations, will assist the Party or Parties so attacked by taking forthwith, individually and in concert with the other Parties, such action as it deems necessary, including the use of armed force, to restore and maintain the security of the North Atlantic area. (The North Atlantic Treaty, Washington D.C.— 4 April 1949)

Instead of automaticity, each signatory will "take such action as it deems necessary." Although it is often mischaracterized as the Three Musketeers' pledge, Article 5 is not "all for one and one for all." That pledge is more akin to the requirement of the Brussels Treaty, and it remained in effect for its members.

The NATO Treaty's Articles 4 and 9 replaced the Brussels Treaty's Article VII clause on consultations. Article 4 states that "the Parties will consult together whenever, in the opinion of any of them, the territorial integrity, political independence or security of any of the Parties is threatened." NATO's Article 4 outlines stricter guidelines, using more traditional military-type descriptions, on what issues required consultation than the wording of the Brussels Treaty's "any situation which may constitute a threat to peace." The NATO Treaty's Article 9 was similar to the first sub-paragraph in the Brussels Treaty's Article VII as both established a council to work out the implementation of the respective treaty and that could meet quickly when it was deemed necessary. Article 9, however, clarifies that each treaty party would be represented in the council, and the writers of the treaty took the further step of expressly giving the council the ability to set up "subsidiary bodies as may be necessary; in particular it shall establish immediately a defence committee which shall recommend measures for the implementation of Articles 3 and 5." Article 3 spelled out: "In order more effectively to achieve the objectives of this Treaty, the Parties, separately and jointly, by means of continuous and effective self-help and mutual aid, will maintain and develop their individual and collective capacity to resist armed attack." As with many of the NATO Treaty articles, Article 3 articulated what was logically implied, but not detailed in the Brussels Treaty. The language in Article 3 is particularly interesting because the phrase "continuous and effective self-help and mutual aid" came from the Vandenberg Resolution. The treaty negotiators were looking for ways to strengthen the case for U.S. Senate approval of the treaty.

The NATO Treaty was signed in Washington on April 4, 1949, by Belgium, Canada, Denmark, France, Iceland, Italy, Luxembourg, the Netherlands, Norway, Portugal, the United Kingdom, and the United States. A few days later, the Brussels Treaty members, as well as Denmark, Italy, and Norway requested military and economic assistance from the United States. The Berlin Blockade ended on May 9, 1949. The NATO Treaty entered into force on August 24, 1949; ironically, the day after President Truman publicly announced the discovery that the Soviet Union had successfully exploded its first atomic bomb. The successful Soviet atomic test occurred approximately three to five years earlier than forecast by U.S. intelligence and was quite a surprise, indicating that the worst-case intelligence estimates were too optimistic. The first North Atlantic Council (NAC) session took place in Washington on September 17, 1949. The anticommunist cause suffered another setback on October 1, 1949, when Mao Zedong proclaimed communist victory in the Chinese civil war and founded the People's Republic of China. In the West, it was easy to tie events together and believe oneself under siege from a monolithic communist movement.

Congress passed the U.S. Mutual Defense Assistance Act of 1949 to authorize the president to provide military assistance to the NATO Treaty signatories and to set funding limits. President Truman signed the act into law on October 6, 1949:

> The President is hereby authorized to furnish military assistance in the form of equipment, materials, and services to such nations as are parties

> to the [NATO] treaty and have heretofore requested such assistance.
> Any such assistance furnished under this title shall be subject to agree-
> ments . . . designed to assure that the assistance will be used to promote
> an integrated defense of the North Atlantic area and to facilitate the
> development of defense plans by the Council and the Defense Commit-
> tee under Article 9 of the North Atlantic Treaty and to realize unified
> direction and effort.

The act provided the authorization for the initial money to support the implementation of the NATO Treaty; however, the United States was clearly
viewing the struggle as worldwide. Congress declared itself "as favoring the
creation by the free countries and the free peoples of the Far East of a" Brussels or Washington Treaty–like joint organization. The act also authorized
continued funding for Greece and Turkey as well as military assistance to
Iran, the Republic of Korea, and the Republic of the Philippines. Finally, the
act provided an emergency fund for the president's use in the general area of
China "in consideration of the concern of the United States in the present
situation in China." The United States was definitely *in*. (See the Timeline
of Illustrative Non-NATO Events in Appendix I.)

The combined effect of the successful Soviet atomic explosion and the
corollary conclusion that the Soviets were on their way to creating thermonuclear weapons as well as the consolidation of the communist victory on
mainland China forced the U.S. government to reexamine its analyses of the
presumed Soviet threat to the United States and the free world. This review,
which began in January, resulted in the first draft of NSC-68 in April 1950.
NSC-68 firmly established the policy of containment against an aggressive,
communist monolith and cast a long shadow over U.S. policy for most of
the Cold War. The June 24, 1950, invasion of South Korea by North Korean
forces during the review contributed to the portrayal of communism as both
monolithic and aggressive. The large-scale entry of Chinese Army units into
the Korean War in late November 1950 gave further cause for alarm. It appeared that the worst-case scenarios were coming true, which reinforced the
importance of worst-case analyses and planning and made it more difficult to
look for alternative explanations for world events.

The culmination of the reviews and part of the implementation of the
recommendations was President Truman's Proclamation of the Existence of a
National Emergency on December 16, 1950. In Proclamation 2914, Truman
declared that "world conquest by communist imperialism is the goal of the
forces of aggression that have been loosed upon the world," and that "the increasing menace of the forces of communist aggression requires that the national defense of the United States be strengthened as speedily as possible."
He also asked all citizens "to keep faith with our friends and allies," elliptically

indicating the importance that NATO was to play in the struggle against communist domination of the world. The classified NSC68/4 of December 14, 1950, acknowledged a divergence between the U.S. and NATO military build-ups. Whereas the NATO Defense Plan of October 1950 had set a target date of 1954 for the nations to provide adequate forces for NATO's defense, after the Chinese entry into North Korea, the United States was determined to speed up its process to meet a new target date of June 30, 1952. NSC-68/4 also proposed various methods to try to increase the speed of the United States's allies' build-ups. The Soviets had to be kept *out* of West Europe.

Question for Consideration

The Soviet Army did not end up invading western Europe, and the Soviets did not rain nuclear-tipped ballistic missiles down on America. Was it because of the power of the NATO Treaty, or was it because the west did not really understand the Soviet Union, China, Korea, or communism?

The German Question

The status of Germany remained a sticking point. The protocol between the victory powers at the Potsdam Conference in August 1945 continued to build upon the wartime agreements. Germany would be divided into zones of temporary occupation, but eventually a government of a unified Germany would sign a final peace settlement for World War II. In the meantime, the occupying powers of Britain, the Soviet Union, the United States (and France if it accepted the invitation to join in the Potsdam agreements) were to treat the Germans in each zone as uniformly as practical. Concurrently, Germany was to be completely disarmed and demilitarized. In addition, the occupying powers were to take reparations from their respective zones, with the Soviet Union additionally receiving a percentage of industrial capital equipment from the western zones. Finally, the Potsdam Protocol agreed in principle to giving the German city and area of Königsberg to the Soviet Union, moved the Polish western border westwards, and gave that part of former German East Prussia not given to the Soviet Union to Poland. (See the Timeline of The German Question in Appendix I.)

However, the victory powers found it difficult to agree on common economic and political policies with respect to Germany as a unit. The differences were partly based on ideology, which pitted the western democratic and capitalist ideals against the Soviet Union's one-party state with a command economy, and assessments of the risk of German resurgence, which correlated to an extent with geographic proximity to Germany and the extent of suffering incurred under German occupation during the war. These factors led to disagreements on reparations, political parties, currency and economic issues, and the role and capabilities of a German state at the end of the occupation. In addition, Germans had differing views on many of these issues. As it was increasingly difficult to reach a consensus on Germany and the victory powers needed to govern their occupation zones, the policies promulgated in the different zones began to diverge. However, the United States and United Kingdom united their zones economically in January 1947, with France joining later. June 20, 1948, the Western powers implemented a currency reform within their sectors. The Soviet Union protested and began the Berlin blockade on June 24, 1948. By July, the Western powers invited the German states (*Länder*) within their zones to draft a constitution. The *Grundgesetz* ("Basic Law," or the provisional constitution pending a constitution for a reunited Germany) was accepted on May 23, 1949, resulting in the founding of the Federal Republic of Germany (FRG) on May 24, 1949. The FRG was still under occupation and not a sovereign state, although it became a full participant in the Marshall Plan. The Soviet occupation zone, minus the Western sectors in Berlin, was declared the German Democratic Republic (GDR) on October 7, 1949.

Konrad Adenauer, the first chancellor of the FRG, saw the benefits of integration with the west and the adoption of a market-based, democratic system as outweighing the costs of postponing the dream of a reunited, democratic Germany. Western integration became the path to achieve the FRG's full sovereignty. Integration was also seen by many countries as a way to bind Germany to its neighbors and thereby reduce the possibility of war. In May 1950 French Foreign Minister Robert Schuman proposed that control of French and German coal and steel production be placed under a joint authority. This would restrict the FRG's ability to produce armaments. Schuman's proposal resulted in the European Coal and Steel Community (ECSC), which was established in the Treaty of Paris, signed April 1951, by Belgium, France, Italy, Luxembourg, the Netherlands, and the FRG. The treaty came into force in July 1952. (See the Timeline of European Integration in Appendix I).

Today the ECSC is widely acclaimed to be one of the key building blocks that led to the European Union. At the time of its negotiation, however, Germany was not a sovereign power willfully giving up control of its coal and steel production to a higher body. France held the German mining and industrial state of Saarland in protectorate status, and the International Authority for the Ruhr (Belgium, France, Luxembourg, the Netherlands, United Kingdom, United States, and the FRG) controlled Ruhr production. The ECSC replaced the International Authority for the Ruhr, and France, after a plebiscite, returned the Saarland to the FRG in 1957.

As the Cold War gathered momentum, it became clear that a resurgent Germany was less of a problem than an aggressive Soviet Union. Occupation, democracy, and economic integration would keep the FRG out of Soviet influence, but with the Korean War, the focus shifted to finding a way to turn the FRG into a positive contributor to the defense of Western Europe. German military forces would go a long way to strengthening the West's paucity of conventional military forces in central Europe. The simple answer would be to have "Germany," that is, the FRG, rearm and to make its military forces available to the West. Politically, however, this was not an easy thing to do. America's Cold War allies were reluctant to let such a recent enemy rearm, and the Soviet Union dabbled with offers of German reunification under the conditions of total disarmament and neutrality for the reunified German state. However, events such as the Soviet and East German military suppression of the June 17, 1953, uprising in East Berlin made it difficult for Western governments and populations to give much credence to Soviet proposals for a neutral Germany.

The apparent success of the ECSC led its members to expand upon the integration model as a method to bind in a rearming Germany. In May 1952, France, Italy, the Benelux, and the FRG signed the European Defense Community (EDC) Treaty in Paris. The concept was that the EDC members would contribute forces to the EDC's integrated land, naval, and air forces. The FRG's military forces would only operate under EDC control, but the other EDC members would cooperate within the EDC but also maintain independent control over their military forces. However, the French National Assembly refused to ratify the EDC Treaty in August 1954; the Gaullists saw the EDC concept impinging on their national sovereignty.

Since the FRG could not be permitted to simply rearm with no external controls, after consultations between the Brussels Treaty signatories, the United States, Canada, the FRG, and Italy, it was decided to invite the FRG and Italy to join the Brussels Treaty, and for the FRG to join NATO. The Brussels Treaty was amended in October 1954 when the organization became known as the Western European Union (WEU). (See the Timeline of European Security Cooperation in Appendix I.) Italy and the FRG acceded to the treaty, and the two explicit references to the dangers of a resurgent Germany were dropped. In addition, the WEU members agreed in the amended Brussels Treaty to "work in close cooperation with" NATO and to rely on NATO for "information and advice on military matters" so as to not duplicate staffs. The FRG acceded to the Washington Treaty in May 1955. The FRG would have control over its new military, but it would be bound to the WEU and NATO. There were also internal constraints on the new *Bundeswehr*. The FRG constitution limited its use to defense against an attack on the FRG or its allies. On May 14, 1955, the Soviet Union, Albania, Bulgaria, Czechoslovakia,

German Democratic Republic, Hungary, Poland, and Romania formed the Warsaw Pact. On December 30, 1955, the Soviet Union and the GDR declared the GDR an independent country. The division of Germany appeared final. The Germans were *down*.

Although pithy, the statement that NATO is about keeping the Russians out, the Americans in, and the Germans down loses relevancy for describing NATO the more time passes from NATO's founding. Nevertheless, it is important to understand NATO's origins in order to better understand the rest of NATO's historical evolution and how NATO works today.

CHAPTER 3

How Does NATO Work?

Rather than jump into NATO's post-founding history as told through the strategic concepts, I decided to insert this chapter on how NATO works first. The primary reason is that once the NATO Treaty was ratified, NATO had to create a working organizational structure, a decision making process and a defense planning process before NATO could actually act in any meaningful way. Consequently, this chapter can be read as a historical continuation of the NATO story or an inserted description of how NATO works. In either case, the emphasis is on how NATO currently works because once established, NATO's basic organizational structure, its reliance on consensus decision making, its methods of defense planning, and the accompanying traditions have remained remarkably constant at the macro level. These processes have in turn shaped NATO's evolution, so knowing how NATO works will be helpful when reading the successive chapters on NATO's evolving strategic concepts. In addition, readers may find the information in this chapter useful for understanding current NATO events and doing outside research.

Questions for Consideration

- If you established an organization of a dozen independent states, how would you set up the organization's governance?
  - How would it make decisions?
- Who would be in charge of the military planning and operations?
  - Is it even necessary to have one person in charge?

- How would you organize the militaries to provide a collective defense?
  - Would they work side by side, or be integrated in some way?
  - How would they communicate?
  - Could they exchange fuel or ammunition?
  - What doctrine would they use?
- How would you know what capabilities each national military has?
  - Would you need to know?
- What language or languages would you use?
  - Would the language(s) used be different for meetings than the language(s) used for military operations?

Basic Organization

The North Atlantic Treaty itself actually provides very little guidance on how the members are to organize the organization's administrative structures. Article 9 states that there should be a council "to consider matters concerning the implementation of this Treaty." Every member state is to be represented on the council, and the council is "to be able to meet promptly at any time." In addition, the council may establish "subsidiary bodies" as necessary, but the treaty specifically directs the council to create a "defence committee which shall recommend measures for implementation of Articles 3 and 5." The reference to Article 3 pertains to developing the "collective capacity to resist armed attack," in other words, combined defense planning. Article 5 deals with the "collective self-defence" of a member under attack, in other words, conducting combined combat operations.

The council, which came to be called the North Atlantic Council (NAC), initially met at the ministerial level, that is, at the level of the members' foreign ministers (e.g., U.S. Secretary of State) with a rotating chairmanship. However, this proved a difficult administrative concept in practice, and by the ninth ministers' meeting in February 1952, the Allies made the NAC a permanent structure comprised of Permanent Representatives (Perm-Reps), typically of ambassador rank, from each Ally. In addition, the Allies selected a Secretary General (SecGen) to serve as a permanent chairman, to coordinate NAC activities, and to oversee the single International Staff supporting the NAC. The PermReps, SecGen, and International Staff are currently located at NATO Headquarters near Brussels. The NAC still meets periodically at the ministerial level, and occasionally at the heads of state (e.g., U.S. President) level at NATO summits, but all NAC decisions carry the same weight regardless of whether made at the PermRep, ministerial, or summit level. The NAC is NATO's senior decision making body. All NATO committees, working groups, organizations, agencies, and military commands fall at least nominally under the NAC.

> NATO Headquarters was initially in London, but moved to Paris in April 1952, first to Palais de Chaillot, and in 1960 to Porte Dauphine. However, the French withdrawal from NATO's integrated military structure forced NATO to relocate its headquarters to Brussels in 1967. Work is underway on a new headquarters complex near the current headquarters.
>
> NATO Headquarters is not to be confused with Supreme Headquarters Allied Powers Europe (SHAPE), which is a NATO military command's headquarters. SHAPE was established in April 1951 as the military headquarters for Allied Command Europe (ACE), commanded by the Supreme Allied Commander Europe (SACEUR). SHAPE was located in Rocquencourt in Versailles, near Paris, in order to be centrally located in continental Europe for better access to its subordinated military forces. SHAPE remained there until it moved to Casteau, near Mons, Belgium, in March 1967 as a result of the French withdrawal from NATO's integrated military structure. The site near Casteau was chosen because it kept SHAPE centrally located on continental Europe, it would be about an hour distant from NATO Headquarters in Brussels, and it was already a Belgium military caserne. SHAPE and SACEUR remain at this location, but the command is now called Allied Command Operations (ACO).

At its initial meeting in September 1949, the NAC established the Defence Committee mentioned in Article 9. The Defence Committee consisted of the Allies' defense ministers (e.g., U.S. Secretary of Defense) or in Iceland's case a representative, since it did not and does not have a defense minister. The Defence Committee also initially had a rotating chairmanship, but also evolved into the NAC model of PermReps, double-hatting the national PermReps to sit in both the NAC and the Defence Committee. The SecGen served as the permanent chair, responsible for coordinating International Staff support through the operative equivalent of the current Defense Policy and Plans Division and the Operations Division. The Defence Committee also met periodically at the ministerial level. When France left the NATO integrated military command structure in 1966, the Defence Committee's name changed to the Defense Planning Committee, and France did not participate. When France reintegrated its forces into the NATO integrated military command structures in 2009, it began to participate in the Defense Planning Committee, which did not change its name. However, in June 2010 NATO dissolved the Defense Planning Committee, with the NAC taking over its responsibilities to oversee the defense planning process.

The Defence Committee was originally tasked to provide the NAC with recommendations on how to implement Articles 3 and 5, and the Defense

Planning Committee continued to perform these functions. With respect to its Article 3 duties, the Defense Planning Committee oversaw NATO's force planning process and provided guidance to NATO's military authorities. In the force planning process, NATO sets its military requirements and then sets unique planning targets for each Ally's contribution to meet those overall requirements. For example, NATO has a standing maritime presence in the Mediterranean Sea, currently called the Standing NATO Maritime Group 2. If NATO were to decide that that group should consist of four frigates, one of which should have anti-submarine capabilities, Italy might be given a force goal to be able to continuously provide such a ship. The Defense Planning Committee approved these force goals and assessed whether each Ally was meeting its unique goals. With respect to its Article 5 duties, the Defense Planning Committee oversaw NATO's integrated military structure, although the Nuclear Planning Group has responsibility for certain nuclear matters. The NAC originally tasked the Defense Committee to establish a military organizational structure that consisted of the Military Committee, the Standing Group, Military Representatives (MilReps), and Regional Planning Groups.

The Military Committee consists of each of the Allies' Chief of Defense Staff (CHODS), who normally are their senior-most serving military officer, usually in the general or admiral ranks. The Military Committee initially met periodically in Washington DC and provided advice upwards to the Defense Committee and guidance downwards to the Standing Group. The Standing Group was a subcommittee of the Military Committee, located in Washington DC, and consisted of a British, French, and U.S. member. The Standing Group operated in permanent session, essentially functioning as the Military Committee when it was not in session, and translated Military Committee guidance into specific policy guidance for NATO's Regional Planning Groups. The Standing Group also had a liaison or representative at NATO Headquarters who attended all meetings of the NAC, even private ones, to maintain close communications between American military authorities, the keeper of the atomic sword, and the NAC. In some ways, this appeared to place the Standing Group above the Military Committee. It also appeared to exclude most Allies from its decision making, although they were allowed to send MilReps with more observer than participant status to the Standing Group.

In 1957, the Military Committee adopted the model of meeting in permanent session at the MilRep level, with periodic meetings at the nations' CHODS level. The MilReps are serving military officers representing their national militaries on the Military Committee and are not the same person as the national PermRep. The CHODS select the Chairman of the Military Committee for a three-year term. The Chairman coordinates Military

Committee activities and oversees the International Military Staff support-ing the Military Committee. France provided a military mission for liaison with the Military Committee when its forces were not integrated into the NATO military structure. The Military Committee is the senior military authority in NATO, and reports to the NAC and the Defense (Planning) Committee. The MilReps, Chairman of the Military Committee, and Inter-national Military Staff are also located at NATO Headquarters. Although the Canada–United States Regional Planning Group is still in existence, the other four original Regional Planning Groups evolved into the NATO major military commands. All reported to the Standing Group until it was dissolved in 1966 and now report to the Military Committee.

The current operating modes are for the NAC in PermRep session and the Military Committee in MilRep session each to meet at least weekly, and more often as necessary. The Defense Planning Committee met as needed at the PermRep level. The PermRep/MilRep and ministerial/CHODS meetings typically occur at NATO Headquarters, although they can take place else-where. The summit-level meetings tend to be hosted by an Ally. The meet-ings vary in format as to how many supporting staff are present, and can be funneled down to private sessions with only the principals (e.g., the SecGen and PermReps) and no note taking to resolve difficult issues. Lower level meetings of boards, (standing) committees, and (ad hoc) working groups are usually open to all Allies. Ministerial level meetings currently occur twice a year, once in the late fall and once in the spring. These break the year into two work cycles, with the intensity increasing during the cycle to complete the "deliverables" for the ministerial sessions. The fall ministerials are fol-lowed by the winter holiday slowdown, and the spring ministerials are followed by summer, which is when most personnel depart and arrive or take summer vacation leaves. The schedule of the meetings echoes through the NATO hierarchy. The Military Committee meets first in CHODS session to resolve any problems and approve the proposals prepared by the Interna-tional Military Staff and reviewed by the MilReps. The Defense Planning Committee met second so that it could conduct its own work as well as re-view and approve any Military Committee documents that required Defense Planning Committee approval. The NAC ministerial is last so that it can review and approve the work of the Defense Planning Committee (through June 2010) and Military Committee in addition to performing its own work. Furthermore, the meeting schedule has become fuller, with a NATO-only session of each type of ministerial meeting, followed by a NATO-Partner, a NATO-Russia, and a NATO-Ukraine version of each committee. The NATO-only meeting precedes the other meetings so that one of the agenda items can be to review or resolve the NATO position before meeting with the others.

Each Ally (i.e., member state) and now Partner (i.e., not a member of NATO, but a participant in the Partnership for Peace program) maintains a national delegation of varying size to support their PermRep and MilRep, or ambassador and military liaison officer. Members of these delegations remain in close contact with their home capitals and represent their nations at NATO Headquarters.

NATO staffs are a mix of NATO civilian employees, who are paid by NATO, and civilian and military personnel seconded by their countries to serve in the NATO positions for periods of time, usually for several years. All personnel so serving are to work in a nation-neutral manner and not advocate their country's positions while working for NATO. This process also occurs in the military staffs of NATO commands at all levels. Military officers assigned to NATO continue to wear their national uniforms.

NATO's official languages are English and French. Major documents are published in both, and higher level meetings provide translation into both. However, communication in working-level meetings and military operations are in English. Consequently, it is not particularly unusual at a working-level meeting for the chairman of the working group, who is a military officer posted to NATO from country X, to have a disagreement in English with a member of the working group, who is a military officer from X's national delegation. The chairman fulfills his NATO role and tries to forge a consensus, while the working group member represents national policy and may be the odd man out. During a military operation, units use their national language internally, but they use English to coordinate with other NATO units. For example, members of a Polish infantry company use Polish to communicate with each other and to communicate with their Polish company commander; however, if they were attached to a Dutch battalion or were coordinating air support, they would communicate with the Dutch battalion staff or with Spanish F-18 aircraft in English. Consequently, many members of NATO staffs as well as national officers and enlisted personnel conducting NATO military operations are not working in their native language.

If one considers that NATO English is British English, the vast majority of personnel serving in NATO billets are using a language not entirely native to them; however, because many Americans use American English spell-checkers on their NATO computers, there appears to be a low-intensity conflict over proper English within NATO, with humor being the primary weapon. For example, a British Navy captain who served as a Deputy Branch Chief within Policy Division at SHAPE presented his boss, an U.S. Army brigadier general, with a British dictionary as a going-away gift to remind him of their frequent good-natured arguments on the correct spellings of words such as *armour* or *kilometre*.

Decision Making through Consensus

Decision making at NATO has traditionally been done through consensus. Consensus is not majority rule. Majority rule systems often leave the minority with no recourse after a vote is taken. The minority may actually oppose a majority decision, and in a group of sovereign countries, it is difficult to force the minority to comply with the majority's decision. Another reason that consensus decision making has traditionally been used at NATO was that the United States was not going to accept other governments dictating actions either through mandatory clauses, as in the Brussels Treaty, or in the form of a majority rule system. In NATO, there is no formal voting of any kind. Consensus is sometimes characterized as a system in which every participant has a veto and consequently, agreement is only to be found at the lowest common denominator. However, since NATO has been operating since 1949, the members are in continuous dialogue over a variety of issues. Instead of treating each new issue as an independent, disconnected zero-sum discussion, continuous dialogue allows for the give-and-take of negotiations and compromises across the range of issues. In addition, it is important that all Allies have a stake in the decision making to increase the likelihood of their participation at some level in the implementation of decisions.

In NATO, consensus is achieved largely through process and procedure. Ideas or proposals can enter NATO a variety of ways, including from individual staff members up the staff chain, national delegations into the staffing process at meetings or via memoranda, and from the NAC down; however, all proposals must enter the process via officially recognized channels. Consequently, an editorial in a newspaper remains outside, unless, for example, an Ally's PermRep were to make the same argument in a NAC meeting and garner support for an evaluation of the proposal. Then, the proposal would enter official channels, be tasked through the International Staff, and out to other NATO organizations with any connection to the subject for study, coordination, and recommendations. Similarly, if a committee or division of the Internationals Staff or International Military Staff was developing a paper that reviews potential options for a particular problem, staff members or national representatives might inject new options into consideration.

In any event, once the idea is captured on paper, the consensus process begins. An ad hoc working group might be formed, or the tasking will be given to a NATO staff section or to an existing working group. Because the end goal is consensus, national delegations might be invited to participate in working groups and make inputs on NATO staff drafts at this informal level. If the proposal is specific, only one NATO staff division might be involved. If it is more complex or has broad implications, the International Staff or International Military Staff may have to coordinate drafts among several staff divisions and a multitude of NATO organizations. Drafts must achieve consensus at the lowest levels before progressing up the chain. An item with military implications, for example, traditionally starts in the International Military Staff, is tasked downward for advice from major NATO commands, is consolidated and then passed through the Military Committee, to the Defense Planning Committee (previously), and then on to the NAC if necessary. All nations' representatives must agree with the wording at each step of the way.

For formal coordination, the NATO International Staff and International Military Staff use what is called the "silence procedure." In this procedure, the NATO staff member who chairs the forum drafts what he believes to be the consensus of the participants, and circulates the draft to the national delegations. This draft comes with a deadline for national delegations "to break silence" and provide additional information, alternative wording, or perhaps justifications for their position if they disagree. Remaining silent, in other words, not breaking silence with an official memorandum, is the equivalent of giving consent to the NATO staff draft in question. If no Ally breaks silence, the draft is finalized and goes up the chain. If one or more Allies disagree, the NATO staff element may revise the draft to attempt to resolve the issue and send the new version out under silence. If there appears to be too big a gulf, the NATO staff element may call a meeting to see if the issue can be resolved in a face-to-face manner, or to discuss possible ways out of the deadlock. In the worst case, a deadlock would be reported up the chain for higher ups to try to resolve.

Because of this tiered responsibility with final decisions usually taken at the Military Committee, Defense Committee, or NAC with full Alliance representation, there often is less need for real discussion at each level as the item progresses up the chain. Most issues are worked from the bottom up, and compromises are worked out at as low a level as possible to achieve consensus. Consequently, few items get to the NAC that require major deliberation. For military issues, for example, each Ally's capital has theoretically seen the issue at the Military Committee, and has had (previously) another chance at the Defense Committee to inject amendments, caveats, or a rejection. It is a rare item that is both so controversial and so important that it is passed to the NAC to achieve consensus or to provide modified guidance for the staffs to rework the issue.

A few examples provide some insights into the decision making process. The first hypothetical case involves an Allied government that adopts a new security policy that includes advocating for Russian membership in NATO. The Ally's foreign ministry would instruct its PermRep to advocate this policy at NATO. The PermRep and his staff might first broach the idea at a series of informal coffee break discussions with colleagues to test the winds, although everyone would soon know it was coming since it would be a major policy shift. The next step might be an oral presentation at a NAC meeting, or an official, written request for NATO to study the matter. In either case, if agreed through consensus by the NAC, it would first go to the International Staff, most likely in a directorate in the Division of Defense Policy and Planning. However, because the issue of potential Russian membership in NATO would impact most of NATO in one way or another, the directorate would need to seek advice from and coordinate the issue with several other directorates across various International Staff divisions. In addition, the Military Committee would be tasked to provide advice. The Military Committee would pass it to the International Military Staff, where it would most likely end up in one of the branches of the Plans and Policy Division. That branch would coordinate the response with other branches and divisions in the International Military Staff, and the Chairman of the Military Committee through the International Military Staff would in turn task the strategic commands, Allied Command Operations and Allied Command Transformation, to provide advice to the Military Committee.

The staff at each command would craft coordinated advice for the International Military Staff, which would then likely consolidate the commands' advice and use that as the foundation of the draft for the Military Committee's response. The International Military Staff branches and divisions would coordinate a draft, and invite staff officers from the national delegations to participate in working groups working on the draft. Because the Military Committee would be offering advice of a military nature on the impacts of such a decision and avoid taking a stance on the political aspects of the issue, it might appear that consensus could be reached, and a draft would be circulated under the silence procedure to the national delegations. If silence was broken, the International Military Staff might try again to develop a draft for another round in the silence procedure. The MilReps might also have a closed, no-notes session to work out a consensus response to send to the NAC (International Staff).

The International Staff would use the Military Committee's advice as an attachment to its study, but the International Staff would have to address not only the technical impacts of Russian membership from its level, but also look at the political issues. National delegations would supply their inputs, and the International Staff would coordinate draft versions of the study. There would likely be opposition from some Allies to offering Russia NATO membership. Because membership is a black-or-white status, in order to achieve consensus in the face of opposition, the staff might try compromise formulations like extending an eventual membership invitation to Russia, increasing efforts at cooperation in the NATO-Russia Council, or even inviting Russia to submit a Membership Action Plan. However, only one nation would need to break silence to hold up the entire matter. If it was only one Ally, or a small group, other Allies might try to pressure the recalcitrant Allies to join a consensus, which might yield a compromise solution, an invitation to Russia to join, or a stalled study with no way forward. The size and power of an Ally might play a role in these negotiations, but in the end, NATO operates by consensus, and one nation, however small, can block consensus.

For another example, if an Allied government felt strongly about eliminating NATO's tactical nuclear weapons in Europe, it might advance this position within the current discussions to develop NATO's next Strategic Concept, expected to be approved at NATO's next summit at the end of 2010. It would generally go through the same process described above. One might think that the onus would be on that Ally to achieve the consensus of all NATO members to implement such a radical change to NATO strategy, and that would be true. However, unlike the Russian membership example, in which an Ally cannot really go its own way and let Russia into NATO, the nuclear issue offers the possibility of a different practical solution. In this case, if the Ally could not persuade the rest of the Allies to form a new consensus and eliminate the tactical nuclear weapons, that Ally could withdraw its practical support for the current concept that Allies share the nuclear load. For example, if the Ally had dual-use tactical aircraft, it could stop training the air crews for nuclear missions. If a nuclear storage site was located on its territory, it could ask that it be removed. Such actions could potentially have major political repercussions on NATO because they would practically erode NATO's common stand, theoretically weaken the U.S. nuclear link (why should the United States provide a nuclear umbrella to protect all NATO members if some free ride and do not pull there share?), and perhaps push other Europeans to follow suit.

It is not a new concept that an Ally may not support a consensus position in practice, and because democratic governments can be voted out, a subsequent government may even appear to hinder implementation of a standing NATO decision. NATO's crisis management role offers a similar problem. That is, all Allies might agree that NATO should intervene with military force in country X, but some Allies might not provide any forces. It has been a long-standing concept of NATO that each member is free to participate as much or as little in NATO operations as that member desires. This flexibility has been a key lubricant to getting beyond what would otherwise become impasses to achieving agreed policy positions and implementing those decisions. It is also inherent in Article 5 of the NATO Treaty that an Ally could agree to a consensus that country Y attacked an Ally, and that NATO should implement Article 5, but then not offer any military forces. It could be the case that none are needed, that the Ally does not have any, as in the case of Iceland, that the Ally needs them at home, or that the Ally is not fully committed to the decision. However, the inaction in the last case is double-edged because it affects Alliance cohesion, and to a certain degree, NATO's power lies in its perceived cohesion. If outsiders do not believe that all NATO Allies would support the NATO words with actions, potential adversaries might seek to exploit the fault lines between Allies. Nevertheless, there is a big difference between not participating and actively undercutting. If an Ally were to consistently undercut consensus positions, the Ally and NATO would both lose credibility, and that Ally would also be reducing its perceived individual benefit of membership. This would be contrary to the individual Ally's long-term interest since Allies have presumably joined NATO to achieve the benefits of common action, achieved through give-and-take discussions.

Finally, it is important to note that the process need not be slow and cumbersome. For example, after the terrorist attack on the United States on September 11, 2001, the NAC called a special session that evening, and on September 12 announced that if the attacks of the previous day were determined to have been directed from abroad, then the attacks would be considered to be covered by Article 5. The United States sidetracked the issue a bit by talking about forming a grand coalition instead of NATO action against terrorism, but by October 2, 2001, the NAC stated that its condition for invoking Article 5 was satisfied, so Article 5 was then operative. On October 4, the NAC announced that it had agreed to adopt eight measures requested by the United States under the auspices of Article 5. These measures were the result of coordination between the United States, its Allies, and NATO staffs. On October 9, the first NATO AWACS (airborne warning and control system) aircraft departed Germany to begin patrolling the skies in the United States, and the NATO Standing Naval Force Mediterranean (STANAV-FORMED) moved into the eastern Mediterranean to display NATO resolve.

Defense Planning

It is hard to overestimate the importance of the Defense (Planning) Committee's work in defense planning in making NATO what it is today. NATO began its annual reviews in 1952. The initial reviews assessed the forces the Alliance had on hand or that Allies had earmarked for the Alliance and established force goals for three years into the future. NATO established a standard planning rhythm of sending detailed questionnaires concerning both military and economic factors of defense to the Allied nations. The nations would respond in the summer and the NATO military authorities and staffs would examine each Ally's responses. The NATO military authorities would also provide an assessment on the Alliance's military posture. The whole packages and recommendations were reviewed up the chain, and then the

NAC ministerial made any required decisions toward year's end. The general steps in the process remain in place today, although NATO has switched to a longer, biannual force planning cycle to allow more time for the various steps.

It is important to understand the formal and informal negotiations behind the whole process. First, there is no point in establishing the overall Alliance defense requirements beyond what the individual Allied nations can afford or are willing to pay for. The resulting gap between supposed requirements and on-hand military capabilities causes problems for NATO. If NATO successfully deters aggression against its members with much lower military capabilities than its supposed requirements, NATO and the requirements process lose credibility with the Alliance's domestic publics. NATO's risk assessment and process for setting the overall defense requirements would appear unrealistic. Consequently, future NATO claims that threats demand an increase in military spending would run the risk of being ignored because the Alliance would appear to be crying wolf (i.e., creating an imaginary threat). A second problem is that some members might provide their force goals, whereas others would not. This imbalance creates friction between the members and tempers the Allies' ability to work together and implement other common goals. A loss of credibility in this way reduces Alliance security because NATO's deterrence is partially based on outsider's perception that the Alliance can and will act coherently if threatened. If outsiders do not believe this to be the case, they might adopt more risky political behavior towards NATO, thinking that NATO would not be able to reach consensus and act cohesively.

The same holds true with respect to giving a nation force goals that it cannot or will not meet. However, NATO force planning can also be used to a nation's political benefit. For example, if a particular government wanted to purchase airplanes or ships in order to stimulate the national economy, keep specific industrial segments working at a higher capacity, or gain political capital in industrial circles, and if the decision to purchase was a politically controversial policy at home, the nation could offer NATO a specific future military capability. NATO could then in turn make that capability one of the nation's force goals. The government could then turn around and sell the spending program domestically as a necessary NATO requirement instead of a political party's unnecessary spending program. The same game can be played in the other direction when, for example, a new party comes to power in a country on a platform calling for reduced defense spending. The new government can ask NATO to reduce certain of its force goals by announcing its intended cuts as part of the on-going or upcoming planning cycle. If NATO eliminates those particular force goals, the government can say building frigate X is a waste of money and not a requirement for NATO or national defense.

While aware of the politics that can occur in the background, NATO military authorities try to determine the correct level of overall Alliance defense requirements and a comprehensive way to use the military capabilities that the various Allies are offering to NATO. Once the NATO military authorities determine what they deem is the best fit of capabilities to requirements, they make recommendations. In addition, the Allied countries pressure each other in various ways because the natural tendency for a country would be to be a *free-rider* and not invest its own money, but still reap the security benefit of being in NATO. Of course, if all Allies tried to do this, NATO would not actually provide any security. Consequently, there are a variety of competing interests and negotiations to keep the overall NATO defense requirements and the individual national force goals at a level that can reasonably be met by each Ally and still afford a general feeling of equity on some level between the Allies. The equity is not that all nations provide an equal number of forces, or even that every infantry battalion have the same combat capabilities. Rather, equity is in the sense of each nation pulling its perceived share of the load based on its economy, its manpower, its military prowess, and its geographic location. Not all of the factors are easily quantifiable, nor is it in the interest of the Alliance to have them so because the lack of total clarity allows the Allies to work out compromises with each other.

Although accepted as common practice today, it was truly amazing that the Allies were sharing such detailed information on their military forces and economies by 1952, given Europe's history. This was especially true when Germany joined the Alliance, but the economic and military weakness of the Western nations, their fear of the Soviet Union, and steady U.S. pressure for European cooperation and self-help contributed to this unprecedented openness. The standardization of the process let both the NATO military authorities and the individual Allies see where the Alliances shortcomings were, a first step for eventual cooperation among Allies in bilateral or in multilateral ways including at the Alliance level. Cooperation also opened the possibility of specialization. If the collective defense was perceived to be credible, Allies could specialize some of their defense spending to fill NATO shortfalls. Instead of creating armies similar to those of their neighbors in order to deter them, Allies could create armies designed to achieve synergy. They no longer had reason to fear their Allied neighbors because they had near total insight into their Allies' military and economic capabilities and plans.

After the Berlin Wall fell, and NATO began increasing its contacts with the militaries of former adversarial states and of neutrals, it became clear that developing something similar to the NATO force planning process for these countries could increase transparency and confidence between NATO and these countries, as well as between the countries themselves. Several of these countries also expressed interest in participating in peace support exercises with NATO, and many joined the Implementation Force (IFOR) and its successor the Stabilization Force (SFOR) that NATO sent under UN auspices to Bosnia-Herzegovina. NATO required planning data, including the manning, equipment, and capabilities of these units, before NATO military authorities could integrate these forces into an exercise or into IFOR/SFOR.

Although it could be done on an ad hoc basis, it was much easier for NATO planners to, at a minimum, have the information provided in NATO formats. From NATO's perspective, a better solution was for NATO to build planning databases for reference during exercise or operational planning. Then, if a country said that it would provide the frigate X, NATO planners would already know its capabilities, including, for example, its communications and radar equipment, whether it had its own helicopters, and what types of weapons it carried. Consequently, they would know how frigate X would communicate with NATO ships, whether its radar might interfere with other radars, and what mission sets it could provide to the exercise or operational task force. NATO created the Planning and Review Process (PARP) within the Partnership for Peace program in December 1994 as an optional program for Partners to provide NATO with planning information, in NATO-standardized formats, on the forces the Partner would be willing to provide to NATO for NATO-led exercises or peace support operations.

Partners were encouraged to share data with their neighbors, and Partners accorded Membership Action Plan (MAP) status provide defense planning information questionnaires to NATO as part of their MAP. NATO does not share its defense plans and defense planning requirements with Partners, although in the course of exercises and operations, Partners see firsthand the capabilities of NATO units. In addition, some NATO members now share their defense questionnaires with the EU, seeing no reason to go to the extra work of providing a separate, smaller response for the EU defense planning process.

Other Factors of Note

The other supporting piece to NATO's ability to plan and conduct missions and exercises alone and in conjunction with Partners is NATO's Standardization Agreements (STANAGs). The STANAGs provide agreed-to, NATO-wide standards across the range of procedures, equipment, and systems. The STANAGs regulate things as varied as radio terminology and the phonetic alphabet ("alpha, bravo, charlie . . ."); grades of diesel fuel and gasoline; standard rifle ammunition requirements (NATO's 5.56 mm round); equipment components; quality control standards; and NATO joint doctrine. Each Ally implements the STANAGs within its national armed forces. For example,

American soldiers and marines talk in terms of *clicks* (kilometers) professionally, even though they live in a nation that measures distances in miles, yards, and feet. In addition, by clearly laying out procedures, doctrine, and equipment standards, STANAGs provide the basic operational and technical knowledge for Partner and other nations to participate in NATO-led exercises and operations. The STANAGs have also become a universal standard for many military operations and technical data beyond NATO. For example, STANAGs eased the integration of the many nations with no direct experience with NATO who joined the United States–led Desert Shield/Storm, and STANAGs contribute to the ease of communication and cooperation between the various national ships participating in the anti-piracy operations near the Horn of Africa.

The combination of common defense planning and STANAGs has also paved the way for Allies to purchase weapons systems from other Allies, common weapons system development and procurement, common training, and in specific cases, multinational manning and operation of aircraft. In the mid-1970s, Belgium, Denmark, the Netherlands, and Norway signed collectively, as the European Participation Group, to purchase U.S. F-16s. The package included industrial offsets, with all four countries producing parts, and the aircraft were assembled in Europe. Turkey later joined the F-16 program, also producing them under license. In addition to the United States and these Allies, Greece, Italy, Poland, and Portugal currently fly F-16s. At the end of the 1960s, Britain, Italy, and West Germany had already decided to go a step deeper and jointly pursue the development and production of a common fighter, the Panavia Tornado, which entered the air forces' of the three countries in different variants by the early 1980s. In the early 1980s, Italy, the United Kingdom, and West Germany established a common Tornado flight training program in the United Kingdom, and a NATO undergraduate pilot training course was instituted in the United States. Italy, the United Kingdom, West Germany, and eventually Spain cooperated again in the development and production of the Eurofighter Typhoon, with deliveries beginning in the early 2000s. The American F-35 Lightening II Joint-Strike Fighter, currently under development, is also the product of international cooperation, with the United Kingdom; Italy and the Netherlands; and Canada, Turkey, Norway, and Denmark participating at different levels. The use of U.S. aircraft facilitates NATO's nuclear weapons sharing program, although the Tornado aircraft, for example, are also capable of delivering U.S. tactical nuclear weapons.

In the late 1970s, the NATO Defense Planning Committee decided to purchase, man, operate, maintain, and base Airborne Early Warning Aircraft. The British provided a national E-3 D AWACS aircraft component, and 12 of the then 15 Allies contributed to the purchase and operation of E-3A AWACS and some support aircraft at the NATO E-3A Component at Geilenkirchen, Germany. The crews, maintenance, and computer software support are all multinationally manned at the NATO E-3A Component. It is the only such organization in the world, where the military crew is composed of airmen from the participating Allied nations, speaking to each other in English. It is the same for the ground crews servicing and maintaining the aircraft and the software teams. The manning is proportional to the percentage that each Ally contributes to the NATO E-3A AWACS Component. The French national E-3F AWACS unit has traditionally coordinated its NATO activities with the NATO AWACS Commander at SHAPE, who has command over the E-3A and E-3D Components. The commanders of the NATO E-3A Component and the NATO Airborne Early Warning and Control Force rotate between German and U.S. generals since they are the biggest contributors. Currently 15 Allies participate in the NATO E-3A Component.

In addition to facilitating common weapons system procurement, the Alliance builds and maintains Alliance common infrastructure projects. Consequently, having a NATO airfield or headquarters on a country's territory can provide economic benefits to the host country in terms of major construction and infrastructure maintenance. There are short-term job opportunities during construction and long-term job opportunities supporting the base and its personnel. Finally, there are also the trickle-down effects of base personnel seeking housing, entertainment, and shopping in the area.

Lastly, the governments and personnel from the NATO nations seem to hold a general belief that when people from different countries must work together in international staffs, their daily interactions promote cooperation, understanding, and friendships.

NATO fosters the development of person-to-person ties between the citizens of its members. Some would argue, with some tongue in cheek, that for most of NATO's history, the intensive planning and meetings at NATO Headquarters and the various integrated military commands were just an excuse to bring the diplomats, and more important, the military members from the Allied countries (from privates to generals and admirals) together for coffee and an occasional stronger drink. It is there that they talk about how they see the world, where they should take their cars for repairs, problems with their children in schools, and so forth. This continuous contact between military and civilian personnel, often including their families, creates the glue that binds the Allies together as well as the lubrication that allows them all to generally get along, overcome difficulties, and work together to solve problems, whether it is planning a staff holiday party, resolving a contentious silence procedure, or planning a combat operation in Afghanistan.

Although this chapter examines a variety of issues, readers using the front-to-back method should be continuing to deepen their understanding of what NATO is by tying the descriptions provided in the first chapter with the origins of NATO contained in the second to the descriptions of how NATO works provided in this chapter. We now move on to how all these factors came together in the creation of NATO's first Strategic Concept.

CHAPTER 4

The First Two Strategic Concepts: Atomic War

The Washington Treaty was written in broad terms. It outlined the general purpose of NATO and laid its foundation, but the treaty did not provide anything along the lines of a strategy or guidance for drafting operational plans for the collective defense of its members. For example, the treaty does not state against whom or what the Allies are collectively defending. Consequently, NATO created the Strategic Concept to lay out its view of the world and the threats it faced as a basis for developing its high-level strategy and to provide objectives and guidance to its military organizations to develop war plans. In autumn 2010, NATO is currently operating under its sixth Strategic Concept and laying the groundwork for the developing the seventh. (See the Timeline of NATO Strategic Concepts in Appendix I.) This chapter begins the examination of the series of strategic concepts as documentation of the evolution of NATO's thinking about the threats that it faced. In short, the strategic concepts periodically update NATO's answer to the question of *why* NATO. In addition, the chapters look at how NATO decided to counter the threats articulated in the high-level strategy, objectives, and guidance it gives to its military organizations.

Questions for Consideration

- Would you expect there to be differences of opinion on the threats facing NATO?
  - Among Allies?
  - Between Allied civilians and Allied military officers?
- What might be some factors that would lead to such differences?
- Is war, or its outcome, predictable?

The First Strategic Concept (DC 6/1, December 1949)

The process for the first Strategic Concept began on October 6, 1949, when the Military Committee tasked the Standing Group in M.C. 2/1 to prepare "an overall defensive concept for the North Atlantic Treaty area." The Standing Group (of the Military Committee) was a standing committee of military representatives from France, the United Kingdom, and the United States, stationed in Washington DC. The Standing Group had oversight for military planning when the Military Committee was not in session. Other Allies could accredit military representatives with the Standing Group but these officers served more in an observer than participant level. The Standing Group provided the inner core of the Alliance's military expertise. The Standing Group responded to M.C. 2/1 with NATO's first draft version of the Strategic Concept (MC 3) to the Military Committee on October 19, 1949: "The aim of this concept is to ensure unity of thought and purpose insofar as the objectives of the defense of the North Atlantic Treaty area are concerned. It has been drawn up in broad terms which take into account both political and strategic considerations."

The Strategic Concept was prepared prior to the establishment of the Supreme Allied Commander Europe (SACEUR) and Supreme Allied Commander Atlantic (SACLANT) integrated military command structures, so the Standing Group's draft was aimed for eventual delivery to two different audiences. The first audience was up the chain of command. The draft would provide high-level guidance for the Military Committee to provide to the Defense Committee and eventually to the North Atlantic Council (NAC) for political approval. The second audience was down the chain of command. The Standing Group would provide the Strategic Concept and "more detailed strategic guidance of a purely military nature" to the five Regional Planning Groups (North Atlantic Ocean, Canada–United States, Western Europe, Northern Europe, and Southern Europe/Western Mediterranean) then in place.

The development of the first Strategic Concept is particularly instructive because it set several markers for later procedures. It captures the very first thoughts on how the military envisioned the collective defense of NATO as well as the early political maneuverings to reach an acceptable final product. It also reveals the interactions between the Standing Group and the Military Committee, as well as between the military and civilian authorities. For example, the Standing Group construct gave the United States, United Kingdom, and France much more input into the military planning process than the other Allies had; however, they were the three biggest military powers and had special victory power responsibilities for Berlin, Germany, and Austria. Practically speaking, NATO could not do anything militarily without their buy-in, and although U.S. atomic bombs would be used to defend NATO, the bombs would remain under U.S. control.

In addition, the process in general could be portrayed as a military usurpation of power since the Strategic Concept was looking at much more than purely military planning issues. The military's claim to be taking political and strategic considerations into account would have been seen as beyond the military's purview had it been done in the individual national political processes. However, the Allies were willing to allow this within NATO as an expediency to fill a void since NATO did not start out with a permanent civilian staff bureaucracy or permanent committees. Nevertheless, leaving the drafting process in the hands of military officers let the military officers set the starting point for later discussions among NATO's civilian political leadership firmly within the militaries' presumed institutional desires to create as big, modern, and well-equipped armies as possible.

The Standing Group's draft Strategic Concept (MC 3) was short, only seven pages, and straightforward. The assumption was that NATO was defensive in nature and would be responding militarily to an enemy invasion along several fronts. The successful deterrence and defense of NATO rested on the prompt use of American atomic bombs. Interestingly, neither the drafts nor the final approved Strategic Concept actually identified the enemy.

MC 3's Preamble started with the wide-ranging statement that "the attainment of the objectives of the North Atlantic Treaty requires the integration by the parties to the Treaty of those political, economic, and psychological, as well as purely military means, which are essential to the defense of the North Atlantic area." The Strategic Concept was to serve as the initial basis of coordination for NATO's common defense. As such, "the objective is adequate military strength accompanied by economy of effort, resources and manpower. It is desirable that each nation be capable of providing for its own defense to the maximum extent possible consistent with a collective strategic plan." The Standing Committee was not developing an integrated plan as much as a coordinated plan. The Preamble concluded with the comment that "the measures required to implement this concept will require constant review." This constant review evolved into the NATO defense planning process as described in the previous chapter, in which both overall requirements as well as individual countries' abilities to meet them are periodically reviewed.

MC 3 also provided *defense principles* as basic guidance for the five regional planning groups. Taken together, the principles placed the responsibility on the individual Allies to create a series of ad hoc arrangements based on geography and capabilities to supplement self-help instead of an integrated NATO strategic plan performing this function. In addition, MC 3 stated that each member should seek comparative advantage, specialize, and prioritize economic over military strength. National contributions were to be individually tailored to each nation's "situation, responsibilities and resources." Further-more, "The military strength of the participating nations should be developed without endangering economic recovery and the attainment of economic stability, which constitute an essential element of their security." The draft MC 3 also provided two major objectives. The first was "to coordinate, in time of peace, our military and economic strength with a view to creating a powerful deterrent." The second was "to develop plans, for use in the event of war, which will provide for the combined employment of military forces."

MC 3 also provided a series of *basic undertakings*, which have the appear-ance of military objectives for war planning. The Standing Group identi-fied the first undertaking as: "Insure the ability to deliver the atomic bomb promptly. This is primarily a U.S. responsibility assisted as practicable by other nations." The Standing Group was straightforward in its assessment that the defense of NATO rested primarily on the United States' atomic bombs. The second undertaking was: "Arrest and counter as soon as practica-ble the enemy offensives against North Atlantic Treaty powers by all means available, including air, naval, land and psychological operations." There was no intent to trade territory for time, and "all means available" would seem to reinforce the inclusion of atomic weapons. Furthermore, MC 3's second undertaking clearly stated, "the hard core of ground power in being will come from the European nations aided by other nations as they can mobilize." The continental Europeans would have to maintain adequate standing ground forces to handle initial enemy offensives, while the United States, Canada, and the United Kingdom were permitted the luxury of mobilization, perhaps because of the anticipated early use of atomic weapons.

The third undertaking was: "Neutralize as soon as practicable enemy air operations." This direction was given with the understanding that "European nations should provide the bulk of the tactical air support and air defense in being, other nations aiding as they can mobilize." The fourth undertaking was: "Secure and control sea and air lines of communication, and ports and harbors, essential to the implementation of common defense plans." However, primary responsibility was assigned to the United States and United Kingdom for this task, with the other nations securing their harbor defenses and coastal sea-lanes, and assisting the United States and United Kingdom as possible. The fifth undertaking was: "Secure, maintain and defend such main support areas, air bases, naval bases and other facilities as are essential to the successful accomplishment of the basic undertaking," i.e., prompt atomic bombing. The nations on whose territory the bases and facilities rested were charged with ful-filling the tasks of securing, maintaining, and defending the bases. The sixth, and last, undertaking was: "Mobilize and expand the overall power of the Al-lied nations in accordance with their planned contribution to later offensive operations designed to maintain security of the North Atlantic Treaty area."

With foresight, MC 3 also recognized and described several *cooperative measures* that would have to be agreed to before collective war plans could be successfully implemented, or perhaps even developed. *Standardization* and *cooperation* were the buzzwords. Standardization, "insofar as practicable," was recommended with respect to "military doctrines and procedures," "maintenance, repair and service facilities," and "military material and equipment for use in operations." Cooperation was recommended "in the construction, maintenance, and operation of military installations of mutual concern," "in arranging for military operating rights, in peacetime, in furtherance of common defense requirements," and "insofar as practicable and within the legal limitations and administrative restrictions of each country, in research and development of new weapons and in the development of new methods of warfare." The Standing Group also recommended combined training exercises, and the "compilation and exchange of intelligence information and data peculiar to the conduct of contemplated Atlantic Treaty organization defense planning and operations resulting therefrom [sic]." Over time, NATO has increased its standardization and cooperation in all of these areas.

The military representatives of the nations not in the Standing Group were not in total agreement with MC 3. It went through two further versions within the Military Committee before being submitted to the Defense Committee. For example, the other Allies wanted explicit recognition that "each nation's contributions should be in proportion to" considerations of its geographic position, industrial capacity, population, and military capabilities. Bigger, more economically advanced nations were to shoulder more of the burden. It was also clarified that each nation was to develop its military strength for the two not quite identical purposes of providing for its own defense as well as participating in the common defense. The significance of economic recovery and stability were downgraded. Whereas MC 3 stated that developing military strength should not *endanger* economic recovery and achieving economic stability, which formed an "essential element" of security, the later versions stated that "the participating nations should bear in mind that economic recovery and the attainment of economic stability constitute important elements of their security." With *important* being less critical than *essential*, the Military Committee changed to the position that military demands could potentially trump economic matters. European Allies also succeeded in tempering the references to European nations providing the "hard core of ground forces" and the "bulk of the tactical air support and air defense." The later versions stated that the Europeans would only *initially* bear these burdens and removed references to the non-European nations' mobilizations. Instead of mobilizations, the non-Europeans were now to "give aid with the least possible delay and in accordance with over-all plans." These last changes implied a lightening of the European load made possible by a speedier appearance of non-European nations' forces.

On November 29, 1949, the final Military Committee version was submitted to the Defense Committee, where it appeared as DC 6, still with the title, "The Strategic Concept for the Defense of the North Atlantic Area." At the Defense Committee meeting on December 1, 1949, the Danish Minister of Defense raised a concern about the explicit linkage of the atomic bomb to the defense of NATO. After some discussion, the Defense Committee agreed to new wording: "Insure the ability to carry out strategic bombing promptly by all means possible with all types of weapons, without exception. This is primarily a U.S. responsibility assisted as practicable by other nations." The successful defense of NATO rested on the American atomic bombs, but this was politically too sensitive to explicitly spell out in the NAC-approved Strategic Concept, even though it was classified. The Defense Committee approved the Strategic Concept on December 1, 1949 (DC 6/1), and the North Atlantic Council foreign ministers approved it on January 6, 1950.

As the Military Committee finalized and sent the Strategic Concept to the Defense Committee at its second meeting on November 29, 1949, it concurrently tasked the Standing Group to develop and provide more detailed and classified Strategic Guidance for North Atlantic Regional Planning to the Regional Planning Groups. The Standing Group developed the Strategic Guidance with military representatives accredited to the Standing Group and sent the final version to the Regional Planning Groups on January 6, 1950 as SG 13/16. This demonstrates the latitude afforded the Standing Group since it sent the Strategic Guidance to the regional planning groups before the Military Committee saw or approved it.

The Strategic Guidance explicitly stated that the planning was for a war initiated by the Soviet Union. The Strategic Guidance and its Intelligence Annex warrant study since the assumptions contained in them guided NATO thinking about the Soviet Union for decades. Their common foundation was the premise that Moscow's goal was to conquer and rule the world. The Strategic Guidance stated that "precise Soviet intentions are not known and cannot be predicted with reliable accuracy. For military planning purposes, however, it is essential to consider maximum intentions and capabilities. The ultimate objective of Soviet policy is the establishment of Communist regimes, directed from Moscow, throughout the world."

The Intelligence Annex stated that whereas the Western countries demobilized after World War II, the Soviet Union reorganized its military forces and kept a standing "powerful military machine," "controlled by a unified command and a single staff system." The Soviet Union's combat power resided primarily in its army and the supporting tactical air forces, but the Soviet Union was increasing its submarine force and long-range air forces. NATO was not to expect warning before an attack, and although the Soviet Union had economic weaknesses, "it would be dangerous to count on a rapid diminution of the Soviet war effort on purely economic grounds." The West also was not to count on potential Soviet "moral failure."

NATO was not just anticipating a war in Europe, but a world war. Assumptions included Soviet air attacks on the NATO Allies in Europe and in the United States, air and naval attacks on the sea lines of communication, blockades of NATO ports, worldwide Soviet-initiated sabotage and subversive activities, and potential atomic weapon use "by either side." The assumptions also provided line-ups of presumed Soviet allies (Eastern European countries, China, Outer Mongolia, and North Korea), likely NATO supporters (Australia, New Zealand, South Africa, Ceylon, and Jordan), as well as neutrals and the likelihood of their becoming NATO supporters. For example, it was assumed that Latin American countries, Greece, Turkey, Iran, Japan, and the Philippines would quickly swing to the NATO camp. India and Pakistan were assessed to likely remain friendly towards NATO but neutral. West Germany, Austria, Iraq, South Korea, and French Indochina were in a special category since they were likely to be sympathetic to NATO, but unlikely to be able to help since "their strategic or political situation will be precarious," that is, they would likely also be targets of Soviet or Soviet-inspired aggression. The Arab world was believed to be willing to provide assistance, short of actual military participation, to NATO. It was assumed that the then traditional European neutrals of Switzerland, Sweden, Spain, and Ireland, as well as Afghanistan, would resist any Soviet attacks on their territories. Israel was assessed similarly, although with the additional assumption that it "may consent under pressure to assist the Allies." Yugoslavia was the only wild card. It was "impossible" to predict its alignment in case of war, although it was thought that the Soviet Army would have to invade before it could use Yugoslav territory for launching further operations. This of course contradicted the view of monolithic, Moscow-directed communism.

It is worth noting that these assumptions were sent to the Regional Planning Groups in January 1950, that is, after China had been "lost," but before the Korean War and the French debacle at Dien Bien Phu. From this point of view, the categorization of South Korea and French Indochina as sympathetic to NATO, but unlikely to be able to help was insightful, but also problematic since it was not clear why the Soviet Union and its allies, the expansionist China and North Korea, would not start the potential world war in Asia. In addition, the Standing Group's inclusion of NATO members' "overseas possessions" in the alignment of countries against the Soviet Union as planning assumptions stands in contrast to Article 6's precise geographic limits to the North Atlantic area and the exclusion of members' colonies. Furthermore, the military's discussion of the wartime alignment of countries like Japan, China, North and South Korea, Ceylon, Afghanistan, Siam, and Indonesia would seem superfluous unless NATO were considering either out-of-area operations or a super wartime alliance.

The expectation of a world war did not exactly match NATO's foundational premise that Western Europe would be the key battleground in the global struggle between the Soviet Union and the West. The Strategic Guidance offered convoluted logic in an effort to unite these two views. On the one hand, NATO regional planners were to craft their plans on the assumption "that the USSR will attempt to defeat the forces of the North Atlantic Treaty nations and reach the Atlantic Seaboard, the Mediterranean and the Middle East." On the other hand, the Intelligence Annex provided a slightly different narrative of the presumed Soviet perspective. The Soviet Union wanted world domination, so it should logically attack the United States; however, such an attack would be foolhardy unless the Soviets had enough weapons of mass destruction to achieve the task. Consequently, it was believed that the Soviets would opt for a phased approach. First, the Soviet Union would dominate Europe, Asia, and the United Kingdom. Then the Soviet Union would consolidate its position militarily and integrate the economic and resource base of Eurasia. Then, from this "impregnable position," the Soviet Union could attack North America with "military forces." Latin America and any other remaining areas of the world would then presumably fall in line.

This narrative contained several inconsistencies. For example, if the Soviet Union went to war to secure the economic and resource base of Western Europe, it would most likely destroy its objective instead of securing it. It also did not explain why the Soviets would see Europe as their first objective. Attacking U.S. forces in Europe (which some argue served primarily as a trip-wire) would bring the United States with its atomic weapons into the war in the beginning, eliminating the possibility of a two-tiered approach. Furthermore, Eurasia might seem "impregnable" to some army officers, but certainly not to air force, navy, or marine officers. Moreover, the narrative ultimately rested on the assumption that the Soviet Union would somehow capitalize on its obvious weaknesses to achieve victory in Asia and Europe and against the United Kingdom and United States. The Intelligence Annex had already highlighted Soviet military weaknesses, primarily in the areas of its surface fleet; its strategic mobility, which was based almost entirely on railroads; and its inexperienced long-range aviation forces. It also projected that Soviet shortages in high-octane fuel, electronics systems, and fire-control systems would continue. These weaknesses would severely limit the Soviet's ability to launch and sustain the presumed strategic offensive.

Nevertheless, the intelligence analysis quickly came to the conclusion that the war could be boiled down to the Soviet's overwhelming ground offensive, supported by tactical aviation versus the West's strategic (including atomic) bombing counteroffensive. Over the long term, the West's industrial base and its naval strength would more than compensate for its reliance on sea lines of communications. Consequently, the Soviets would have to get control of or neutralize Western strategic airbases by using "political action or actual warfare." "However, they would realize that the Western Powers would not permit significant areas to be overrun singly but, regarding the conflict as world-wide, would probably attack the Soviet Union from wherever possible. The Soviet's leaders therefore would probably decide to launch full-scale offensives in a number of areas concurrently."

Consequently, the Standing Group's scenario developed an avalanche of spiraling worst cases to come to the opinion that if the Soviet Union were to decide to go to war, it would not after all be a sequenced effort, but a multi-front, global war. The Intelligence Annex finally supposed that "the Soviet plan would probably include the following operations:

a. 1. Subversive activity and sabotage against Allied interests in all parts of the world.
   2. A sea and air offensive against Allied sea communications.
   3. A campaign against Western Europe, an objective which would appear to be the easiest to attain.
   4. An aerial bombardment against the British Isles.
   5. Campaigns against the Near and Middle East.
   6. A campaign against Yugoslavia and Italy.
   7. Attacks against key installations in Canada, the United States and Alaska.
   8. Campaigns with limited objectives in the Far East.

b. If essential to Soviet plans, a campaign against Scandinavia.
c. If possible, a campaign to overrun the Iberian Peninsula, and secure the Straits of Gibraltar.
d. Air attacks against Allied bases."

In fact, the Intelligence Annex stated: "It is believed that the Soviet Union, subject to economic calculations and limitations and to the morale of its population, would have sufficient armed forces to undertake all the campaigns listed above and still have adequate reserves." Nevertheless, since it was a NATO assessment after all, the annex continued: "It is probable, however, that the bulk of the Soviet ground forces immediately available would be launched at Western Europe." The Soviet Union would be able to do this, however, partly because the "Chinese Communist forces may undertake campaigns against neighbouring countries in South East Asia."

The Standing Group provided the Strategic Guidance to the Military Committee on March 3, 1950, as MC 14, Strategic Guidance for North Atlantic Regional Planning, and the Military Committee approved the document at its third meeting on March 28, 1950. The Strategic Guidance stated that since the end of the Second World War, Allied military power had atrophied, while "the USSR has maintained, if not increased, her technical, military, and economic capabilities." NATO would have to walk a tightrope between the number of forces required and what the NATO nations could actually provide, and "special emphasis must be laid on the necessity for developing methods to compensate for numerical inferiority, " which was another veiled reference to the importance of the atomic bomb in NATO planning. The Strategic Guidance required two levels of plans. Short-term plans would be reviewed annually, with the first review set for September 1, 1950. The Strategic Guidance was primarily aimed at the medium-term plans, with a planning date of July 1, 1954. This would give the Allies time to build up their military capabilities without overstretching their economies. The regional medium-term plans were to provide by February 1950 target requirements for the buildups to achieve by the summer of 1954. The document contained specific sections for the individual Regional Planning Groups.

The Strategic Guidance also contained a compilation of NATO's defense policies and principles. It acknowledged that NATO forces would be outnumbered; however, NATO would counter this through a combination of maintaining its technical edge, training, coordination, standardization, and sharing "planning, intelligence, and technical information." It also stated the rather obvious policy that if war occurred, "special emphasis must be placed on the defense of Europe, since its loss might well be fatal to the defense of the North Atlantic territories as a whole." The document also noted, rather strangely, that the regional planning groups were to draft plans to achieve Allied war objectives that were not yet decided by the NATO nations, except for the obvious goal of "defeating," without defining the term, the Soviets as soon as possible. As far as actual regional plans, the various groups were instructed to defend their regions, giving a special emphasis to items required for counteroffensive operations and air offensive operations. Interregional coordination was stressed, as were the sea lines of communication, including convoys and shipping requirements. The regional groups were also specifically instructed to plan guerrilla operations in the enemy's rear areas and to coordinate psychological operations against the Soviet Union and its satellites.

The Regional Planning Groups developed initial plans and requirements and forwarded them to the Standing Group, which combined them into a consolidated NATO Medium Term Defense Plan. The Standing Group provided this to the Military Committee, which approved the 1954 Defense Plan and submitted it to the Defense Committee, where it was approved as DC 13 on April 1, 1950, just a few days short of the first anniversary of the signing of the Washington Treaty. DC 13 incorporated DC 6/1, NATO's Strategic Concept, MC 14's Strategic Guidance, and the Regional Planning Groups' inputs into a single document, setting the initial military requirements NATO wanted in place by July 1, 1954.

DC 13 produced some nuances different from the Standing Group's threat assessment in its planning guidance. There were differences in how the military officers in the Standing Group and their superiors saw the world. DC 13 stood in contrast to MC 14's formulation that the Soviet Union could simultaneously begin attacks in Europe and Asia, and against the United Kingdom while the Soviets were building up a nuclear weapons stockpiles for eventual action against the continental United States. Whereas the Strategic Guidance (MC 14) raised the specter of a surprise Soviet attack, DC 13 stated: "It is improbable that the Soviets would deliberately venture any actions which would involve them in open war" until they believed that they have adequate atomic and conventional superiorities over the NATO nations to win. DC 13 also placed more emphasis on ideology, psychological operations, and morale. It was not necessarily all about military forces:

> The Soviet Union may be expected to further its political aims by all of the measures implied in the term "cold war," i.e., threat of military aggression, political and economic warfare, propaganda, subversion, sabotage, and other clandestine activities. It may be expected that these methods will be developed to a degree without precedent in history. They particularly belong to a conflict which is envisaged by the Soviet Union as a revolution in which the communist movement, an international political movement with a long tradition of subversion and clandestine resistance to authority, will fundamentally be engaged.

In fact, Western governments had to pay particular attention to the possibility that the Soviet satellite states would try to enlist expatriates in the West to act as spies, saboteurs, or propagandists. The insidious threat of the "fifth column," members of the communist parties in the West, was even more important. The fifth column could be expected to deliver propaganda, create strikes and riots, assassinate leaders, spy, conduct sabotage, conduct paramilitary operations, seize specific points, and coordinate their special operations with Soviet airborne or other forces.

On the other hand, nationalists in the Soviet Union's satellite states might be exploitable over the long term to conduct sabotage and guerrilla operations in the Soviet rear, but would need support and guidance from NATO to be truly effective. DC 13 also opened up the possibility of exploiting nationalist elements in the Soviet Union, as well as developing propaganda activities in peacetime to convince the Soviet population that NATO military action would be targeted against the totalitarian system and not against the people, in order to lower morale within the Soviet Army during war.

The DC 13 sections on the Soviet economy provided more details on major problems in Soviet industry, strategic resources, and transportation that would be difficult to overcome for anything more than a short war. Consequently, NATO's analysis was that the Soviets could only conduct a short war, whereas NATO specifically would want a long war in order to make use of its greater industrial, mobilization, and transport capabilities as well as to have a higher probability of serious resistance developing within the satellite and Soviet populations. However, the paradox within this analysis was that the Soviet Union was unlikely to be able to achieve its presumed war aims in a short war.

The more developed section on Soviet military factors started with the statement that the size and composition of the Soviet military would not change much "during the next few years," although it might improve its weapons or create new ones that could increase its combat power. The satellite armies were all rated poorly, yet credited with being able to make contributions to Soviet combat power by 1954. "The material maintenance and operational efficiency are considered to be relatively low in the Soviet Navy," and with respect to the Soviet air forces, the emphasis was that the trends indicated that they would get better equipment and training. Consequently, whereas MC 14 with its worst-case perspective made Soviet victory, and therefore, war, appear possible, DC 13 stated, "a major military action in 1954 against the NATO countries would entail considerable risk."

Questions for Consideration

- Why do you suppose the NATO military authorities were so focused on the worst case?
- Why do you think the NATO military and civilian leaders left contradictions in the documents?
- Who do you think was more correct in their assessments—the NATO military authorities or the civilian officials?
- Based on these documents, do you think that war was likely when NATO wrote them in the spring of 1950?
- Was the Soviet Union in a position to actually attack and win in 1950?
- What about in 1954, NATO's projected date to implement its plans?
- Why didn't the United States use nuclear weapons in the Korean War?

  - Why didn't the Soviet Union, the People's Republic of China, or North Korea seem concerned that the United States might use nuclear weapons?

With respect to defense planning, DC 13 remained true to the general gist of its guiding documents. NATO's defense, and therefore, deterrence, against a Soviet-initiated world war was the initial use of nuclear weapons, backed over the long term by the NATO nations' ability to mobilize their superior economies. "The overall strategic aim of the North Atlantic Treaty Powers, should [they] be drawn into war, is, in cooperation with their Allies to destroy by a strategic offensive in Western Eurasia the will and capabilities of the USSR and her satellites to wage war. In the Far East the strategic policy will be defensive."

However, DC 13 introduced a deeper level of analysis and planning. The plan outlined a four-phase concept of operations, with DC 13 actually only covering Phase 1, the period starting with the initial Soviet attack through whenever NATO managed to halt ("stabilize") the Soviet offensive. The key component of Phase 1 was the Allied air offensive with nuclear and conventional weapons. Phase 2 was the period between the stabilization of the Soviet offensive through the beginning of NATO major offensive operations. Phase 3 was "Allied initiation of major offensive operations until Soviet capitulation is obtained." Phase 4 was "Final achievement of Allied War Objectives."

The overall strategic plan was remarkable on several accounts. NATO, in peacetime, determined that the European theater would take precedence over Asia in the potential world war. On the one hand, this eliminated the need for a wartime conference similar to the Arcadia Conference (December 1941–January 1942), in which Franklin D. Roosevelt and Winston Churchill agreed to the "Europe First" strategy in World War II. On the other hand, it seems strange that the NATO nations, which in the Washington Treaty geographically limited the treaty's applicability, appeared to agree that NATO (i.e., the organization and all Allies, not just *some* NATO Allies) would be involved in a Far Eastern theater of operations. In addition, the NATO Treaty Powers appeared to anticipate alliances and cooperation with other nations in the great offensive. The Northern European Region's plan, for example, pointed out the importance of Sweden and the desirability of having Sweden's full cooperation for the region's defense, even if it did not eventually join NATO,. Also since Nazi Germany had been unable to destroy "the will and capabilities" of the Soviet Union despite reaching Leningrad, the outskirts of Moscow, and Stalingrad, the NATO offensive could reasonably be assumed to have strategic objectives as distant as the Urals, the presumed easternmost portion of Western Eurasia, behind which lay much of the Soviet industrial base.

Furthermore, NATO's strategic air offensive with nuclear weapons in Phase 1 was not seen as sufficient to compel victory. The great, primarily ground, counteroffensive was the harbinger of final victory. Politically, one might argue that this was necessary to keep all the NATO nations involved and spending enough on defense to field respectable conventional forces. This remains a central tenet for NATO defense planning. Militarily, one might question the need for atomic war, or at least the practical and physiological ramifications of the affects of atomic war on the great ground offensive. It also indicated a bias within NATO's military representatives for conventional, ground operations. Finally, it is noteworthy that Soviet capitulation (Phase 3) was not synonymous with final achievement of the Allied war objectives (Phase 4).

NATO faced a strategic dilemma. If its defense truly rested on American atomic bombs and airpower, there would be no compelling reason for the other NATO Allies to invest heavily in military capabilities. Even if the Soviets launched a high-powered military offensive in 1954 or later, Soviet tanks could not attack American atomic bombers until the tanks occupied the bombers' airfields, but American bombers could bomb Soviet tanks on the North German Plain or in factories in the Soviet Union. The Soviet tanks would never get to U.S. bases in the United Kingdom, United States, or North Africa, and would take days or weeks just to drive to U.S. bases on the periphery of Europe. However, the United States' original demand was that European nations contribute to their own defense. The United States was not interested in totally underwriting the worldwide containment of communism and still had troops stationed in Europe and Asia. NATO politically needed not only a credible justification for a conventional defense of Europe, but also a credible belief that the Soviets placed immense importance on conquering Western Europe. Consequently, the NATO military authorities' worst-case planning in MC 14, with the assumption of simultaneous attacks in Europe, Asia, and the United Kingdom, required modification. NATO needed the vaunted "fifth column" to put at least some American air bases at risk. Furthermore, the Soviets would be attributed the capability to build a large intercontinental bomber force as well as a large and competent strategic air defense force. For example, DC 13 stated: "The increase in the Soviet long-range air capabilities by 1954 against the NATO regions diminishes neither the vital importance of Western Europe to Soviet aims nor the threat of attack to this area."

The NATO military planners worst-case planning presented a Soviet Union that wanted to attack, conquer, and subjugate Western Europe as its first priority—regardless of the facts or the logic of arguments to the contrary. The planning scenario did not allow simple weapons of mass destruction exchanges between the United States and the USSR. The Soviet Army would attack, and West Germany, Denmark, the Benelux (Belgium, the Netherlands, and Luxembourg), and France would, therefore, have to be held not only in order to protect these territories, but to keep the flanks from falling and Europe from collapsing, as well as to protect the United Kingdom and to provide a base from which the counteroffensive would start. The military forces in Western Europe would throw everything into the fight in order to defend their territory, and blunt, slow, or stop the Soviet offensive, so that reinforcements from the North American Allies could arrive for the grand counteroffensive behind the strategic air offensive. This apparent contradiction between a reliance on a nuclear defense and the need for large defense spending on conventional forces remains an inherent source of tension within NATO.

At the same time, the military of each Ally would presumably be institutionally motivated to create large military forces. DC 13 provided an amalgamated list of all the regions' requirements to meet the defense plan for 1954. With respect to naval forces, the planners required 951 major surface combatants; 12 fleet aircraft carriers; 19 escort aircraft carriers; 107 submarines; 2,382 carrier aircraft; and 882 shore-based aircraft; as well as additional ships. Required land forces came to over 71 infantry divisions, just short of 19 armored divisions, and one-third of an airborne division. The plan required 8,004 interceptor, fighter, light bomber, and reconnaissance aircraft, as well as 672 cargo aircraft. Heavy bombers (i.e., those used for strategic conventional and atomic bomb delivery) were not included in the total NATO requirements since this was almost exclusively a U.S. function. By way of comparison, the U.S. Air Force had approximately 2,000 fighter, interceptor, attack, and reconnaissance aircraft and approximately 2,400 cargo aircraft in fiscal year 1950. By fiscal year 1954, the USAF had approximately 6,000 fighter, interceptor, attack, and reconnaissance aircraft and approximately 3,600 cargo aircraft; however, it was largely the Korean War that drove these increases. The approximate number of U.S. Air Force bombers went from 800 to 1,500 over the same period.

The North Korean invasion of South Korea in June 1950 caused considerable consternation within NATO. After all, DC 13 stated that the Soviets might launch limited campaigns in the Far East simultaneously with major campaigns in Europe. That North Korea attacked without Soviet forces could only be to the Soviet Union's benefit since it could retain even larger reserves. The whole situation could have been read as evidence that DC 13's Estimate of Enemy Capabilities and Possible Courses of Action was very accurate indeed. However, the implication of such a conclusion would be that Western Europe, the Soviet's primary campaign objective, was next. Several Allies, especially the United States, wanted to speed up the creation and deployment of NATO forces, while others maintained that their economies could not support any acceleration. This eventually made the idea of rearming West Germany to provide manpower for the Alliance more palpable. The Standing Group also entered exploratory planning liaisons with Greece and Turkey to strengthen NATO's southern flank. In addition, the United States led and other Allies participated in the UN force repelling the North Korean invasion, drawing off forces that potentially would have defended or reinforced the defense of Europe. The Soviet Union, however, did not attack Western Europe.

Although it was remarkable that NATO had gone from the basic treaty to DC 13 within the course of a year, the Medium Term Defense Plan was more of an exercise in trying to set and justify force goals for the nations to meet than an actual plan. The organizational structure based on the Regional

Planning Groups was conceptually vague. There was no clear chain of command within the regions, between the regions, or above the regions. The Standing Group and the Military Committee, operating by consensus, were adequate to request, draft, and approve studies and amorphous plans, but they could not substitute for the clear military lines of command necessary in wartime.

Discussions in the summer and fall of 1950 led the NAC to create a centralized NATO military command structure. On December 19, 1950, General Dwight Eisenhower became the first SACEUR in charge of Allied Command Europe (ACE). On December 20, 1950, the Western European Union (WEU) decided to merge its existing military organization into the new NATO command structures being developed by General Eisenhower and his fledgling headquarters, Supreme Headquarters Allied Powers Europe (SHAPE). On April 2, 1951, SHAPE was officially declared operational, and the three European Regional Planning Groups were disbanded. On June 19, 1951, the NATO members signed the NATO Status of Forces Agreement regulating the status of Allied military forces on each other's territories, and on September 20, the Allies signed a similar document regulating the status of civilians serving in NATO staffs as well as those representing their nations at NATO institutions. In January 1952, Vice Admiral Lynde McCormick became the first SACLANT in command of Allied Command Atlantic (ACLANT). ACLANT subsumed the duties of the North Atlantic Ocean Regional Planning Group, leaving only the Canada–United States Regional Planning Group in existence. In February 1952, Admiral Sir Arthur John Power became the first Commander-in-Chief Channel (CINCHAN), commander of the (English) Channel Command, a third major NATO command. SACEUR, SACLANT, CINCHAN, and the Canada–United States Regional Planning Group were independently subordinated to the Standing Group of the Military Committee and directly to the Military Committee when the Standing Group was disbanded.

In addition to developing internal structures, the NATO members invited Greece and Turkey to accede to the Washington Treaty. In October 1951, the Protocol to the North Atlantic Treaty on the Accession of Greece and Turkey was signed, modifying the NATO Treaty to include Turkey, and on February 18, 1952, Greece and Turkey acceded to the Washington Treaty.

The Second Strategic Concept (MC 3/5, December 1952)

Given the new military structures and members, in 1952 the Standing Group reviewed, updated, and merged NATO's high-level planning documents. It issued a new Strategic Concept (MC 3/5) and new Strategic Guidance (MC 14/1), which were approved by the Military Committee and NAC in turn in December 1952, as the Defense Committee had been absorbed into the NAC. MC 3/5 updated DC 6/1 to reflect the new command structures. Both the previous Strategic Guidance (MC 14) and Medium Term Plan (DC 13) were merged into MC 14/1. MC 14/1 pushed the planning date back two years to 1956, updated the intelligence estimate, and incorporated NATO's expanded defense obligations with Greece's and Turkey's memberships.

In MC 14/1, the NATO military authorities still saw the Soviet Union as starting a world war with Western Europe as its most important objective. NATO would still be defensive in the Far East, but MC 14/1 also forecasted the development of a NATO-like organization in the Middle East that would join with NATO against the Soviet Union. Yugoslavia was portrayed as much more likely to swing to the NATO camp, even if not attacked by the Soviet Union. "Viet Minh Forces," which were battling the French for independence in French Indochina, were added to the Soviet Bloc's scorecard. Japan, Nationalist China, and West Germany were listed under "Western Powers," which also included Australia, Latin America, Ceylon, New Zealand, and South Africa in addition to the NATO members.

Although written primarily to consolidate and update the previous guidance to conform to the new command structures, there were several new points in NATO's new strategic documents. MC 3/5 opened the possibility that during peacetime, members could step in and implement military preparations for wartime needs in a country that did not want to or could not implement them, provided the involved countries agreed. MC 14/1 specifically tied this to "the obligation to defend German territory which will result from the creation of the European Defense Community." However, the European Defense Community failed to materialize when French public opinion turned against the largely French creation. Nevertheless, NATO's clearly stated new obligation to defend Germany was quite extraordinary given that Germany was not a member of NATO.

Perhaps the biggest change, however, dealt with atomic warfare. MC 14/1 did not see a need to change any planning for the 1953–1954 period, but by the 1954–1956 period there could be significantly more weapons and delivery systems so at that time NATO might be able to get by with less conventional forces. However, since NATO conventional forces were already so short of their force goals in 1952, the members were to continue their buildups with an eye to reexamining their 1956 requirements later. The military authorities were leery of resting too much of the defense on the atomic bomb, and it was important for all members to contribute. In comparison with its predecessor documents, MC 14/1 downplayed for the most part the threat of Soviet airpower at both the tactical and strategic levels. Simultaneously, MC 14/1 highlighted the importance of non-NATO countries in Northern Africa and the Middle East in providing bases for the strategic (atomic) air campaign. Nevertheless, the NATO military authorities were very keen to develop NATO's conventional forces. The general concept was to have "the maximum forces available at the very outset or at least ready to come into action in the first few weeks" and "to insure that forces which are to bear the brunt of the initial attack are preponderantly those which have the *greatest stopping power* (emphasis in original)." The conventional defense was to be forward, and the troops on the presumed front lines were to be well equipped, well trained, and in a high state of readiness. NATO could not rely on mobilizations to provide the forces, training, and equipment. In addition, airpower would be critical to slowing and then stopping the Soviet offensive.

MC 14/1 pointed out another coming change in the nuclear arena. The United States and Canada had previously maintained that they were willing to accept the risks inherent in not trying to provide defenses against attacks that were unlikely to significantly degrade their capacities to wage war. "However, in 1956 the Soviet Union may have a formidable atomic potential against North America, and an adequate defence for this area thus becomes essential in order to permit NATO to accomplish its military objectives."

The threat of Soviet atomic weapons and delivery systems striking the United States and Canada was important for several reasons. For one thing, it provided the U.S. and Canadian governments with a NATO justification for the heavy U.S. and Canadian investment in air defense in the 1950s. NATO still assessed that the Soviets were unlikely to attack Western Europe unless they could counter the threatened retaliatory U.S. strategic (atomic) air campaign. If the Soviets judged that they could inflict serious damage on the United States, this would mitigate their fear of U.S. retaliation because the United States would not want to risk its cities a nuclear exchange. Consequently, in this worst-case scenario, the Soviet Union would be free to attack Western Europe. Therefore, stronger North American air defenses made an attack in Europe less likely. Nevertheless, NATO would logically have to prepare its forces for war on short notice at any time, and MC 14/1 made this a military planning condition.

It was also not clear what the presumed defense of North America could be. U.S. Air Force ideology was still that the bomber would always get through, so air defenses were by definition porous. If the Soviet Union attacked conventionally, NATO would clearly rely on atomic bombs to redress its inferiority in conventional military power. If the Soviets attacked with nuclear weapons, NATO would also rely on atomic bombs. However, as the Soviets developed more nuclear weapons, the United States would have to keep a quantitative or qualitative superiority for this strategy to make any sense. A nuclear arms race was in the making.

Questions for Consideration

- If NATO nations had limited resources, then the presumption would be that spending on conventional forces would decrease in order to fund the nuclear arms race; however, if the United States was the only nation paying for its nuclear weapons, how could the other Allies practically or demonstrably share the burden?
- On the practical side, if NATO's grand plan rested on North America providing not only the strategic air offensive but also the manpower and industrial base of the alliance for the eventual counteroffensive, and the Soviet Union could attack and significantly weaken the United States' ability to provide the strategic air, the manpower, and the resources, could NATO win?
- Do you see a difference between tactical, or non-strategic, nuclear weapons (i.e., those designed to be used on the battlefield) and strategic nuclear weapons (i.e., those to be used deeper in the enemy's territory against command and control facilities, economic targets, and cities)?

NATO continued to look at the issues regarding nuclear warfare, as U.S. and Soviet nuclear weapons stockpiles increased. NATO's members were not going to be able to meet the agreed-to force goals. DC 13 had called for 90 divisions by July 1954 and the requirement was rising as the NATO military authorities placed more emphasis on an in-place, forward defensive strategy. The United States had adopted NSC 162/2 in October 1953, increasing its reliance on nuclear weapons to reduce the defense budget and permit a post-Korea reduction in forces. As foreshadowed in MC 14/1, perhaps the time had come to do the same in NATO and reduce conventional force requirements. In December 1953, the NAC requested the Military Committee to study the gamut of issues. The Military Committee provided its report in November 1954 as MC 48, *Report by the Military Committee to the North Atlantic Council on the Most Effective Pattern of NATO Military Strength for the Next Few Years*.

MC 48 used 1957 as the war start date for the assessment, and was a further evolution of the basic strategic concept and planning guidance process. MC 48, however, did place a new emphasis on nuclear deterrence. NATO "must convince the Soviets that: a. They cannot quickly overrun Europe. b. In the event of aggression they will be subjected immediately to devastating counter-attack employing atomic weapons." The NATO military authorities considered the development of conventional forces a critical part of condition *a*, as if condition *b* did not exist. The NATO military authorities also indicated their intent to expand the range of their atomic weapons by defining "atomic weapons" in a footnote as including atomic as well as thermonuclear weapons "delivered by aircraft, guided missiles, rockets and artillery." The discussion was no longer limited to the United States' strategic air offensive dropping some atomic bombs. This new scenario announced the proliferation of nuclear weapons across the tactical and strategic landscape, used by both NATO and the Soviet Union. However, this new scenario also placed some nuclear weapons in the NATO conventional ground forces. NATO's ground forces were not going to lose their importance in nuclear warfare.

MC 48 examined the issue of air defenses and concluded that counter-air operations (e.g., attacking the enemy's airfields) were the most effective defense. The NATO military authorities then briefly explored the potential parallel to nuclear operations (i.e., the idea of a preventative or preemptive attack as a form of defense) before categorically ruling out a NATO-initiated war in Europe. The Soviets would have to attack first. MC 48 also looked at "the remote possibility" of a Soviet conventional attack without nuclear weapons in order to keep NATO from using its nuclear superiority. However, MC 48 stated that NATO could not stop the Soviets from rapidly conquering Europe without using both strategic and tactical nuclear weapons from the very beginning. Furthermore, MC 48 argued that since the Soviets would clearly see the same outcome, they would also conclude that there was nothing to be gained by not using nuclear weapons in their initial, surprise attack. Consequently, the presumed war would consist of two phases. The first would be largely nuclear, aimed primarily, but not exclusively, at the enemy's atomic capabilities. This phase would presumably be relatively short in duration until one side, the presumed looser, exhausted its stocks of nuclear weapons. The side still in possession of nuclear forces would then initiate the second phase to achieve the final war aims, in which it could still use nuclear weapons, but with a heavier reliance on conventional forces.

Therefore, the military authorities argued that NATO should develop large nuclear weapons stockpiles, as well as conventional forces that could operate in a nuclear environment and use nuclear weapons. In addition, these "forces-in-being," highly trained and ready to go to war at any time, would need to be based in such a way that they could survive enemy nuclear attack, yet still be able to conduct immediate nuclear and conventional operations themselves. The forces would need to be dispersed for survival, but able to be concentrated when necessary for conventional-type operations. NATO was also to invest in intelligence, warning, and communications as well as in establishing a common tactical doctrine to integrate the combined operation of these highly trained, mobile conventional and nuclear forces. The military was responding to its own worst-case formulations without regard to their economic implications.

Finally, the NATO military authorities were clear that "the importance of obtaining a German contribution to these forces cannot be too strongly emphasized." This statement was partially a result of the Allied governments' failure to establish the European Defense Community, but the military authorities went a step further and indicated essentially that the previous planning documents were wrong. There could be no realistic defense of Western Europe without both the German troops and the immediate use of large numbers of nuclear weapons. The implication of this statement was that NATO's decision to greatly expand its reliance on tactical and strategic nuclear weapons would not result in less demand for conventional troops. The Germans were foreseen as additional required forces, not replacements for those already included in the planning force goals.

MC 48 did not present the move towards a deeper reliance on the range of nuclear weapons as a choice. It was simply the way the world was going. NATO had no choice. If deterrence failed, NATO must fight a nuclear war. In order to deter the Soviet Union, NATO must be ready to immediately counterattack with strategic and tactical nuclear weapons. That was the world as seen from the members' militaries. The Military Committee did not stop to think that a Soviet thermonuclear surprise attack on Europe might destroy the original justification for a Soviet attack on Western Europe postulated in MC 14. Previously, it was thought the Soviet Union was to attack Europe because it needed the West European economies and resources to create a single Eurasian economic system under Moscow's control before attacking the United States. Now, under worst-case scenario planning, the NATO military authorities presumed the Soviets simply wanted to destroy both Western Europe and North America.

The NAC, in ministerial session, approved MC 48 in December 1954, noting that it was approving the *planning* of the immediate use of nuclear weapons, but not the actual immediate use of nuclear weapons if attacked. The Allied governments, not the military commanders, would make the decisions concerning when and how to implement the plans. It was an important caveat, but nevertheless MC 48 created an interesting situation. The Eisenhower administration had adopted its New Look defense policy to reduce costs by emphasizing strategic atomic bombing and strategic air defense while cutting conventional forces. This was presumed to provide sufficient deterrence and save money over the course of the potentially long Cold War. NATO's military planners, on the other hand, did not just want the strategic atomic bombing. They wanted more ground forces in terms of both quantity (the Germans) and quality with the forces-in-being concept (i.e., highly trained, well equipped, mobile, in a high readiness state, deployed in depth, and with either their own tactical nuclear weapons or the capability of integrating operations with nuclear weapons). The new evolution in the strategy would not result in cost savings. The NATO military authorities were not following Eisenhower's New Look.

If one follows the logic of the military argument, the Soviet Union could overrun Western Europe whenever it wanted to, that is, not just in the planning date of 1957, but also in 1954 since at the time there was no German army and the NAC was not going to let the military automatically use nuclear weapons upon initiation of hostilities. NATO's current and planned conventional defenses were not deterring the Soviet Union from attacking. At the same time, it is worth noting that MC 48 was also useful to politicians trying to explain the creation of a new German army to their suspicious publics, since the politicians could say that the NATO military authorities said it was a military requirement for the defense of all NATO Allies.

The NAC requested the Military Committee to continue to study and develop planning guidance for the required military strength necessary given the NATO Strategic Concept, Soviet capabilities, and military developments. The Military Committee approved MC 48/1, The Most Effective Pattern of NATO Military Strength for the Next Few Years, Report No. 2, as a supplementary report to MC 48, in September 1955 and sent it to the NAC, which approved it in November. MC 48/1 stood by the concept and conclusions of MC 48, but pointed out that because the NAC had relaxed the force goals, NATO would not be able to implement the forward strategy outlined in MC 48 until mid-1959 (i.e., two years late). The German issue was not resolved as quickly as the military had forecast, and it would take time for the German forces to become fully ready. In addition, the minimum military measures listed in MC 48 were not being implemented very fast, and there were some issues to be worked out concerning NATO military advice to the NATO nations during the Annual Review of their respective forces to be assigned or earmarked for NATO. The Military Committee indicated that it would not be able to actually defend Western Europe successfully until 1959, with the civilians unwilling to fund defense at the level recommended by the military. Resources were tight, and the implication was that the civilians did not rate the danger of a Soviet attack as highly as the military did.

In fact, in MC 48/1, the Military Committee specifically mentioned a Soviet-announced reduction in its military forces. The Military Committee concluded that even if the Soviets were to reduce as announced, Soviet forces would still outnumber NATO forces. Furthermore, the Soviets would continue to improve their forces' quality and atomic war–fighting capability. More importantly, the NATO military authorities took credit for the announced reduction, writing that NATO's growing strength "has served as a major deterrent to USSR aims and has contributed significantly to the apparent change in tactics of Soviet foreign policy." Consequently, NATO nations needed to press ahead and increase their forces to the level that they agreed to in the 1953 Annual Review. In fact, "NATO's military position" was "jeopardize[d]" by the delay in fielding German forces, some members' announcements that they intended to lower their force contributions, and the temporary redeployment of some forces that were planned to be in place when the Soviets attacked. The implication was that despite the military's best attempts to ensure an adequate defense, the Allied governments were putting NATO at risk.

MC 48/1 also provided information on a variety of studies that were not completed prior to MC 48. For example, MC 48/1 gave firmer information on the anticipated two phases of the potential war. The initial phase, marked primarily by "intensive atomic exchange" would last 30 days or less. The second phase would be marked by a shift to more conventional operations with less emphasis on atomic air operations. NATO members were to establish and train civil defense organizations in order to reduce reliance on military forces in national recovery after an atomic attack so that the military forces could begin the counteroffensive. In addition, Allied governments were to develop plans for decentralized operations so that they could still direct the war effort after such attacks. With respect to naval forces, the Military Committee advocated a defense based on almost immediate offensive operations to destroy the Soviet naval forces. This would require a forward maritime defense to bottle the Soviet naval forces near their Arctic Sea, Baltic Sea, and Black Sea bases. Similar to the land and air forces, this would require high readiness states for the NATO naval forces-in-being and patrols near the Soviet naval access points to the North Atlantic and Mediterranean. This in turn would also require NATO member governments to make provisions to give major NATO commanders immediate operational control over their naval forces upon Soviet attack. NATO also would need immediate control over members' merchant marine fleets. Finally, the NATO military authorities pointed out that the NATO members were not provisioning their war stocks at the agreed level, and that a forward defense in a nuclear war required the forces-in-being to be fully provisioned, the war reserves to be dispersed, and adequate systems to be in place for resupply of the forward forces.

The Military Committee was increasing its resource requirements while the civilian governments appeared to be reducing the forces that would actually be provided, relying on the atomic bomb as a deterrent, force multiplier, and cost-saving strategy. The military saw the force requirements for 1956 established in the 1953 Annual Review as the barest of minimums necessary, while civilian governments increasingly saw them as unachievable, or perhaps exaggerated, goals. In addition, the NAC's approval of MC 48 and then MC 48/1 created a divergence between NATO's strategic documents. On the one hand, NATO's strategic concept (MC 3/5) and its associated planning guidance (MC 14/1) relied on NATO's strategic atomic bombing capability to deal with a primarily conventional Soviet military attack. The MC 48 series, on the other hand, called for expensive, mobile, dispersed, high readiness conventional and nuclear forces-in-being to immediately counterattack a predicted massive Soviet nuclear surprise attack and then follow up with a more conventional force phase involving tactical nuclear weapons. The Military Committee set out to resolve these differences and to bring NATO's strategic documents into line.

CHAPTER 5

The Third and Fourth Strategic Concepts: Coping with a Changing World

Several threads were being pushed and pulled in different directions during the period between NATO's approval of its second strategic concept in December 1952 and the approval of the third strategic concept in May 1957. For example, the Soviet Union had proposed joining NATO, but was rejected, in the spring of 1954. In February 1956 Nikita Khrushchev, the First Secretary of the Communist Party of the Soviet Union, made his "Secret Speech" to the 20th Party Congress in which he denounced Stalin for his excesses. This speech signaled the possibility that the Soviet Union might change into a less authoritarian system; however, the speech was a contributing factor to a worker's revolt in Poznan, Poland, in February as well as to the larger political revolution in Hungary in October 1956, which the Soviets brutally suppressed. Soviet forces invaded Hungary in November after the Hungarian government announced its intention to leave the Warsaw Pact. (See the Timeline of Illustrative Non-NATO Events in Appendix I.)

Questions for Consideration

- Did German membership and the German divisions tip the tide and deter the Soviets from attacking NATO?
- If the Allies were having a difficult time meeting their defense requirements, what would be the potential impact if one or more pulled military forces out of Europe to fight somewhere outside of Europe?
- How confident could the non-U.S. Allies be in a Strategic Concept that rested on U.S. nuclear weapons, when the United States did not share many details on the weapons or their planned use?

- Why didn't NATO intervene militarily when the Soviets crushed the Hungarian Revolution?
- What is a *limited* war? How does a country go about fighting such a war?
- What does mutually assured destruction mean?

In the West, the colonial world was changing, and the Suez Crisis proved very troubling for NATO. The Suez Crisis began when Egypt nationalized the Suez Canal in July 1956 in response to the withdrawal of the British and U.S. offer to finance the building of a dam at Aswan. The crisis peaked in October and November of 1956 when British, French, and Israeli forces invaded Egypt to seize the canal. The crisis dramatically demonstrated an already acknowledged deficiency in the organization. In May 1956 the North Atlantic Council (NAC) had established the Committee of Three Wise Men to make recommendations on how to improve and deepen the scope of inter-Ally political consultations and increase Alliance cohesion on matters beyond military planning in Europe. Some Allies saw NATO affairs in isolation and wanted to maintain freedom of action outside of NATO confines, whereas others believed that Allied actions outside of the NATO area could have relatively direct consequences for all NATO nations. In the Suez Crisis, the British and French did not share with the Allies their full intentions or operational plans for coordinated military action with the Israelis against Egypt after it had nationalized the canal. The United States was committed to countering communism, but was ideologically opposed to colonies. The United States had condemned the repression in Hungary, was more concerned about a major war with the Soviet Union, and did not portray Egyptian President Nasser as a communist. In addition, the United States was trying to save defense dollars by relying more on nuclear deterrence (assured destruction of the Soviet Union) and less on conventional forces. In the end, the United States did not support the British and French action and pressured the United Kingdom in particular with economic threats as the Canadian government developed a ceasefire plan, thereby establishing the model for future UN peacekeeping missions.

In addition, Britain and France told NATO in August 1956 that they would be pulling personnel and units that were assigned to or earmarked for NATO, thereby reducing NATO's military capabilities to implement its maritime and continental defense plans as the Soviet Army went into Hungary. Furthermore, after the British and French troops landed in Egypt, the Soviet Union threatened to attack Britain and France as a way to show its support for Egypt. If the Soviets were to actually attempt to carry out their threats, their military forces would have had to cross Allied territory. This would have forced an Article 5 decision. Finally, with decolonization increasing, it was clear that the British and French, as well as other Allies, could expect to encounter other Soviet-supported revolutionary movements or governments in the third world. Other NATO members were not keen on being drawn into nuclear war because of some Allies' adventures outside of Europe. That was not what the treaty was designed for. One outcome of the Suez Crisis was the broadening and deepening of Allied consultations within the NATO structures. This atmosphere in turn was conducive to the negotiations of the Treaties of Rome in 1957 establishing the European Economic Community and European Atomic Energy Community.

On December 13, 1956, the NAC issued guidance to the NATO military authorities in the form of C-M (56) 138 (Final), Directive to the NATO Military Authorities from the NAC. The directive was an assertion of civilian control over the military, and it changed the strategic planning process. Instead of letting the military provide an intelligence analysis of the threat and then develop planning guidance based on that assessment for NAC approval, the NAC chose to more specifically bind the military's imagination with political and economic reality before the military drafted the new strategic guidance and associated documents.

The NAC Directive's Analysis of Soviet Intentions addressed the Khrushchev changes with respect to decentralization and democratization, but concluded that these changes were not major in character. The Soviet and Warsaw Pact intervention in Hungary showed that there were clear limits as to what the Soviets would permit in Eastern Europe, although the events also indicated that the Soviets would also potentially have problems with their satellites if the Soviets were to go to war with the West. The rising Soviet economic power could lead Soviet leaders to believe that they might achieve their objectives without going to war, and the Soviet Union was now capable of offering economic assistance and weapons to nationalist and neutralist movements in the Middle East, Asia, and Africa (i.e., in the current and former European colonies).

Nevertheless, the NAC was confident that although the Soviets were developing nuclear capabilities to attack both Europe and North America, the threat of Western retaliation that would destroy the Soviet Union was sufficient to keep Soviet aggression in check. In fact, the NAC believed that the threat of nuclear retaliation was sufficient to deter nuclear or conventional attacks against NATO and furthermore implied the same with respect to even conventional attacks by the Soviets, Communist Chinese, or satellites beyond the NATO area. The NAC's statement in this regard appeared to ignore recent events in Asia: the Communist Chinese victory (1949), the North Korean invasion (1950), and the Viet Minh's success in Vietnam (1954). The United States' preponderance in nuclear capability had not appeared to produce any effective deterrent value in any of these cases.

To the NAC, given its sense of confidence in its threat of nuclear retaliation, the problem had become one of how to keep the Soviet Union from
initiating war through miscalculation or misunderstanding. For example, the
Soviets might think the West would not react to a certain Soviet action, or
the Soviets might misconstrue Western actions into believing an attack on
the Soviet Union was imminent. Although these arguments rested at least
as much on how the West managed its balance of projected bellicosity as
on how the Soviets interpreted it, the NAC developed a series of scenarios
for the military authorities to consider, in which the Soviets might launch a
conventional attack that could inadvertently lead to general nuclear war. For
example, the Soviet leadership might decide to initiate a conventional-only
attack in the belief that NATO would not be the first to use nuclear weapons,
that the West might believe the nuclear exchange would hurt it more than
the Soviet Union, or that the Allies were in disagreement on how to respond,
for example, over whether to use nuclear weapons. The Soviets might also
believe that the West would not support a non-NATO country if the Soviet
Union invaded it or pressured it into the Soviet bloc. The Soviet Union
might also stumble into major war by supporting guerrilla forces in noncom-
munist countries, or by being forced to resort to large-scale operations to
control its satellites.

These scenarios did not deal so much with fighting a war as much as they
did with preventing a war through the deterrent threat of massive retaliation. Part of the deterrent obviously rested on the weapons systems and the
military's credibility; however, the political cohesion and decisiveness among
the NATO members' governments played a bigger part in these scenarios.
Consequently, the drafting of C-M (56) 138 (Final) reflected the degree of
dissention between NATO members over the recent Suez Crisis and its resolution. Western militaries did not make a stellar showing, and the differences
in opinion between the United States on the one hand, and the British and
French on the other, was quite open. The last scenarios in the document also
captured some of the disagreement over another issue within the Alliance.
The scenarios implied that the military authorities should be making plans
for events occurring outside of the NATO area as far away as Asia, which
reflected the stand of some members, whereas the second part of the directive
negated planning for such events and simply called for their observation.

The NAC directed the military authorities that in order to deter the Soviets from attack and to win the war if attacked, despite Soviet surprise and
advantage in numbers, NATO must maintain and protect "a fully effective
nuclear retaliatory force." In addition, NATO must have land, sea, and air
forces in order to demonstrate its military commitment, "to deal with inci-
dents such as infiltrations, incursions or hostile local actions," "to identify Soviet or Satellite aggression (on land, sea or air)," and "to protect and maintain

sea communications." NATO's forces must also be prepared to handle larger attacks, using forward defense and the immediate use of nuclear weapons to initiate and maintain a strategic counteroffensive. In the cases of infiltrations, incursions, and local hostile actions, NATO's military forces must be able to react without necessarily using nuclear weapons. Of course, it was still the responsibility of the national governments' representatives in the NAC to decide whether to implement the plans and use nuclear weapons.

NATO's governments were subtly telling the NATO military authorities to reduce the conventional force side of their defense plans and to rely more heavily on nuclear weapons, more along the lines of the Eisenhower New Look. Nevertheless, the NAC told the military to plan on Canadian, U.K., and U.S. forces still being stationed in Western Europe, although the military authorities were also to take into account that "certain NATO countries" may need to redeploy some of their NATO forces outside of NATO to counter the ever-changing Soviet-inspired worldwide communist threat. The NATO military authorities were not to count on all the forces actually being in place at any given time, buttressing the case for reliance on nuclear weapons. In addition, only the early warning and nuclear retaliation forces were to "be kept in constant readiness at all times." Keeping all forces at this level added unnecessary cost and complications. Furthermore, NATO military authorities were to observe events occurring outside the NATO area for possible threats to NATO, but they were not to plan for events that were not covered by Articles 5 and 6 of the NATO Treaty. Finally, the NAC reminded the military that economic stability was a key part of the security of NATO nations, and that "few, if any, NATO countries can be expected to make a substantial increase in the proportion of their resources devoted to defense." The military authorities were to provide a new report on how to achieve the most effective defense, with respect to both the Alliance's as well as individual members' contributions, "within the resources likely to be available."

The Third Strategic Concept (MC 14/2, May 1957)

The Military Committee responded to the NAC direction with MC 14/2, A Report by the Military Committee to the North Atlantic Council on Overall Strategic Concept for the Defense of the North Atlantic Treaty Organization Area, and MC 48/2, Report by the Military Committee to the North Atlantic Council on Measures to Implement the Strategic Concept. MC 48/2 was to cover the period from its approval through 1962. These two new documents officially replaced MC 3/5(Final), MC 14/1(Final), MC 48 (Final), and MC 48/1(Final). The Military Committee approved MC 14/2 and forwarded it to the NAC in February and MC 48/2 in March 1957.

MC 14/2 and MC 48/2 addressed some of the issues relating to out-of-area military deployments. For example, MC 14/2 stated that NATO's security rested to a degree on the ability of some Allies to send forces or honor defense commitments beyond the NATO area. NATO military authorities would not plan out-of-area operations, but they openly stated that NATO's security depended on certain members not only defending NATO from within but also retaining the capability to send forces far afield to counter Soviet influence. The NATO military authorities were lobbying for certain Allies to maintain or increase their non-NATO defense capabilities, and potentially justify the need for others to increase military spending in order to be able to backfill them. In addition, MC14/2 stated, "it is vital to the Alliance" to keep certain non-NATO nations out of Soviet influence, implying either a strong NATO defense commitment with accompanying NATO military planning or more support for non-NATO defense spending in certain countries to take on these tasks. MC 14/2 also stated that NATO members should not neglect their NATO commitments when embarking on such adventures "short of general war," but since they were deemed vital and essential, it is not clear how this was to be worked out, or how the forces were to avoid general war in Asia, for example.

The Military Committee agreed with the NAC that the Soviet Union would not deliberately start a nuclear war. A war caused by Soviet miscalculation or misunderstanding was more likely, but in the end, the Soviets were most likely to either continue the cold war or conduct limited, conventional operations as a way to avoid nuclear destruction. However, since the consequences of general nuclear war most threatened the survival of the NATO nations, military planning had to be geared for deterrence and, if such a war were to break out, winning. The war was still forecasted to be in two phases, with the massive nuclear exchange lasting 30 days or less. NATO would depend on its well-trained, well-supplied, dispersed, yet mobile in-place forces for a forward defense, which apparently was not going to suffer the same losses expected to be inflicted on the Soviet Army formations. There would be some sort of regrouping, and then in a longer, more conventionally fought war. The West would prevail because of the head start gained from winning the first phase of the war, its industrial base, its organized home front, and its eventual command of the seas.

MC 14/2 made clear that if the Soviets stumbled into a conventional war, or purposely tried to fight a limited conventional war, NATO could not stop the Soviet Army from overrunning Europe. Consequently, the Military Committee concluded that NATO had to resort to immediate use of both strategic and tactical nuclear weapons. Although the Military Committee included the NAC's direction to have a capability to defend in such cases without necessarily using nuclear weapons, NATO's ability to defend without nuclear weapons was practically nil. Even in the case of Soviet infiltrations or support of local hostile acts, the NATO military authorities stated that if they believed the Soviets were trying to broaden or prolong such an incident, NATO would have to go nuclear. The risk of being overrun was simply too great. From the military authorities' viewpoint, NATO did not and could not have a concept of fighting a limited conventional war against the Soviet Union. NATO would have to turn to nuclear weapons early. In fact, MC 14/2 made clear that even if the Soviets were not directly involved, or their involvement could not be determined, in an attack on a NATO member, NATO would use "all appropriate military measures" to win quickly. Nuclear weapons were an option in this case too. The emphasis had clearly shifted to a defense based on the immediate use of nuclear weapons at both the strategic and tactical levels.

In MC 48/2, the NATO military authorities stated that the Soviets were not likely to initiate a war as long as they could get what they wanted "by other means," instead of the litany that the Soviet Union was afraid of nuclear war. Although this was in recognition of the Soviet Union's growing economic and diplomatic power, there was also a slight hint of a veiled critique of the NATO governments' not fully supporting a strong NATO military capability to project a strong stance against the Soviet Union. MC 48/2 also added a new scenario under the model of war due to Soviet misunderstandings. If the Soviets thought that they had achieved "a scientific breakthrough" that would minimize NATO's ability to retaliate, they might decide to attack. This elliptical reference to potential Soviet long-range ballistic missile developments indicated that the NATO military authorities believed that Soviet missile success might indeed be revolutionary and dramatically alter the military balance between NATO and the Soviet Union in the Soviet's favor.

Although MC 48/2 parroted the NAC instructions on readiness levels, the military authorities argued that NATO's military forces needed to be physically and mentally prepared to launch their strategic nuclear weapons at the initiation of a Soviet attack. NATO's nonstrategic land, air and sea forces-in-being must be in forward positions, equipped for immediate use of tactical nuclear weapons, and sufficiently supplied to conduct operations for some time. NATO naval and air forces would destroy enemy air and naval threats at their source as the best means of defense. The NATO governments should conclude their ongoing discussions, implement a warning system, and develop a more integrated NATO air defense system. In addition, for the first time in the strategic planning documents, MC 48/2 highlighted the obvious, but previously not mentioned fact, that the nuclear retaliatory forces were primarily long-range bombers under national, not NATO command.

Both MC 14/2 and MC 48/2 generated considerable debate, especially with regard to the statement that NATO would not fight a limited, conventional war. The NAC approved both documents on May 9, 1957. However, when the Military Committee released the final approved versions two weeks later, the cover sheets contained the caveat that any member delegation could subsequently request a reconsideration of any part of either report, and indirectly NATO's strategy; the caveat was an indication of how shallow the consensus actually was.

NATO could not, and just as important for deterrence, would not, fight a limited war against the Soviet Union. This was not just a nuclear matter, but also a military-political necessity. If the Alliance were to truly fight a limited war, it would lose the ability to escalate to nuclear weapons or to broaden the scope of operations by, for example, counterattacking in other regions. To do so would broaden the limited war into the general war that was already NATO's default option.

In addition, a limited war would place the Alliance under immense strain since it would confine military operations to a particular country, countries, region or regions, and would not directly affect all members the same way. This would place a very heavy burden on the particular country or region, but allow members in other regions to ponder the possibilities of cutting their own or NATO's losses in the affected region. Given the choice between, say, a relatively small loss of Greek territory and thermonuclear war across Europe and North America, some members might be more inclined to yield another Ally's territory.

Furthermore, developing conventional forces necessary to fight limited wars would raise the defense requirements for the members. Since the Soviets might start a limited war in any of NATO's regions, each frontline member would need more conventional forces to offset the Soviet superiority, while rear area members would need more forces to serve as conventional reinforcements. Finally, the ideal training, equipment, and location for forces fighting a limited war might not be the same as for those fighting a campaign using tactical nuclear weapons as an integral part of a larger war effort. The one big war was more likely to strengthen the Alliance bonds, and spur more uniform defense investments.

The strategy contained many potential weaknesses and papered over potential differences of opinion, but it was the best that NATO could come up with in 1957. Moving to a new strategy would require consensus among all 15 members, and this consensus was slow to develop. NATO's discussions did not take place in a vacuum. Several noteworthy events occurred that potentially supported one argument or another.

For example, the Soviet Union's successful launch and orbit of Sputnik heralded potential major changes in the balance of power through the practical development of nuclear-armed intercontinental ballistic missiles (ICBMs). The United States' heavy investment in strategic air defense against the

Soviet bomber fleet that never quite materialized would soon be obsolete. It had no capability against ICBMs. The United States' heavy investment in strategic atomic bombers would also come into question. ICBMs would travel halfway around the globe in half an hour to hit cities or military forces un- hindered, but bombers would be flying half day or longer missions, and a per- centage would be shot down. In addition, some Allies wondered if the United States would so staunchly extend its nuclear umbrella over NATO's European members when American cities were realistically and directly threatened. The fact that the United States owned the vast majority of "NATO's" nuclear weapons and delivery systems and did not place them under NATO control was another factor in this argument.

Nevertheless, in the Final Communiqué from the heads of state NAC in December 1957, NATO announced that it had "decided to establish stocks of nuclear warheads, which will be readily available for the defence of the Alliance in case of need." In addition to the warheads, the NAC "has also decided that intermediate range ballistic missiles will have to be put at the disposal of the Supreme Allied Commander Europe [SACEUR]." SACEUR was dual-hatted as both the senior U.S. military commander in Europe and the senior NATO commander, so placing nuclear missiles under his com- mand kept them under American control; however, the communiqué stated that "the deployment of these stocks and missiles and arrangements for their use will accordingly be decided in conformity with NATO defence plans and in agreement with the states directly concerned." The United States and its NATO Allies were moving to a more cooperative arrangement on nuclear weapons. The United States was already training European military officers and technicians for the Nike-Hercules surface-to-air missile and Matador surface-to-surface missile, both of which could carry nuclear warheads. In NATO's concept of nuclear sharing, the United States retained control over the nuclear warheads prior to launch, but stored them on the territory of Al- lies, and the Allies actually manned and fired the weapons. This was done in Canada as well as in Europe.

The concept is still operational today, but the Intermediate-Range Nu- clear Forces (INF) Treaty signed in 1987 eliminated the last NATO surface- to-surface nuclear missiles (Pershing II and ground-launched cruise missile). The United States has withdrawn nuclear artillery shells, leaving only aircraft delivery as a means for Allies to launch tactical (or nonstrategic) nuclear weapons. Currently the Tornado and F-16 aircraft of European Al- lies are reportedly capable of delivering U.S. nuclear bombs. This Alliance burden-sharing served to complicate Soviet targeting. At the same time, it strengthened cooperation within NATO since it eventually gave the non- nuclear Allies more information and say on nuclear issues since the weap- ons were stored on their territories, their crews operated and maintained the delivery systems, and their crews had to know the targets and technical data on the weapons in order to train for the nuclear missions.

Questions for Consideration

- What are the implications of having nuclear weapons stored or on quick reaction alert status aircraft or missile crews when a coup occurs such as in Greece or Turkey?
- How do you think NATO's nuclear sharing concept fits into the Nuclear Non-Proliferation Treaty?

The Berlin Crisis of 1958–1962 was another significant event that shaped Allied views on the Soviet Union. In November 1958, Khrushchev initiated a Berlin crisis, demanding that Britain, France, and the United States agree to leave the occupied city. The crisis lasted until 1962, marked by periods of negotiation, ultimatums, and saber rattling. The United States federalized part of its Air National Guard and deployed large formations of aircraft to Europe during one point in the crisis. Large numbers of East Germans were migrating to West Berlin, and the East Germans surprised the world when they started building the Berlin Wall in August 1961. East German attempts to limit British, French, and U.S. access to the Eastern, Soviet sector resulted in a tank standoff at Checkpoint Charlie, the transit point between the Western and the Soviet occupation zones for military forces in Berlin. It was clear that strategic bombers backed the small number of tanks at Checkpoint Charlie, but it was also clear that neither the United States nor NATO really had the capability to diffuse such a crisis by threatening the use of credible military forces somewhere between the two extremes of a handful of tanks and total thermonuclear war. In the end, the United States and Soviets agreed to withdraw their tanks simultaneously from Checkpoint Charlie, bringing the world back from the brink of nuclear war. The creation of the Berlin Wall itself froze the situation into a permanent stalemate with Britain, France, and the United States continuing to occupy the Western Sector, to patrol the Soviet Sector, and to deal with the Soviets for access. The Soviet military also continued to patrol the Western Sector.

As the crisis in Berlin ebbed and flowed, Khrushchev visited the United States in September 1959, during one of the less tense, negotiation-focused periods of the crisis. It was the first such visit for a major Soviet leader. This period of relaxation of the Cold War tension did not last, however. Francis Gary Powers, flying a CIA high-altitude spy plane, was shot down over the Soviet Union and taken prisoner in May 1960. It was now clear to the world that the United States was conducting such flights. The Eisenhower reciprocal visit to the Soviet Union was cancelled. The CIA-sponsored Bay of Pigs invasion of Cuba fiasco followed in April 1961, and the U.S.-Soviet Cuban Missile Crisis occurred in October 1962. The specter of nuclear war, presumed to end in mutual destruction, tended to turn any incident into a crisis that could end the world. As the Soviet Union increased its nuclear capabilities, the outcome of the West's construct of massive retaliation evolved towards mutually assured destruction.

Questions for Consideration

- The Kennedy administration changed U.S. strategy to flexible response in the early 1960s, but NATO did not change until several years later. Do you think that the United States followed two different strategies (flexible response for the United States and massive retaliation for NATO)?
- Does a strategy of flexible response cede the initiative to the opponent, or does it give new flexibility, and potentially the initiative, to the responder?
- What were NATO's three categories of responses, and how were they different?
- Was the U.S. war in Vietnam connected to NATO?
- Why didn't NATO participate as NATO in Desert Shield and Desert Storm?

The series of crises in the late 1950s and early 1960s revealed the weakness of massive retaliation under mutually assured destruction conditions. It was a hollow threat. There was an extensive range of conditions under which the United States was unlikely to start a nuclear war that could lead to its demise. In addition, a U.S. strike on Moscow was unlikely to affect Chinese actions, and expending nuclear weapons on China or other countries would reduce the number of weapons assigned to the Soviet Union. The United States was also unlikely to launch nuclear strikes on Moscow in response to communist-inspired revolutionary movements during the era of decolonization. At the same time, the United States wanted to be able to respond to saber rattling, demonstrations of force, and low-level use of force by the Soviet Union or its allies, and be able to escalate U.S. levels of force to achieve satisfactory resolution of crises short of total thermonuclear war. This flexibility might also allow limited use of tactical nuclear weapons as an escalatory stage that might be sufficient to resolve a crisis. Consequently, the Kennedy administration replaced massive retaliation with flexible response. Flexible response also provided a theoretical framework that supported the initial use of U.S. special operations forces in Vietnam and the later buildup of conventional forces after the Gulf of Tonkin incident in August 1964 to fight the Soviet-sponsored North Vietnamese government without bringing the United States and Soviet Union directly to the brink of nuclear war.

The U.S. change in strategy did not lead to an automatic change in NATO strategy, despite the obvious and very pragmatic problem that the United States provided the vast majority of the nuclear weapons that would be used in NATO's defense. The consensus agreement of all NATO members was required to change MC 14/2 and MC 48/2, and it would not be a minor change that might be papered over with new interpretations or a simple amendment. Adoption of a new NATO strategy akin to the United States' flexible response strategy would require increases in the whole range of NATO members' special operations and conventional forces, and explicit recognition that NATO needed to be able to fight limited wars with the Soviet Union or its allies. These concepts directly contradicted MC 14/2 and MC 48/2. Not all the Allies were enamored with the economic and political-military consequences of such a strategy change.

The French, in particular, saw flexible response as a way for the United States to try to separate and protect its homeland from a Soviet strategic nuclear strike while the United States waged a "small" or combined conventional and tactical nuclear war isolated to Europe. The French also questioned whether the United States would really extend its nuclear umbrella to Europe since the Soviet Union was perceived to be able to effectively attack the United States with nuclear weapons and cause great destruction. The French also disagreed with the concept of fighting a limited nuclear war with tactical weapons, believing instead that *all* nuclear weapons were strategic because their use would radically change the nature of the war. In addition, the French were already developing their own nuclear weapons and delivery systems. France withdrew from the NATO integrated military command structure in 1966 and requested all foreign troops to depart France. France, however, remained a member of NATO, continued to have a Permanent Representative (PermRep) on the NAC, and continued to participate in nonmilitary activities. The Defense Planning Committee assumed political oversight of the Military Committee upon France's departure. The Defense Planning Committee was composed of the PermReps of the members with militaries participating in the NATO integrated military structure, (i.e., all members but France).

It was also becoming clear that the vision of a monolithic Soviet-led block was wrong. The Soviet Union's problems with Tito's Yugoslavia were long known, and by the early 1960s, major Chinese-Soviet disagreements were becoming more apparent. The recall of the Soviet advisors from China, the growing ideological disputes, which evolved into explicit condemnation of each other's leaders, and the Chinese-initiated Sino-Indian War, which had occurred about the same time as the Cuban Missile Crisis, were clear indications to the Western world that there was no longer a worldwide, Moscow-directed communist movement, if indeed there ever had been one.

The NAC Ministerial authorized a study in December 1966 on NATO's future. Among the reasons for the study were the French announcement of its withdrawal from the integrated military command structure, changes in Soviet-Chinese relations, a general acceptance that security in Europe was grounded in the mutually assured destruction stalemate, and public perceptions that the Soviet Union was becoming less of a threat to NATO nations. The study, known as the Harmel Report, was provided to the NAC Ministerial in December 1967.

The Harmel Report naturally concluded that NATO was indeed necessary for European stability and security, that NATO would be critical to bringing peace to Europe, and that the time was ripe to look beyond the current stability achieved via the mutually assured destruction scenarios to a future peace. Since the United States and the Soviet Union both had a second-strike nuclear capability, building more nuclear weapons would not bring more security. It would only foster an arms race that would be expensive and illusory. NATO's reliance on tactical nuclear weapons to backstop its conventional forces also appeared to create a stalemate. Since the West would have an advantage in an arms race, it was thought that the Soviets might be amenable to move to a paradigm where arms control and disarmament initiatives would replace the arms race and provide security in Europe at less cost than the array of forces on each side of the divide across Germany. This could possibly eventually lead to an acceptable solution to the German question, which was still the root cause of the European security problem. However, in order to achieve this vision, the Allies had to continue to exhibit solidarity and resolve, and invest in their military forces. In a sense, the Harmel Report offered a new vision with carrot and stick to both the Soviet Union as well as to Western voters questioning the need for NATO and the need for national military expenditures. The path to peace lay through NATO-coordinated negotiations, conducted from a position of strength buttressed by continued Allied military expenditures, but the Harmel Report subgroup working on NATO's future security policies also noted that the Soviets were unlikely to engage with NATO on troop reductions if it perceived that such activities were designed to allow the United States to draw down in Europe as it built up in Vietnam.

The Harmel Report subgroup working on NATO's future security policies also addressed a number of other issues beyond strengthening NATO's military forces while beginning to explore arms control seriously. For example, it mentioned the need to better integrate NATO's nonnuclear members into nuclear planning. This was particularly important as NATO moved to a more flexible strategy that might, paradoxically, lower its threshold for using tactical nuclear weapons in support of conventional operations on the territories of nonnuclear members. After all, only the United States and United

Kingdom had nuclear weapons for NATO planning; France's nuclear weapons would not be at NATO's disposal. Since NATO was moving to a defense against the more likely, lower end spectrum of Soviet-inspired conflict, it would also be important for NATO to continue to consolidate its abilities to consult during crises.

The report also acknowledged the technology gap between members and saw that it was likely to increase as military equipment continued to increase in both cost and capability. Consequently, the report recommended increased cooperation in research and development as well as in production of military equipment to give the members with smaller and less technologically advanced economies the opportunity to continue to have a hand in the military-industrial complex. Countries in such a position might be more likely to continue to arm themselves if they were investing in their own economies. Finally, the report also expressed NATO's concern over the weakness of its southern flank in Europe, partially because of the increased Soviet Navy presence in the eastern Mediterranean and the Soviet support to the Arab countries during the Six-Day War in June 1967.

The Fourth Strategic Concept (MC 14/3, January 1968)

While the Harmel study was ongoing, the French departure from NATO's integrated military command structure opened the opportunity for a new strategic concept. In its May 1967 ministerial, the Defense Planning Committee tasked the NATO military authorities (via DPC/D[67]23, Decisions of the DPC in Ministerial Session) to revise NATO's Strategic Concept. The new Strategic Concept was "to allow NATO a greater flexibility and to provide for the employment as appropriate of one or more of direct defence, deliberate escalation, and general nuclear response, thus confronting the enemy with a credible threat of escalation in response to any type of aggression below the level of a major nuclear attack."

The Defense Planning Committee commented that the Soviet Union appeared to be behaving more cautiously in Europe, although it was actively seeking to take advantage of every situation outside of Europe in order to threaten NATO if it came to war. The guidance also observed that as long as NATO maintained the capability to catastrophically damage the Soviet Union even after a surprise Soviet nuclear strike, the Soviets were unlikely to start such a war. Consequently, NATO must have a secure second strike nuclear capability. In addition, the Soviets were unlikely to start a limited war against NATO if NATO continued to make clear that such an action risked a NATO escalation to nuclear war. For this plan to work, however, NATO must keep its military forces in a high state of readiness, and NATO must remain cohesive and resolute. The Defense Planning Committee recognized that its flank regions were particularly weak militarily, but saw value in being able to potentially deploy reinforcements during a crisis or in the case of a possible Soviet attack in order to show NATO's resolve, while simultaneously making use of the escalatory construct. Although the Defense Planning Committee wanted forces to be able to deter, and if deterrence failed, to counter Soviet aggression on three levels—strategic nuclear, tactical nuclear, and conventional forces—the guidance made it clear that many of its conventional forces were "organically supported by tactical nuclear weapons," thereby severely limiting the option of a lengthy conventional war.

As usual, the Defense Planning Committee did not forecast a rosy economic future for its members. It predicted that the members' economic contributions to defense were unlikely to be higher in 1975 than they were in 1965, so there was no expectation of increased conventional forces to create the desired flexibility at the lower, conventional end of the potential spectrum of conflict. In fact, since the cost and capabilities of military equipment were both increasing, NATO military authorities were tasked to use systems analysis tools to compare the effectiveness and efficiencies of forces fielding different weapons mixes, considering things like costs in terms of acquisitions, operations, maintenance, and personnel. This paralleled the approach of the U.S. Secretary of Defense Robert McNamara, who had overseen the United States' adoption of flexible response; emphasized civilian control over the military; and relied on data, models, and analytic methods for decision making in the Pentagon.

In September 1967, the Military Committee forwarded the proposed new Strategic Concept (MC 14/3) to the Defense Planning Committee, which approved the new NATO Strategic Concept at its December ministerial. Both committees approved MC 14/3 with the caveat that if there appeared to be any differences between MC 14/3 and DPC/D(67)23, the DPC document prevailed. The NATO military authorities deferred publicly to a NATO version of civilian control of the military.

MC 14/3 redefined some very critical words. NATO's military authorities defined *conventional forces* as "those forces employable in a non-nuclear role, although they may have a nuclear capability." Although it was important to note that some conventional forces had nuclear capabilities (since NATO's nuclear sharing concept was nearing its peak), previous reports had placed the emphasis on a force's primary mission and the force's capabilities to determine whether the force should be labeled as conventional or nuclear. This was quite different from the new definition of nuclear-capable forces as *conventional* because they *could be used* conventionally. For example, U.S. B-52 bombers were previously considered strategic nuclear bombers, but now could be labeled conventional under the new NATO definition since some were being used conventionally in Vietnam. If war with the Soviet Union occurred, the Soviets would not know if a particular U.S. B-52 carried nuclear or conventional bombs until it dropped them, but the Soviets would probably assume it was nuclear. This blurred the distinction of *conventional* forces and reinforced the idea that the adoption of the flexible response Strategic Concept was a minor papering-over of NATO's inherent reliance on first use of nuclear weapons as the foundation of its defense. MC14/3 also differed stylistically from its predecessors in referring to the threat as the "Warsaw Pact," instead of the previously ubiquitous "Soviets" or "Soviet Union."

In their threat assessment, the NATO military authorities concluded that "the Warsaw Pact leaders probably believe that they now possess sufficient military power to deter NATO from resorting to all-out nuclear war except under extreme threat to its vital interests." That is, the Soviet Union's secure second-strike capability should keep NATO from attacking with nuclear weapons as long as the Warsaw Pact did not put the survival of NATO's members at risk. Consequently, the Warsaw Pact, as seen by the NATO military authorities, should stop developing further military capability. To the NATO military authorities, the Soviet Union's continued investment in its navy; nuclear, chemical, possibly biological weapons; and unnecessarily large conventional forces indicated that the Soviets were seeking military advantage over NATO. Nevertheless, although the Warsaw Pact was attributed capabilities for a wide range of military activities ranging from harassment of West Berlin traffic to major worldwide nuclear attack, "the more probable actions appear to be those at the lower end of the spectrum."

Alliance cohesion would be as much of a target in Warsaw Pact plans, with one possible scenario being that the Warsaw Pact would conduct some limited action, achieve their objectives, then call for negotiations before NATO's military was actually engaged. In the end, NATO's new Strategic Concept was based on deterrence, achieved through three tenets. First, the Warsaw Pact had to believe that NATO had a credible military capability. Second, the Warsaw Pact had to believe that NATO's members would resolutely use that capability if necessary. Third, the Warsaw Pact would not be able to predict with any degree of certainty how NATO might respond to Warsaw Pact aggression. This uncertainty in the enemies' minds, coupled with the ever-present threat to destroy Soviet society with nuclear weapons, was the real *flexibility* in NATO's flexible response in MC 14/3.

The NATO military authorities followed the DPC/D(67)23 lead and offered three military responses if deterrence failed. The three responses were not mutually exclusive, and one or more could be used simultaneously. Direct defense was the first response, but it contained a mix of ideas, some in apparent contradiction. The basic idea was that NATO would use its forces-in-being to counter whatever the Warsaw Pact might try, ostensibly ceding the initiative to the enemy and fighting at whatever level he chose to fight. To actually implement this plan fully, NATO would need a massive investment in conventional forces, placed on the border in a high level of readiness, ready to counter anything from harassing Berlin transit traffic to covert action to a large-scale conventional Warsaw Pact offensive along several fronts. Since such a massive investment in conventional forces would be too expensive, the Military Committee placed several caveats in the concept of direct defense. First, it only applied to Warsaw Pact attacks that were not major nuclear attacks. Second, the intent was only to "initially" meet the attack with direct defense. Successful direct defense was defined as either repulsing the enemy, or "placing upon the aggressor the burden of escalation," that is, NATO would just have to make a good showing of trying to stop the attack, and then it could pull out the nuclear weapons and blame the Warsaw Pact for forcing NATO to use them. Furthermore, direct defense was explicitly not limited to a purely conventional defense. "The direct defense concept includes the use of such available nuclear weapons as may be authorized, either on a pre-planned or case-by-case basis." Consequently, to the NATO military authorities, the direct defense response could easily result in NATO resorting to nuclear weapons and not fighting "on the level at which the enemy chooses to fight."

The second possible NATO response was deliberate escalation. It was difficult to draw a clear line between direct defense and deliberate escalation since direct defense already included nuclear escalation. In addition, the explanation of deliberate escalation confused the issue. It provided a list of example actions, but then added the caveat that these would only be examples of deliberate escalation "provided they have not previously been used as part of a direct defensive system." The key differences appeared to be that in deliberate escalation, NATO would emphasize that it was deliberately escalating the level of combat, yet still trying to control it, and that the NATO response would not necessarily be tied to repulsing the specific enemy attack. NATO might open another front, demonstratively use nuclear weapons, or strike targets further in the enemy's rear with nuclear weapons. NATO would be sending political signals with its escalation and weakening the enemy's will to continue the fight. However, this theoretical exercise in political signaling could have been read to imply that NATO might have been willing to settle for something less than the *status quo ante bellum*. That in turn would directly contradict the military objective of preserving or restoring "the integrity and security of the North Atlantic Treaty Area." This discussion paralleled U.S. practices on using the escalation of conventional force as political signaling in Vietnam. In the U.S. case, civilian leaders tended to favor the concept, whereas the military did not.

The third possible NATO response was the old standby of general nuclear response. This would involve massive nuclear attacks on Warsaw Pact nuclear forces, military forces, and industrial centers (i.e., cities). This "can be forced upon NATO by a major Soviet nuclear attack." This actually was a major break with the past, since it implied that a major, purely conventional Warsaw Pact attack would be met with one of the other two responses. Those responses could easily involve tactical nuclear weapons, but NATO's first use of nuclear weapons at the tactical level was now separated from the concept of a massive nuclear retaliation against Soviet society as a response to a conventional attack; however, Soviet use of tactical nuclear weapons would still run the risk of NATO escalation to a general nuclear response.

Although the NATO military authorities were still committed to the forces-in-being forward defense, the new strategic concept echoed DPC/D(67)23's ideas that NATO must place more emphasis on being able to reinforce its flanks as well as on mobilizing reserve forces since both might be needed. Mobilizing reserves or deploying reinforcements could serve as political signals of NATO's determination in a crisis and as necessary measures to support the direct defense or deliberate escalation responses. The Strategic Concept also called for NATO to be able to use chemical warfare on a limited scale to retaliate if the Warsaw Pact used chemical warfare. NATO was also to prepare passive defenses against chemical and biological warfare. In addition, there was a call for better integration of national and NATO nuclear planning, indicating a degree of unhappiness with the United States' and the United Kingdom's coordination of their nuclear plans. Nobody could actually predict what the U.S. president would do if war broke out, but the Allies were interested in knowing more about the plans and what his options might be since their military forces would be carrying out the plan under NATO's nuclear sharing concept.

One of the fears that sparked NATO's rewrite of the Strategic Concept was that a crisis or low-level Warsaw Pact *aggression* could result in NATO members breaking ranks, which would cascade into a new Munich, that is, the West would yield to Soviet demands or territorial gains in order to appease the Soviets and preserve the peace as Chamberlain had done with Hitler prior to World War II. MC 14/3's method to avoid this scenario was to create relatively automatic responses for the high-end and the low-end cases of Warsaw Pact aggression. At the high end, in the event of a massive Soviet strategic nuclear attack (the most unlikely scenario), NATO, primarily in the guise of the U.S. nuclear arsenal, would respond with massive retaliation almost immediately and with little to no consultation with its NATO Allies. At the low end, in the event of a small Soviet conventional attack or border incursion, which was presumed to be the more likely scenario, NATO would initially counter the Warsaw Pact aggression with conventional forces-in-being. If the NATO forces encountered difficulty halting the aggression, and the military authorities wanted to use tactical nuclear weapons, the NATO members would probably have time to consult on the issue first.

With NATO's responses to the high and low ends relatively clear and noncontroversial, the problem remained as to what to do in cases that fell in the middle of the spectrum, that is if the Warsaw Pact launched a major conventional invasion along several fronts, which tended to be unlikely, or if NATO chose to move up the escalatory ladder to gain control over what was originally a lower end Warsaw Pact aggression. The NATO military authorities would press for permission to use tactical nuclear weapons, and the members would need to consult, which could potentially fracture the Alliance. However, MC 14/3's relatively automatic choices at the high and low ends gave the illusion that the unwanted middle outcomes were insulated from becoming reality.

Furthermore, the key to avoiding the middle was to invest in conventional forces, and to develop mobile, deployable reinforcements and mobilizable reserves in order to delay nuclear decisions as long as possible. Therefore, the logic was that if a segment of the population did not like the idea of using nuclear weapons or did not want NATO to actually run the risk of needing to consult on nuclear weapons employment, that segment should push for more expenditures on conventional forces and capabilities. That, of course, ran counter to NATO's original premises that relying on nuclear weapons would be cheaper and that the economic growth of the European countries was critical to their long-term security.

Two significant events occurred outside of NATO between the Military Committee's approval of MC14/3 in May 1967 and the May 1969 approval of supporting document MC 48/3, Measures to Implement the Strategic Concept for the Defence of the NATO Area. The first event was the communist Tet Offensive in January 1968 in Vietnam. The Tet Offensive became a major turning point in the U.S. prosecution of the war because it shook the American public's confidence in the U.S. government's policies with respect to Vietnam. The government claims that the United States was winning the war were shattered by television coverage of the initially dramatic communist gains. Americans became disillusioned with the U.S. government and its foreign policy. At roughly the same time, the Eastern Bloc gained sympathy in the West due to the Prague Spring, which began when the Dubček government took over in Czechoslovakia in January 1968 and began instituting liberal reforms in his "socialism with a human face" program. However, when the Prague Spring came to a sudden end with the Soviet-led invasion in August 1968, the effect of the invasion was a general disillusionment in the West with the Soviet Union and its foreign policy. The Soviets justified their intervention with what came to be called the Brezhnev Doctrine, which was that the Soviet Union had the right and duty to intervene if one of its allies appeared to be leaving the communist fold. It took some time for NATO to analyze the implications of the Soviet action; the Defense Planning Committee did not approve MC 48/3, the Measures to Implement the Strategic Concept, until over a year after the Soviet invasion of Czechoslovakia.

MC 48/3 highlighted the importance of NATO and its members building up several capabilities in order to be able to implement the new strategic concept. For example, NATO would need a very robust and modern command, control, and communication system for military operations. In addition, NATO would need a "rapid, survivable, secure and reliable communications" between NATO military authorities, NATO political authorities, and the members' national authorities in order to have the discussions on authorizing the use of tactical nuclear weapons by the direct defense forces or if NATO were to decide to deliberately escalate the level of military operations. Training requirements would also increase because the new strategic concept required conventional forces to be able to shift quickly between conventional and nuclear operations. Of course, the constant training on nuclear weapons deliveries by dual-capable aircraft or ground units would lead the Soviet military planners to assume that NATO was willing and ready to use tactical nuclear weapons in the event of war. The effect was that NATO could walk the fine political line between telling its public that it would first try to counter lower end aggressions with conventional forces, while indicating to the Warsaw Pact that NATO's defense was really based on nuclear weapons. This provided deterrence at the risk that the Warsaw Pact might then not see any advantage to avoiding the use of tactical nuclear weapons were they to initiate combat operations.

Many of the other implications of the new Strategic Concept were relatively straightforward. Allies would have to improve the conventional forces-in-being, develop rapid reinforcement forces and provide for their transport, and put more effort into developing available and well-trained mobilizable reserve forces. The rapid reinforcement forces would consist of two types of forces. The rapid reaction deployable multinational forces, whose primary task would be to demonstrate NATO's cohesion and resolve in times of tension, would not actually provide much combat power. The more balanced, national reinforcement forces were to be capable of fighting. The NATO military authorities were also willing to accept different levels of readiness among its forces, depending on their mission. However, nations were also asked to prepare the capability to bring their NATO-assigned and NATO-earmarked forces up to higher readiness levels in a crisis before NATO actually declared specific alert levels since waiting for specific alert levels could mean that forces would not be able to get ready in time. NATO would also have to develop an integrated air defense system, tying in all aircraft, surface-to-air missiles, and antiaircraft artillery. A new, and somewhat ironic, wrinkle was that NATO would also have to develop a purely offensive capability since deliberate escalation could require a region not under attack to initiate offensive (not counteroffensive) operations across enemy borders.

With respect to the general situation, MC 48/3 still identified the Central Region of Allied Command Europe as the "heart of NATO Europe." However, since France had withdrawn from the integrated military command, the region lost depth, leading to NATO ground, and in particular, air, forces being more densely packed on fewer bases, which was a new risk. In addition, since Denmark and Norway did not allow permanent stationing of foreign forces or nuclear weapons in peacetime, and their national forces were small in peacetime, NATO would have to push reinforcements quickly to the Northern Region for a show of force or if the Warsaw Pact initiated some form of aggression. In the Southern Region, NATO would also have to push reinforcements quickly to Greece and Turkey. Naval forces in the Atlantic and the English Channel were instructed to be ready to harass Warsaw Pact nonmilitary ships in retaliation for Warsaw Pact actions on NATO merchant, fishing, or oceanographic shipping. Finally, there was a reminder that there was no overall NATO military commander responsible for the Canada-United States Regional Planning Group region. Nevertheless, the national, bilateral, and regional plans were to be meshed with other NATO strategic plans.

MC 14/3 and its supporting MC 48/3 remained in effect for a remarkable period, just under 24 years, until the NAC approved NATO's post–Cold War Strategic Concept in November 1991. One might include the concepts contained in the Harmel Report as well, because its interlocking twin pillars of a strong defense and dialogue with the Warsaw Pact established the basis for détente from the NATO perspective. The Final Act of the Conference on Security and Cooperation in Europe (the Helsinki Final Act) signed in the summer of 1975 was one of many manifestations of this policy. Another was NATO's dual-track decision in December 1979 to simultaneously pursue deployment of new U.S. intermediate-range nuclear missiles while seeking to negotiate an arms control agreement with the Soviet Union to eliminate all intermediate-range nuclear missiles from Europe. This decision was very contentious within NATO as well as between NATO and the Soviet Union. Despite domestic disagreements over the decision and large public demonstrations against the new U.S. missile deployments, the NATO governments remained firm. Although Gorbachev played a key role in changing Soviet perspectives, the resultant Intermediate-Range Nuclear Forces (INF) Treaty signed in Washington DC in December 1987 in many ways validated the concepts of the Harmel Report. The Treaty on Conventional Armed Forces in Europe (CFE) between NATO and the Warsaw Pact provides a final example of the realization of the Harmel Report concepts. The CFE Treaty's purpose was to limit the size and offensive ability of forces stationed between the Atlantic and the Urals (ATTU), by establishing ceilings for different types of equipment (tanks, aircraft, artillery, attack helicopters, and armored combat vehicles) by bloc, region, and nation; establishing a reporting mechanism; and conducting inspections to verify the reports. Actual negotiations began in March 1989, and the treaty was signed in Paris in November 1990.

MC 14/3 also weathered many events beyond the negotiations. The U.S. military forces withdrew from Vietnam in 1973, but Saigon did not fall to the communist North until 1975. In autumn 1973, the Arab-Israeli Yom Kippur War increased tensions between the United States and Soviet Union. The OPEC Oil Embargo, which produced the 1973 oil shortage, followed the war as punishment for U.S. and Western support for Israel. Within NATO, relations between Greece and Turkey hit an all-time low during the Cyprus crisis, culminated by the Turkish invasion of Cyprus in 1974. Greece then withdrew its forces from NATO's integrated military command structure, and did not return them until 1980. The United States and the Soviet Union fought a proxy war in Angola. The Soviet Union invaded Afghanistan in December 1979, and the United States eventually supported, through the Pakistani military and intelligence services, the mujahideen guerrillas battling the Soviet Army. The rise of the Solidarity trade union in Poland in 1980 appeared to create the conditions for another application of the Brezhnev Doctrine, but the Polish government's imposition of martial law diffused the international situation. The United Kingdom fought the Falklands war against Argentina in the spring of 1982, and Spain acceded to the Washington Treaty and NATO membership in May 1982. In September 1983, the Soviet Union's Air Defense Forces shot down a Korean airliner (KAL 007) as it flew over Soviet airspace due to a navigational error. In 1986, the accident in the Chernobyl nuclear reactor illustrated a new, nonmilitary security threat to NATO.

In the summer of 1989, a Soviet pilotless Mig-23 fighter aircraft actually flew across Germany and the Netherlands before crashing in Belgium after its pilot bailed out over East Germany because of problems controlling the aircraft. NATO military authorities intercepted and monitored the Mig-23's flight and did not interpret it as military aggression. Nevertheless, this highlighted a standing problem for NATO civilian and military authorities, that is, how to strike the right balance between fear and complacency. Every exercise or force deployment by NATO or the Warsaw Pact could potentially be camouflage for a surprise attack on the other. Consequently, the other side had to try to quickly ascertain the motivation behind the exercise or deployment. Doing nothing would place one's forces at a disadvantage, but taking to steps to counter the adversary's actions could start an escalation spiral towards war where none was called for.

The Berlin Wall fell in the fall of 1989. On August 2, 1990, Iraq invaded Kuwait, leading to the UN-mandated Desert Shield and Desert Storm operations. NATO was not specifically involved in the war, but NATO did respond in various ways: It allocated more NATO Airborne Warning and Control System (AWACS) sorties to monitor its southern flank. It deployed NATO naval forces to the eastern Mediterranean to monitor and potentially protect shipping. It provided logistics support to Turkey, and it deployed the aviation portion of the Allied Command Europe (ACE) Mobile Force to Turkey. These actions demonstrated Alliance commitment and was designed to deter any Iraqi intentions to attack Turkey, which was supporting the UN operations. In addition to the United States, the United Kingdom, France, Canada, the Netherlands, Spain, Belgium, Greece, Denmark, and Norway participated in Desert Storm. The United States also led, and the United Kingdom and France participated in, Operation Southern Watch over southern Iraq; and the United States, United Kingdom, and Turkey conducted Operation Northern Watch over northern Iraq. The Soviet Union did not participate, being busy with the political situation at home and having previously been a backer of Saddam Hussein. The Soviet military press originally predicted that Desert Storm would be a drawn-out war with heavy casualties, but after the war, it critiqued the Iraqi implementation of Soviet doctrine and its misuse of Soviet equipment.

The world changed dramatically between when the NAC approved NATO's second Strategic Concept in 1952 and Desert Storm. Communism was no longer seen as a Moscow-based monolithic threat. In fact, the Soviet Union itself was crumbling, and Germany was once again unified. NATO had moved from a strategy of massive retaliation to one of flexible response, although both were still fundamentally based on the U.S. nuclear umbrella deterring the Soviet Union from aggression in Europe. Furthermore, the process of creating the third and fourth strategic concepts demonstrated the effects of consensus decision making. The United States could not always get NATO to agree to its national strategy, and NATO's adoption of flexible response was not possible until after the French left the integrated military structure.

The Committee of Three Wise Men, established in 1956, had pointed out that cohesion, achieved at least partly through continuous and close consultations, was critical to NATO's success, and the Harmel Report and the dual-track decision established that NATO could successfully negotiate with the Soviet Union from a position of strength. NATO and the Soviet Union had survived the Korean War, Soviet interventions in Eastern Europe, Berlin crises, NATO's nuclear sharing, mutually assured destruction and the Cuban Missile Crisis, the U.S. intervention in Southeast Asia, the Soviet intervention in Afghanistan, and peaceful protests in East Berlin, to name but a few events that, had they unfolded in different ways, could have had catastrophic consequences. In spite of the underlying risk of thermonuclear war, NATO and the Warsaw Pact had become largely predictable adversaries.

The NATO military authorities were no longer the legends from World War II, towering over their civilian counterparts, but the new generations of NATO military leaders still relied on worst-case planning since they were responsible to win the war should it occur. Furthermore, the conventional warfare aspects of flexible response let them establish high requirements for conventional forces and their capabilities. Despite the high requirements for conventional forces, the politicians rated the likelihood of war as very low. In addition, the mutual confidence-building aspects of détente in general and the arms control treaties in particular had reduced the risk of the Soviet Union starting a war accidentally or because of a misunderstanding. Military spending was important, but national survival did not appear at stake. In retrospect, the relationship was comfortable. The question then became which of NATO's lessons learned from the Cold War could be taken forward to the new era of uncertainty dawning in Europe.

Questions for Consideration

- The Allies have consistently failed to meet their defense requirements and the desired 2 percent of GDP spending on defense—why didn't the Soviet attack?
- Could NATO have gotten by with lower defense requirements?
- Did the West win the Cold War?

CHAPTER 6

The Post–Cold War World and 9/11: Questions of the Past and of the Future

The Strategic Concept (MC 14/3) and its supporting MC 48/3 remained operative until the North Atlantic Council (NAC) approved NATO's post–Cold War Strategic Concept in November 1991. During this 24-year period, the selection of Mikhail Gorbachev to become the General Secretary of the Communist Party of the Soviet Union in 1985 was perhaps the event with the most impact on NATO, the Soviet Union, and the Warsaw Pact. Gorbachev's perestroika and glasnost reforms had the potential to lead to major unrest in Eastern Europe, but his decision to reject the Brezhnev Doctrine led to relatively peaceful transitions of political power in the Warsaw Pact countries. The fall of the Berlin Wall in November 1989 highlighted another potential crisis in the long history of the German question, but it was resolved with the Treaty on the Final Settlement With Respect to Germany, also known as the Two Plus Four Treaty, signed in Moscow on September 12, 1990. West Germany and East Germany were the *two*, allowed to participate in the process by the *four* European Victory Powers from World War II to finally resolve the German question. Meanwhile, nationalist sentiment grew in the various Soviet republics, creating crisis upon crisis, with demonstrations initially suppressed by force. In August 1991, there was a coup against Gorbachev. Although he was freed after three days, it was clear that his power and the existence of the Soviet Union were both rapidly coming to the end.

Questions for Consideration

- Counterfactuals:
  - What if there never had been a NATO?
  - Would Germany have remained divided forever?

> - Would Germany have united, but been neutral and demilitarized?
> - Would the Soviet Union have lasted longer?
> - What would have happened to Western Europe?
> - In your opinion, should NATO have continued after 1991?
> - What were the policy options for dealing with Russia, what would you have chosen to do, and why?
> - In your opinion, did NATO have a credible deterrent against any type of attack through its capability to launch a counterattack with nuclear weapons in 1991?
>   - Who was NATO deterring, and how?

The Fifth Strategic Concept (1991)

When the 1991 Strategic Concept was adopted at the NATO Summit in November 1991, Germany was unified, the Warsaw Pact had disbanded a couple months earlier, and the days of the Soviet Union were numbered. The Harmel Report had indicated that solving the German question would bring security to Europe. Many began to wonder why NATO should continue to exist. NATO, after all, had "won" the Cold War. However, there was a great deal of uncertainty as to what would develop in the political spaces that had once been the Soviet Union and the Warsaw Pact. Pessimists argued that it was too early to tell where the changes might lead and whether they would become permanent. The Soviet Union and Eastern Europe might fall into chaos, perhaps leading to new dictatorships. Consequently, the Allies were not quick to disband the organization and structures that had proved to be so helpful in building commonality of effort and purpose, created over years of discussions, and in deepening relationships, mutual trust, and information sharing.

The 1991 Strategic Concept was the first Strategic Concept that was unclassified, and not coincidentally, was the first that did not start in NATO military circles. It was a new era. However, its corresponding Military Committee Directive for Military Implementation of the Alliance's Strategic Concept, MC 400, published in December 1991 was, and remains, classified.

The 1991 Strategic Concept reflected the uncertainties of the times. It highlighted a mix of threats and opportunities, capturing NATO's uncertainty over what the future might bring. It also implicitly tried to answer the question of "why NATO?" The Conventional Armed Forces in Europe (CFE) treaty was noted because "its implementation will remove the Alliance's numerical inferiority in key conventional weapon systems." The fixation on the conventional force balance between NATO and the Warsaw Pact seemed out of place since the Warsaw Pact had already dissolved. In addition, the logical conclusion from the statement would have appeared to be that NATO could breathe easier, and tactical nuclear weapons would soon be a thing of the past because NATO would not need them to equalize the Warsaw Pact's superiority in conventional weapons. This was not exactly to be the case, though, because as the Strategic Concept pointed out, the Soviet Union's conventional forces under CFE remained the largest in Europe.

In addition, Soviet nuclear "capabilities have to be taken into account if stability and security in Europe are to be preserved." The 1991 Strategic Concept also highlighted that the Soviet Union's nuclear capability was still on par with that of the United States. The Soviet Union was still a major threat to the security of the European Allies. NATO's military authorities would continue to plan for worst-case scenarios involving Soviet major attacks using the full range of conventional and nuclear weapons. NATO had to maintain "the strategic balance in Europe." The Soviets were still being kept out. In this respect, the 1991 Strategic Concept did not appear that different from previous NATO strategic concepts: "Nuclear weapons make a unique contribution in rendering the risks of any aggression incalculable and unacceptable. Thus they remain essential to preserve peace." NATO did not give up its potential first-use philosophy.

The former Soviet satellites could be subtracted from the Soviet side of the balance of power equation, but this was not necessarily a completely good thing. The 1991 Strategic Concept stated that Eastern Europe faced major economic, social, and political problems, among them potential territorial disputes fueled partially by ethnic tensions. These problems could erupt into crises or wars that could directly affect the security of NATO's members.

Furthermore, NATO was no longer arguing that Germany would be the main battleground in a future war. NATO announced in the Strategic Concept that it would reduce its tactical nuclear forces in Europe and actually eliminate the nuclear artillery and short-range surface-to-surface nuclear missiles, which were always the most problematic technically and politically. Technically, these systems would be fired from behind NATO conventional forces, fly over them, and land near them. The concept generated questions about the survivability of the forward NATO troops, their ability to conduct combat operations if the Soviets were also firing nuclear artillery, and their long-range health prospects. Politically, if NATO forces retreated sufficiently before firing such systems, the nuclear detonations would occur on enemy-occupied, but NATO, territory and would affect Allied citizens. These issues would be mitigated by NATO's reliance on longer range, dual-capable aircraft to provide the tactical nuclear war–fighting capability. This would continue to provide the politically important linkage between the U.S. strategic nuclear weapons and the European NATO members by distributing the storage and delivery of U.S. tactical nuclear weapons across several European nations' territories and air forces. This European participation also dovetailed with European members' participation in NATO nuclear planning and decision making. "Off-shore systems" would supplement the dual-capable aircraft.

Conventionally, NATO would reduce the size of its overall military forces, reduce the readiness levels of some forces, and in the central European region, no longer rely on forward, in-place, linear defenses. However, the commitment to reduce forces was not as grandiose as it might seem, considering that the reductions were tied to the CFE Treaty; the unification of Germany had "moved" the old NATO positions from the front line to the rear overnight; and the Two Plus Four Treaty prohibited stationing non-German forces, nuclear weapons, or nuclear weapons carriers in the former East Germany. The unification of Germany shifted the major military focus out of central Europe. NATO was now concerned about the potential instability as well as the military forces of the nations bordering NATO's southern region.

Furthermore, even as the forces were being reduced, NATO needed its conventional forces to become more flexible and more mobile, and Allies to be able to augment, or reinforce, other NATO forces since NATO's military forces would now play a role in managing crises in addition to their traditional deterrent and Article 5 roles. Conceptually, certain NATO forces would need to be able to be quickly built up, deployed, drawn down, and redeployed in carefully orchestrated responses as NATO political authorities managed crises. The Strategic Concept did not explicitly state where these forces might be deployed. It did state that the forces must be capable of reinforcing "any area at risk within the territory of the Allies and to establish a multinational presence when and where this is needed." The possibility of deploying crisis reaction forces beyond NATO territory was left open.

NATO also announced a new characterization of its conventional forces. Henceforth, NATO's conventional forces would consist of available forces, main defense forces, and augmentation forces. The available forces would consist of immediate and rapid reaction forces, designed to be well trained and well equipped, maintained at higher readiness levels and in sufficient numbers to deter limited attacks or defend NATO territory in the case of surprise or limited attacks. They would also serve as crisis reaction forces. The main defense and augmentation forces were to consist of a mix of active-duty and mobilizable elements. The main defense forces would be the core of the forces defending NATO territory, and the augmentation forces would serve as reinforcements. The ground forces in the main defense and augmentation forces would be at lower readiness levels and rely on reserves and mobilization to bring them to their full combat power. As the Soviet conventional forces were collapsing, NATO wanted to move to more mobile, better trained, and better equipped forces at higher readiness states. In addition, NATO emphasized the concept of large mobilizable reserve force.

The 1991 Strategic Concept also broadened NATO's approach to security: "Alliance security must also take account of the global context." Furthermore, "NATO's essential purpose, set out in the Washington Treaty, . . . is to safeguard the freedom and security of all its members by political and military means." Instead of referring to the Article 6 geographic restraints, the Alliance was looking beyond Europe to risks to European security such as the "disruption of the flow of vital resources," weapons of mass destruction proliferation, and terrorism. Many of these threats appeared to be tied to the Middle East and North Africa, and the Strategic Concept stated that "the stability and peace of the countries on the southern periphery of Europe are important for the security of the Alliance, as the 1991 Gulf War has shown." NATO had deployed the Allied Command Europe Mobile Force (Air) to Turkey in January 1991 to increase Turkey's security and demonstrate NATO's commitment to Turkey in case Iraq decided to take any action against Turkey during Operation Desert Storm. The multiple references to Article 4 consultations on security issues that might be beyond NATO territory paralleled the post–Suez Crisis Committee of Three Wisemen's report that NATO nations should use NATO forums to consult on a wide range of security-related issues. The collapse of the Warsaw Pact seemed to set conditions that would allow the Alliance to contemplate actions in 1991 that had ended in fiasco for two of its members in Suez in 1956.

For the first time in a Strategic Concept, NATO acknowledged that the European Community (EC), Western European Union (WEU), and Conference on Security and Cooperation in Europe (CSCE) existed and played important roles in Europe. However, NATO was unique. None of the other organizations tied American nuclear weapons to the defense of the European Allies. The Strategic Concept also addressed several complementary internal NATO initiatives such as the "development of a European security identity" within the EC and the "strengthening of the European pillar within the Alliance." The inclusion of these ideas seemed to cloud the issues. For example, increasing the capabilities of European Allies' defense forces and their ability to cooperate within a European context would serve to achieve EC goals as much as NATO's while concurrently making the EC more like NATO.

Nevertheless, the positive statements about the development of a European security identity stood in juxtaposition to the apparent concern that Allies might retreat from their high level of cooperation. Consequently, there were several statements highlighting what the Allies should continue to do. For example, Alliance solidarity required continued "widespread participation" by European Allies in nuclear planning, basing, and consultation arrangements. The Allies realized that their continued reliance on nuclear weapons would be met by a degree of skepticism among some of their publics. NATO would also increase its dependence on multinational forces because doing so would demonstrate political solidarity, let Europeans work together to strengthen the European pillar, and allow savings through specialization. In addition, multinational forces would be more capable than the national forces of most members.

Finally, there was the old argument that one advantage of NATO's collective defense planning was to "prevent the renationalisation of defense policies." NATO was not only about collective defense from external threats. The Alliance's collective military planning process had increased the confidence and trust between the members, contributing to stability and peace within the Alliance as well. Consequently, the members should not be too hasty to reduce their integration via NATO since security was not only about the Soviet Union. In fact, if the Soviet Union no longer was the bogeyman and Allies were looking for the peace dividend through reduced defense spending, there was a fallback reason for NATO to remain strong. Eastern Europe was a dangerous place that could directly affect Alliance security.

Optimists wanted to recognize the dramatic changes that had taken place in Europe and to foster their continuation. It was an opportunity to overcome the division of Europe and bring peaceful stability and economic growth across the continent. NATO had extended the "hand of friendship and cooperation" to the Warsaw Pact members at the NATO Summit in July 1990, indicating a new direction for NATO. NATO's buzzwords for positively reacting to the new strategic situation were *dialogue* and *cooperation*. However, NATO had to remain strong in order to negotiate with "confidence" and achieve its "desired results." Dialogue and cooperation were specifically tied to arms control and disarmament objectives, with the goal of getting other nations to reduce their forces so that NATO could do the same. However, dialogue and cooperation had new possibilities as well. NATO had established diplomatic and military contacts with former Warsaw Pact members and sought to "increase transparency and predictability in security affairs" in order to increase stability across Europe. In addition, cooperation now specifically included working together with former adversaries to prevent or manage crises. Several of these former adversaries had participated in Desert Storm.

The 1991 Strategic Concept was very prophetic with respect to the risks of war in Eastern Europe as well as to the benefits of friendship and cooperation. The evolution of the 1991 Strategic Concept's ideas of crisis management and cooperation were easily discernable during the 1990s in NATO's Balkan operations and Partnership for Peace (PfP). (See the Timeline of Major NATO Military Operations in Appendix I.) The Balkan wars, in which NATO military forces had for the first time engaged in combat, had perhaps the biggest impact on NATO during that decade. In fact, as the heads of state and government were sitting down at the 1999 summit in Washington DC, NATO aircraft were engaged in combat again in Operation Allied Force, attacking targets in Serbia and Kosovo. NATO began its Balkans operations in the summer of 1992, putting ships in the Adriatic to monitor the UN's maritime embargo to prevent the shipping of arms into former Yugoslavia under Operation Maritime Monitor. NATO continued to increase its involvement, eventually enforcing the UN no-fly zone over Bosnia-Herzegovina, during which NATO forces shot down several Serbian fighter aircraft in February 1994. This was NATO's first combat experience. In August and September 1995, NATO aircraft bombed Bosnian Serb positions. NATO's military presence was a factor contributing to the Dayton Agreement, and in December 1995, NATO provided the peacekeeping force (Implementation Force [IFOR]) to implement the Dayton Agreement. Seventeen non-NATO nations, including Russia, participated in IFOR. IFOR's successor, Stabilization Force (SFOR), continued under NATO command through 2004 in Bosnia-Herzegovina. NATO conducted Operation Allied Force, bombing Serbia without a UN Mandate, from March through June of 1999. NATO then led the UN-mandated Kosovo Force (KFOR) to implement the peace. As with IFOR/SFOR, non-Allies, including Russia, participated in KFOR. NATO also deployed a logistics command center to Albania to support its KFOR operations.

NATO created the Partnership for Peace (PfP) program in 1994. PfP let former Warsaw Pact states, former Soviet republics, and European neutrals each create a bilateral relationship with NATO, in which each country could participate as much or as little as it desired in NATO PfP opportunities. NATO also began the Mediterranean Dialogue in 1994, creating something similar to PfP for select Middle Eastern and North African countries. The Balkan wars and PfP were interrelated since Partners participating in the operations wanted more say in the decision making and the conduct of NATO operations, in which Partners sometimes provided more troops than some Allies did. Although reluctant to grant more authority to Partners, NATO did see the potential planning advantages of having more information on Partner military capabilities. Consequently, NATO created the Planning and Review Process (PARP) within the PfP framework in 1995.

In 1997, NATO created the Euro-Atlantic Partnership Council as a forum for all PfP participants to meet with the NATO Allies. NATO also signed special, individual agreements with Russia and Ukraine, which created the NATO-Russia Permanent Joint Council and the NATO-Ukraine Commission. In March 1999, Poland, the Czech Republic, and Hungary became the first former–Warsaw Pact states to join NATO. This was done at a separate event prior to the summit in order to reduce the risk of the enlargement issue being a stumbling block to Russian participation at the summit itself. At the 1999 summit, NATO also announced the Membership Action Plan, establishing a clear program for future prospective members wishing to follow the path of Poland, the Czech Republic, and Hungary.

The Russian Federation underwent tremendous change during this period. It faced economic turmoil at home for most of the 1990s, with a major economic crisis in 1998. Russian forces participated in the civil war in Tajikistan from 1992 to 1997, and fought the First Chechen War from 1994 to

1996, the Second Chechen War from 1999 to 2000, and have continued to intermittently battle a Chechen insurgency ever since. Russia participated with NATO in IFOR, SFOR, and KFOR. In addition, Russia joined PfP, and signed the NATO-Russia Founding Act in 1997, establishing the Permanent Joint Council and permanent Russian representation at NATO Headquarters. However, Russia froze its relations with NATO when it became apparent that it had no real power to dissuade NATO from bombing Serbia because of its actions in Kosovo in 1999. Russia was also not enamored with the idea of continued NATO enlargement.

Questions for Consideration

- How much of the 1999 Strategic Concept appears to you to be retroactive justification for what NATO did in the 1990s?
- Would you put any bounds on NATO engagement, cooperation, or operations beyond the borders of its members?
  - If yes, how would you conceptualize these boundaries for future decisions on whether NATO should get involved in particular areas or whether it should respond to particular crises?
- Is it possible for the Allied nations to meet the range of missions laid out in the 1999 Strategic Concept?
  - Can each of the types of missions be met equally well, or should they be prioritized?
  - If you think prioritization is necessary, how would you prioritize the missions?
- How do you see the future of PfP?

The Sixth Strategic Concept (1999)

NATO's 50th Anniversary Summit provided an impetus to review NATO's experience with European security in the decade or so since the end of the Cold War and to make course corrections for the future. The dramatic changes in Europe in the 1990s, the growing controversy over Kosovo, and all the potential publicity practically demanded the release of a new Strategic Concept. Since 1991, NATO had stretched its definition of security from the collective military defense of NATO territory to conducting combat operations in places that had not directly threatened NATO countries with conventional or nuclear forces. Nevertheless, there was a line of perspective members waiting for an opportunity to join the new, *transformed*, NATO.

The introduction of the 1999 Strategic Concept stressed that NATO was *indispensable*, and as in the 1991 version, that NATO "must maintain collective defence and reinforce the transatlantic link and ensure a balance that allows the European Allies to assume greater responsibility." NATO's contin-ued reliance on nuclear weapons was also subtly referenced in the introduc-tion: NATO "must, above all, maintain the political will and the military means required by the entire range of its missions." NATO defined its purpose in the 1999 Strategic Concept along the same expanded lines that it used in 1991: "To safeguard the freedom and security of all its members by political and military means." However, in the 1999 version, this had become NATO's *enduring* purpose, and, as a reflection of Operation Allied Force, it was no lon-ger directly linked to the UN Charter. Instead, in 1999, NATO's purpose was based on "common values of democracy, human rights and the rule of law," which was an emerging mantra for use in enlargement decisions.

Whereas the 1991 Strategic Concept mentioned NATO's need to main-tain the strategic balance in Europe, the 1999 version stated: "The Alliance does not consider itself to be any country's adversary." There was no longer any country or group of countries to counterbalance. The Soviet Union's successor, the Russian Federation, was no longer considered an adversary. There was, of course, evil still lurking in the world. NATO must remain strong: "Notwithstanding positive developments in the strategic environ-ment and the fact that large-scale conventional aggression against the Al-liance is highly unlikely, the possibility of such a threat emerging over the longer term exists." One would think that this would be difficult to plan for without the additional inclusion that "the existence of powerful nuclear forces outside the Alliance also constitutes a significant factor which the Al-liance has to take into account if security and stability in the Euro-Atlantic area are to be maintained." Russia was clearly the point of this veiled refer-ence. Nevertheless, the conditions under which NATO would have to con-template using nuclear weapons were assessed to be "extremely remote."

As with the 1991 version, Russia was important, but not the only po-tential security problem facing NATO in 1999. Instead of limiting internal difficulties and potential instability to central and Eastern Europe, the 1999 Strategic Concept expanded to "some countries in and around the Euro-Atlantic area" where internal difficulties could lead to instability, which in turn could affect Euro-Atlantic stability and potentially lead to armed con-flict. The 1999 version also inserted the phrase "human suffering" into the jargon, highlighting a new potential reason for NATO intervention beyond its members' borders. This new reason retroactively justified NATO's Balkan operations. It also expanded the potential for NATO military operations well beyond the restraints of Articles 4, 5, and 6. The 1999 version continued the need to "take account of the global context." However, in 1999, weapons of mass destruction and their delivery means were connected with non-state ac-tors. The spread of technology across the globe could lead to the proliferation of advanced weapons, and "state and non-state adversaries may try to exploit the Alliance's growing reliance on information systems through information operations designed to disrupt such systems" and thereby counter "NATO's superiority in traditional weaponry." NATO had finally achieved superiority in conventional weapons over its potential adversaries, only to discover a new vulnerability in what would eventually be called *cyberspace*. In addition, NATO added organized crime and mass migrations to the litany of terrorism, sabotage, and disruption of the flow of vital resources, as examples of "other risks of a wider nature" affecting Alliance security. In fact, the 1999 strategic concept stated "that the Alliance's forces and infrastructure must be protected against terrorist attacks."

The four core security functions of the 1991 Strategic Concept morphed into five fundamental security tasks in the 1999 version. The first task, security, was almost the same, except that instead of being limited to Europe as in 1991, in 1999, NATO provided a foundation for the "Euro-Atlantic security environment." The second task, consultation, was also almost the same, but in 1999, NATO became an *essential* transatlantic forum for Article 4 consultations. The third task, deterrence and defense, was also quite similar to the 1991 version; however, instead of the more forward-leaning defense of *the territory* of any Ally, the 1999 version returned to traditional caveats: "As provided for in Articles 5 and 6." Article 5 does not provide an automatic common military response, and Article 6 limits the application of Article 5 to specific geographic limits. Whereas the 1991 version's fourth function was to maintain the strategic balance in Europe, in 1999, NATO no longer considered itself any country's adversary.

The 1999 version's fourth task, crisis management, and fifth task, partnership, were categorized as benefiting non-NATO nations by enhancing "the security and stability of the Euro-Atlantic area." Crisis management was tied to Article 7 (rights and obligations under the UN Charter and UN Security Council responsibilities), perhaps giving it more legitimacy, while stressing that NATO's participation would be on a case-by-case basis, and of course, through consensus. NATO felt a need to declare how the Washington Treaty covered military operations conducted under the rubric of crisis management since Article 5 is limited to the case of an armed attack against a member, and Article 4 specifically permits a member to call for consultations when its territory, independence, or security is threatened. The 1999 strategic concept emphasized the *non–Article 5* nature of crisis response operations while simultaneously using the parallels to Article 5 operations as the reason for using common Alliance structures and procedures to plan, train, and execute non–Article 5 crisis response operations. The term *partnership* added "the capacity for joint action with the Alliance," in recognition of how PfP had already evolved. NATO committed itself to "increasing the role the Partners play in PfP decision-making and planning, and making PfP more operational."

In addition, NATO offered a quasi Article 5 commitment by using Article 4–like wording to undertake "to consult with any active participant in the Partnership if that Partner perceives a direct threat to its territorial integrity, political independence, or security."

A decade after the fall of the Berlin Wall, NATO appeared much more secure in its role within the architecture of the European security system. The issue was no longer one of justifying NATO's continued existence, but defining how NATO interacted with the UN, the Organization for Security and Cooperation in Europe (OSCE, formerly CSCE), the European Union (EU, formerly EC), and the WEU. The EU's development of a Common Foreign and Security Policy (CFSP) was linked to the European Security and Defense Identity (ESDI) within NATO, and NATO's agreement to make "available NATO assets and capabilities for WEU-led operations." Specifically, NATO agreed to:

> Assist the European Allies to act by themselves as required through the readiness of the Alliance, on a case-by-case basis and by consensus, to make its assets and capabilities available for operations in which the Alliance is not engaged militarily under the political control and the strategic direction either of the WEU or as otherwise agreed, taking into account the full participation of all European Allies if they were so to choose.

The 1999 Strategic Concept gave the NATO military authorities quite a wide range of planning and force structuring responsibilities. At the high end was the enduring nuclear deterrence against unnamed potential adversaries. This deterrent continued to rest on NATO's perceived ability to initiate a major strategic nuclear weapon counterattack, which in turn rested partly on weapons and training, and partly on Alliance resolve to resort to that option if necessary. In addition, the practical aspects of the military planning process for this event required a potential adversary, even if NATO had no adversaries.

The next level of military force below a strategic nuclear exchange was Article 5 conventional operations supported by tactical nuclear weapons. This level of military force was somewhat problematic since NATO now admitted it had conventional superiority over all nations in the area, and NATO's justification for the possession and potential use of tactical nuclear weapons previously rested on NATO's conventional inferiority in Europe. However, NATO stated that the fact that its capability "to mount a successful conventional defense has significantly improved" allowed it to reduce its sub-strategic nuclear forces since the conditions under which NATO would have to contemplate using nuclear weapons was assessed to be "extremely remote." In addition to having already eliminated the nuclear artillery and ground-launched short-range nuclear missiles as promised in the 1991 Strategic Concept, NATO reduced the readiness level of its nuclear forces, terminated "standing peacetime nuclear contingency plans," and stated that its "nuclear forces no longer target any country."

Nevertheless, NATO would maintain sub-strategic nuclear forces in Europe to reinforce the transatlantic link. Simultaneously, NATO stated that its remaining sub-strategic nuclear forces included "a small number" of British Trident submarine-launched ballistic missiles in addition to the dual-capable aircraft noted in the 1991 Strategic Concept. Nevertheless, as with strategic nuclear weapons, NATO military authorities would need potential targets in order to conduct practical military planning and to develop force structure options. In addition, the NATO military authorities were instructed to be able "to deter and defend against the use of NBC [nuclear, biological, and chemical] weapons," improve missile defenses, and protect not only NATO troops on NATO territory, but also troops deployed beyond NATO territory so that they could fight effectively "despite the presence, threat or use of NBC weapons."

Article 5 scenarios that would be completely fought with only conventional weapons were the next level of military force; non–Article 5 crisis response operations, which NATO was already conducting in the Balkans, formed the lowest level of employment of military force. The 1999 Strategic Concept reinforced the likelihood of NATO crisis response operations. National forces had to be prepared to deploy "beyond the Allies' territory," an issue that was very problematic in the initial Balkan operations, but which had since become accepted practice. NATO also moved to a forward defense with respect to crises in the 1999 Strategic Concept: "An important aim of the Alliance and its forces is to keep risks at a distance by dealing with potential crises at an early stage."

Although it may have been assumed in 1991, the 1999 Strategic Concept removed any doubt and clearly tasked the NATO military authorities to retain the capability for Article 5 operations while conducting non–Article 5 crisis response operations. This indirectly buttressed the need for the tactical nuclear weapons as a substitute for forces deployed to crisis management operations beyond NATO's territory. In addition, the tasking to deter and defend forces deployed beyond NATO's border from NBC weapons further justified NATO's nuclear forces since NATO ruled out a biological or chemical warfare capability beyond defensive measures, leaving conventional and nuclear weapons as the weapons of mass destruction deterrent. However, the implications of this for basing or deploying tactical nuclear weapons if such a threat were to occur were not addressed. In addition, NATO's political authorities also levied the requirement "that the Alliance's forces and infrastructure must be protected against terrorist attacks."

In addition to the four levels of military force described above, NATO forces would also have to cooperate and exercise with Partner forces, and in some cases with military forces that were not from Allied or Partner nations. This also impacted NATO force structure and planning. In addition, the European members would have to be given opportunities to develop force structures capable of eventually conducting exercises or operations under WEU political direction. Forces to support WEU operations were to be "separable but not separate capabilities." Each asset or unit lent to the WEU would be one less for potential NATO operations. The NATO-led PfP exercises and operations as well as the WEU exercises and operations would be based on NATO's integrated military structure as supplemented by cooperation agreements with the individual Partners, with the ESDI Allies, or with the WEU. In addition, the NATO forces could conduct "operations in support of other international organizations." NATO military forces were also expected to participate in military-to-military contacts and other PfP events, as well as similar NATO-Russia, NATO-Ukraine, and Mediterranean Dialogue events. Finally, although not strictly falling under the partnership, the 1999 Strategic Concept also highlighted the importance of civil-military cooperation in combating the less defined threats to security such as cyberspace, organized crime, and mass migrations, where the military's role was unclear. The NATO military forces faced very wide-ranging and flexible demands.

NATO also changed the categorization of its force structure in the 1999 Strategic Concept because of its Balkan experiences. NATO would still need high readiness forces for immediate or rapid use in Article 5 and non–Article 5 operations. However, the term *main defense forces* was dropped because these forces were not only the primary forces for Article 5 collective defense operations, they were also the forces that provided reinforcements to a particular region, and more importantly, provided forces in rotation for a sustained crisis response operation. The problem was that the mobilizable reserve forces (i.e., those that would only be needed "for the worst case— but very remote—scenario of large scale operations for collective defense") had the lowest readiness and required the longest buildup times. From the military point of view, they were too hard to integrate into crisis management operations, and from the political perspective, it was too difficult to call them up for a crisis. *Crisis* implied a short duration event, and the public associated large-scale reserve call-ups of indefinite length with mobilization for major war. Reserve forces, which had been for decades the backbone of NATO's large-scale Article 5 defense, were verging on unimportance. Many Allies had converted from conscription-based militaries, which had served partially to create and train a large reserve pool, to professional militaries using high technology equipment, whose higher personnel costs tended to be offset by personnel reductions and reductions in spending on reserves. For most nations, the reserves were generally not useable in crisis response operations or as quick reaction forces-in-being to defend against a surprise attack on NATO territory, and there was no plausible scenario for a long buildup period prior to a massive Article 5 operation.

NATO military forces had to cover these wide-ranging mission sets in the face of the perpetual counterargument that NATO's security also rested on its members having sound economies, so defense spending must be kept to a minimum. The Balkan missions provided experience that pointed to the solutions. IFOR/SFOR relied on multinational forces, the addition of Partner and other nations' forces, and the development of ad hoc combined and multinational headquarters, sector, and unit command and control structures. NATO's Combined Joint Task Force (CJTF) concept was to provide the structure and doctrine for future tailorable, deployable multinational and combined command and control structures. A CJTF would be developed under the NATO integrated military command structure, but could also be chopped (transferred) to WEU command or control if necessary.

Multinational forces allowed cost savings in Allied national personnel and equipment while concurrently allowing specialization, which could support specific task force formulations and ESDI concerns. This would allow the Alliance to have access to a broader range of capabilities than most members could ever fund in their individual national forces. A consequence, however, is that some Allied militaries are not able to function independently. Perhaps more importantly, an Ally that provides a crucial specialized skill can inflate its political weight within NATO if NATO could not conduct an operation without that specific Ally's participation. Partner and other non-NATO forces added further manpower, equipment, and potentially niche capabilities that together could offset NATO active duty reductions and replace NATO reserves. PARP and the Balkans experience facilitated this. The participation of Partners and other nations also added legitimacy to the NATO operations.

The trick, of course, was that integrated defense planning required detailed information on each participant's defense capabilities; standardization of procedures and doctrine; and interoperability of equipment, not just across the Allies, but also across the Partner militaries and any other nation's forces that might wish to join a specific operation. In addition, since NATO took on the crisis management mantle for out-of-NATO-area operations, NATO needed more deployable and more mobile forces, transport capabilities, and planning processes to take into account force rotation as well as the logistics sustainability of deployed NATO forces. In many cases these were new requirements. A country like Germany, for example, had not considered or equipped its forces to deploy significant numbers outside of Germany, let alone outside of NATO territory prior to NATO's Balkan operations. Consequently, the

1999 Strategic Concept's emphasis on multinational operations also high-lighted the need to use multinational funding, which included NATO fund-ing via the Military Budget and NATO Security Investment Program (NSIP) to acquire and maintain at least some of the newly required capabilities and equipment. It also provided external justifications, from NATO, the WEU, and indirectly the EU, for Allies to continue to spend on defense.

This chapter concludes the examination of NATO's strategic concept se-ries as documentation of the evolution of NATO's thinking about the threats that it faced and the responses NATO chose to counter perceived threats. The first two strategic concepts, approved in 1949 and in 1952, were NATO's first cuts at its collective defense. NATO saw itself as outgunned by the Soviet Army so it developed plans to increase its collective military capabilities. The outbreak of the Korean War gave impetus to the perceived need to increase NATO's defenses, but in the end, both strategic concepts relied on U.S. stra-tegic atomic bombers as the ultimate weapon to defend Western Europe from Soviet aggression. By the third Strategic Concept, approved in 1957, NATO was looking at heavily integrating tactical nuclear weapons with conven-tional forces. The NATO military authorities were convinced that NATO could not stop Soviet aggression without using both tactical and strategic nuclear weapons in addition to conventional forces. NATO could not fight a limited, conventional war with the Soviet Union and win; however, since the Soviet Union was developing ICBMs that would eventually be able to attack North America, NATO's threat of massive retaliation was loosing its credibility. The French departure from NATO's integrated military structure was another factor in NATO's decision to adopt flexible response as its fourth Strategic Concept in 1968. NATO remained with this strategic concept and its still heavy reliance on nuclear warfighting capabilities until adopting the fifth Strategic Concept in 1991 at the end of the Cold War.

In 1991, NATO was unsure how things would develop in the Soviet Union and Eastern Europe. The Soviet Union was still a potential nuclear and con-ventional force threat to Western Europe, and Desert Storm indicated that modern warfare could be fought in the Middle East oil region at a level be-yond the capability of many Allies. Nevertheless, NATO's justification for its continued existence and defense spending requirements were meeting some resistance. Taxpayers were looking for a peace dividend after the Cold War, and European integration was both deepening and widening. NATO demon-strated its utility in managing the crises in former Yugoslavia with the help of its new Partners. In 1999, NATO adopted its sixth Strategic Concept, which incorporated many of the lessons of its peacekeeping operations in the Bal-kans, while NATO embarked on its first peacemaking operation in Kosovo, again with Partner support. NATO found that it needed its conventional forces to become more responsive and that it also needed more command

and control and transport capabilities to support crisis management operations. Simultaneously NATO was establishing conditions and procedures for sharing such assets with the EU as the EU moved towards more military integration among its members. Although the sixth Strategic Concept had a large focus on crisis response operations, NATO stood by its requirements to maintain both strategic and sub-strategic nuclear forces.

CHAPTER 7

NATO's Next Strategic Concept

As this book goes to print, NATO is still operating under its sixth Strategic Concept (introduced in 1999); however, NATO is far along the process of developing its seventh Strategic Concept. Following the spirit of the 1991 and 1999 strategic concepts, NATO has opened the development process to broader public scrutiny than ever before. At the 2009 NATO Summit in Strasbourg/Kehl, the heads of state and government tasked the secretary general to lead the development of a new NATO Strategic Concept and provide it along with implementation proposals at the next summit, scheduled for late 2010. The Alliance leaders were clear in their assessment that NATO will continue to have a mix of conventional and nuclear forces. They also instructed the secretary general to gather a group of experts that would consult with all the Allies in order to develop the new Strategic Concept. The group of experts, under the chair of Madeleine Albright, former U.S. secretary of state, conducted a series of meetings, conferences, consultations, and seminars that generated considerable discussion. The group released its final report, *NATO 2020: Assured Security; Dynamic Engagement*, in May 2010. The report is not the new Strategic Concept, but it sets to paper preliminary perspectives, boundaries, and wording for further discussion within NATO. One can logically assume that a good part of *NATO 2020* will end up in the final version of the new Strategic Concept. This chapter begins with a review of world events leading up to the decision to develop the new Strategic Concept, and then provides an analysis of *NATO 2020*.

9/11 and the Changed Environment

To many the terrorist attacks of September 11, 2001, appeared out of the blue, and the 1999 Strategic Concept's mention of terrorism appears quite prophetic. However, the drafters of the 1999 Strategic Concept were aware of the 1998 attacks on the U.S. embassies in Nairobi and Dar es Salaam and the U.S. retaliatory missile strikes in Afghanistan and Sudan. Regardless, the 9/11 terrorist attacks and their aftermath certainly dominated the first decade of the new century. The tragedy of 9/11 led to an outpouring of sympathy and offers of assistance from U.S. Allies, and indeed much of the world. There was discussion of invoking Article 5 almost immediately. In the end, however, the North Atlantic Council (NAC) decided to wait until the United States could determine that it had been attacked by a foreign entity, so NATO's first invocation of Article 5 did not occur until October. Although the Washington Treaty was not written in these terms, the general understanding up to that point had always been that NATO was a mechanism to allow the United States and Canada to assist the European Allies in their defense. There were no common planning scenarios offering cases in which the Europeans would reinforce and support the United States. The United States provided most of NATO's strategic capabilities such as airlift, air-to-air refueling, and nuclear weapons. NATO, as an organization, and the European Allies had rather limited capabilities to offer the United States. Consequently, there were no obvious contingency plans to rely on for initial use in coordinating a NATO response.

Politically, NATO had not invoked Article 5 or intervened militarily in defense of France during the Algerian insurgency, or against various smaller scale terrorist attacks and insurgencies such as those led by the Irish Republican Army (IRA) in the United Kingdom, the Red Army Faction (RAF) in West Germany, the Red Brigades in Italy, or Basque Homeland and Freedom (ETA) in Spain. Consequently, there was a need to show the difference between these and the U.S. 9/11 case, since the attack was not a conventional assault by a nation-state. The United States was also not immediately sure that the added legitimacy of a NATO Article 5 decision would counterbalance the implied need for more Allied consultations and inputs in determining its response to 9/11. From the non-U.S. Allies perspective, as the source of the attacks became known, the implications of invoking Article 5 became clear. Although Article 5 does not require Allies to actually provide any specific type of assistance, at a minimum, its invocation would be interpreted as the Allies at least symbolically supporting the U.S. response, including military operations in Afghanistan.

NATO invoked Article 5 and provided NATO airborne warning and control system (AWACS) aircraft to assist in U.S. airspace surveillance and control. NATO also expanded its naval presence in the Mediterranean to protect Allied shipping; however, NATO was still running Stabilization Force (SFOR) in Bosnia, Kosovo Force (KFOR) in Kosovo (approximately 8,000 Allied troops still served in the 10,000-man KFOR in February 2010), and operations in Macedonia, so it was already stretched militarily. Long-term plans to turn peacekeeping operations in Europe over to the Western European Union (WEU) or European Union (EU) were successful with SFOR and Macedonia, but this did not free up significant NATO capabilities since European forces were still involved under the EU auspices.

In addition, the United States and other Allies were content to use NATO forums for consultations and coordination, but not for command over U.S. operations. Instead, the United States used the coalition-of-the-willing-under-U.S.-leadership concept, employed successfully in Desert Storm. The U.S. operation in Afghanistan was called Operation Enduring Freedom (OEF). Partnership for Peace (PfP), Partnership for Peace Planning and Review Process (PARP), and the years of experience in IFOR/SFOR and KFOR had already made NATO Standardization Agreement (STANAGS) the lingua franca for such international military operations, and had established the pattern of a UN-mandated force moving in and peacekeeping after combat operations ended. Allies participated and continue to participate in OEF as well as in the establishment in December 2001 of the International Security Assistance Force (ISAF) in Afghanistan. NATO did not assume command of ISAF until August 2003, when asked by the UN and Afghan government because it was apparent that the original ad hoc system of rotating command and the headquarters infrastructure every six months between volunteering nations was breaking down. The United Kingdom, Turkey, and Germany had provided the first three non-NATO ISAF commanders, and after NATO took over ISAF, Germany, Canada, France (EuroCorps), Turkey, Italy, the United Kingdom, and the United States provided commanders. Initially only in the Kabul region, ISAF gradually increased its area of responsibility to all of Afghanistan in October 2006.

As the ISAF mission expanded geographically and in responsibilities, the commander of ISAF became a dual-hatted American, serving also as the commander of the United States' OEF so that U.S. and NATO operations could be better coordinated. U.S., Allied, and Partner forces along with forces from other countries have served and continue to serve in OEF or ISAF. NATO was able to increase its commitment in Afghanistan even as combat operations were increasing in intensity. One factor is that U.S. troops make up part of the NATO troop contingent, but another is that other Allies besides the United States have been attacked or threatened. For example, terrorists conducted the Madrid train bombings on March 11, 2004, and the London transportation system was attacked on July 7, 2005. The war in Afghanistan has a direct connection to 9/11. In April 2010, ISAF troops numbered approximately 100,000 from 46 different countries to parallel the U.S. OEF surge in Afghanistan. Nevertheless, changes in the ISAF mission tasking and the intensity of operations have resulted in rising tolls of dead and wounded, as well as economic costs, and many Allies' publics have become less supportive of the mission. This in turn, has made it increasingly difficult to man ISAF.

In addition, national caveats restricting the types of missions the various national forces can perform cause friction among the Allies. For example, some units may only be allowed to use weapons to return fire in their own self-defense, but not to participate in combat operations. Although the national caveats and their implications first became evident in NATO's Balkan operations, the level of combat intensity is significantly higher in Afghanistan. Consequently, the impact of a nearby unit's inability, or perceived unwillingness, to come to the rescue of other Allies' troops engaged in a nearby firefight is much higher. It also complicates commanders' planning and decision making, but the caveats are a byproduct of relying on voluntary troop contributions. It is better to have troops with caveats than no troops. It is also clear that the level of participation varies across the pool of Allies and Partners. In addition, each nation's level of participation has also varied during OEF and ISAF.

In November 2002, in the midst of the various operations, the Allies decided to further consolidate the NATO military command structure. Instead of the two strategic operational commands of Allied Command Europe (ACE) under SACEUR (Supreme Allied Commander Europe) at SHAPE (Supreme Headquarters Allied Powers Europe) and Allied Command Atlantic under SACLANT (Supreme Allied Commander Atlantic) in Norfolk, Virginia, NATO shifted to a single operational headquarters, Allied Command Operations under SACEUR at SHAPE, Belgium. The former SACLANT headquarters in Norfolk, Virginia, became Allied Command Transformation, tasked to develop doctrine and help prepare NATO militaries to adapt to the new environment and their new missions.

The U.S. decision to invade Iraq in 2003 was quite controversial within NATO. Many Allies did not see the connection that the United States drew between invading Iraq and 9/11. As in Afghanistan, Operation Iraqi Freedom was a coalition-of-the-willing-under-U.S.-leadership concept, with some Allies, Partners, and other nations participating, but not NATO. Nevertheless, NATO conducted Operation Display Deterrence to once again demonstrate its solidarity with Turkey in the face of possible Iraqi action in the lead-up to and during the U.S. invasion. Over time, the U.S. was able to persuade its Allies to agree to NATO establishing a Training Mission for Iraq in 2004, with the actual training conducted both in Iraq and in other countries.

The list of NATO missions has continued to grow. NATO provided additional security for the Olympics and Paralympics in Greece, the soccer World Cup in Germany in 2006, and provided airlift support to the African Union Darfur peacekeeping mission from 2005 through 2007. In 2005, NATO forces also supported the U.S. effort after Hurricane Katrina as well as provided humanitarian assistance after the earthquake in Pakistan. NATO continued the KFOR mission, although it turned the SFOR mission over to the EU in 2004. NATO had also conducted Operation Essential Harvest and several follow-on missions in Macedonia to quell ethnic unrest from 2001 to 2003, when this operation was also passed to the EU. NATO naval forces also set up antipiracy operations off the Horn of Africa, and have continued their increased monitoring of Mediterranean shipping that had begun shortly after 9/11.

NATO also continued to adapt its PfP programs, and went through two more rounds of enlargement. The Baltic states (i.e., the former Soviet Republics of Estonia, Latvia, and Lithuania) were part of the 2004 round, or *tranche* as it was frequently called, subtly implying further rounds of NATO enlargement and that the new members were returning to the whole of Europe. This was particularly galling to Russia, which under Putin had reversed the economic problems of the 1990s, had supported the U.S. response in Afghanistan to 9/11, and was generally becoming more assertive in foreign policy. NATO-Russia relations had returned to a degree of normalcy by NATO's 2002 Rome Summit, during which the new NATO-Russia Council replaced the Permanent Joint Council. It was more than a name change. The format was also changed from a "19+1" (all of NATO's members as one unit with Russia as a separate participant) to a "20" format where each NATO nation represented only itself in discussions. However, a series of contentious issues continued to hinder the development of NATO-Russia relations. These issues included Kosovo, NATO enlargement, and the, to the Russians, somewhat associated *color revolutions* in former Soviet republics, the U.S. invasion of Iraq, and the United States' cessation of the Anti-Ballistic Missile Treaty as part of its National Missile Defense policy. Russia played its *defensive* invasion of the Georgian autonomous regions of Abkhazia and South Ossetia in August 2008 as the same case as NATO's actions in Kosovo and as a warning about further NATO expansion into former Soviet republics. The missile defense issue was worked around by the United States canceling its plans to deploy parts of a missile defense system in Poland and the Czech Republic and through a new U.S.-Russia Strategic Arms Reduction Treaty (START) signed in 2010.

Allied publics are becoming somewhat weary of the operations. Afghanistan is distant, and the economic problems of 2008–2010 eroded support for defense spending. The future of the EU continues to be in question, with some believing more integration is in order, and others looking for a pause, or even a roll-back in some areas in the process. The Russian threat seems to many to be more economic in terms of controlling the gas and oil spigot to the rest of Europe, although the 2007 cyber war in Estonia and the August 2008 military operation in Georgia give some cause for concern. In addition,

Allied politicians and public commentators have begun to muse on whether NATO's future should include tactical nuclear weapons.

The Allies sensed the need to once again reexamine their strategic concept and reorient it to the current and prospective security environment. At the 2009 NATO Summit in Strasbourg/Kehl, the heads of state and government tried to make sense out of the decade so far and issued a Declaration on Alliance Security that highlighted several areas of concern. The declaration emphasized the global nature of most threats, such as terrorism, weapons of mass destruction (WMD) proliferation, and cyber attacks; however, it also mentioned energy security and climate change as security issues and specifically mentioned NATO's willingness to work with Russia to address the challenges. The Alliance leaders were also clear in their assessment that NATO will continue to have a mix of conventional and nuclear forces.

Questions for Consideration

- Does it make sense for NATO to continue to put a threat analysis in its new Strategic Concept, or should it adopt a different structure?
  - If not, what structure would you recommend?
- If you went with the threat analysis structure, what threats would you include in NATO's next Strategic Concept?
  - Russia?
  - Europe, European periphery, or global?
  - The Middle East?
  - North Africa?
  - Oil/gas/energy supplies?
  - WMD proliferation?
  - The proliferation of advanced weapons?
  - Human suffering?
  - Terrorism?
  - Organized crime?
  - Mass migrations?
  - Cyber security?
  - The world economy?
  - Global warming?
- How would you address the issues associated with ISAF in Afghanistan?
- Should NATO Allies and Partners let Russia join NATO? Under what conditions, and what would be the ramifications?
- In your opinion, does NATO have a credible deterrent through its capability to launch a counterattack with nuclear weapons?
  - Who is it deterring, and how?

NATO 2020: Assured Security; Dynamic Engagement

The issues addressed in *NATO 2020* certainly merit discussion and resolution within NATO circles, but not all appear to be of the type that should go into a new Strategic Concept for the Alliance's approach to the outside world. Examples of such issues are the calls to reduce costs and increase the economic efficiency of NATO structures. Of those issues that appear on the level of a strategic concept, the most innovative is the proposed reconceptualization of partnerships, and the most controversial are the proposed reinterpretation of Article 5, the advocacy for expeditionary and preemptive operations, the pressure on Allies to continue to back nuclear burden sharing, and the call for changing NATO decision making away from a totally consensus-based model. These issues were examined in greater detail within the structure of the report.

The report consists of two parts. The first part is the "Summary of Findings," and the second is "Further Analysis and Recommendations." This chapter begins with the second part and returns later to the "Summary of Findings" to capture the style of the document. The "Further Analysis and Recommendations" section is written in a straightforward manner with six chapters. The first chapter, "The Security Environment," is the equivalent to the old intelligence assessment. It concludes that "Conventional military aggression against the Alliance or its members is unlikely but the possibility cannot be ignored." If the possibility could be ignored, or NATO chose to not use worst-case military planning for this requirement, NATO's force structure might look very different. The top three "most probable threats to Allies in the coming decade are unconventional." The first is a conventional or nuclear-armed conventional missile attack. The second is terrorist attacks, and the third is cyber attacks. The lower tier threats of "disruptions to energy and maritime supply lines, the harmful consequences of global climate change, and the financial crisis" are also listed. It should be noted, however, that the characterization of the threats to NATO is not entirely consistent throughout *NATO 2020*, but these discrepancies will be addressed later.

The problem NATO faces is that only two types of attacks—missile attacks, and perhaps terrorist attacks—easily fit current conceptions of an Article 5 attack. The Alliance does not consider daily cyber attempted intrusions or the cyber attacks on Estonia in 2007 as Article 5 situations. NATO did not view the 1973 oil embargo or the more recent temporary Russian stoppages of gas through Ukrainian pipelines as Article 5 cases. NATO's antipiracy operations are also not viewed as Article 5 cases. It is still hard to define what NATO's range of responses to the harmful effects of climate change might be, and even the Allies would not turn to NATO for assistance in overcoming the current global financial crisis. Furthermore, NATO and individual Allies are expending considerable resources in ISAF, but NATO is not leading ISAF in Afghanistan as an Article 5 mission in response to terrorist attacks.

This leaves the NATO military authorities setting requirements for defense against a conventional attack that NATO admits is unlikely, for missile defense and retaliatory capabilities against a relatively small number of conventional or nuclear-armed ballistic missiles, and perhaps for defense against, or remediation of, terrorist attacks. Unless NATO were to change its interpretation of what might justify Article 5 operations or the NATO military authorities artificially inflate the requirements against the conventional attack or the ballistic missile attack, there does not appear to be a direct correlation between the perceived threats and the actual defense requirements, which include ISAF. These should further correlate in some fashion to NATO's actual troop strengths, which currently consist of the combination of NATO's Article 5 defense forces; NATO's forces conducting ISAF, KFOR, anti-piracy operations, maritime patrols, and NATO's other ongoing operations and exercises; and perhaps those forces in predeployment training. Although Allies do not have to assign or earmark all their forces for NATO operations, most nations are no longer capable of fulfilling their NATO/EU requirements and still maintaining enough capability for independent national operations. NATO can ostensibly maintain its current Article 5 defenses and conduct its various ongoing operations; however, the participation of Partners and other troop-contributing nations certainly helps.

The second chapter outlines NATO's core tasks, and the group of experts recommends that NATO highlight four core tasks. The first is no surprise. "The Alliance must maintain the ability to deter and defend member states against any threat of aggression." Deterrence against any threat indicates the need to keep strategic and tactical nuclear weapons. In addition, the report states that NATO should stress its basic Article 5 commitment, and also points out that Article 5 threats in the new era "could arise either inside or outside the Euro-Atlantic region." Since the new, unconventional threats do not fit as nicely into the Article 5 box, NATO must prepare and train to be able to react to them. This section appears to condone preemptive NATO strikes. Instead of looking at the uncertainty of whether a completed terrorist attack would be considered an Article 5 case, it uses the example of "evidence that terrorists are planning a strike" as a case where it is not clear where Article 5 would be triggered. If it is within the realm of possibilities that Article 5 would indeed be triggered by evidence of a planned attack, "the defence mechanisms of Article 5" would appear to be preemptive. A strategy incorporating preemptive strikes would be a major change for NATO, which ruled out preemption throughout the Cold War.

The second task is "to contribute to the broader security of the entire Euro-Atlantic region." This entails cooperation with other organizations such as the EU, UN, and Organization for Security and Cooperation in Europe (OSCE), as well as with other non-NATO partner states. The third task is "to serve as a transatlantic means for security consultations and crisis management along the entire continuum of issues facing the Alliance," since NATO is "the only contractual link between North America and Europe." The increased emphasis on broadening the interpretation of Article 4 consultations is another way to work around the currently perceived weak linkages between the threats and an Article 5 response. In addition, U.S. intelligence, deployments, strategic lift, expeditionary capabilities, and expeditionary mindset are critical to NATO's ability to "undertake crisis response operations within, along, or beyond its borders." The fourth task is "enhancing the scope and management of partnerships," even though this is acknowledged as really being a means to achieve the other tasks, and not an end in itself.

The third chapter, "Partnerships," provides a compilation of suggestions for what to do with old Partners, details of partnership aspects of lessons learned from current operations, and a vision of partnering across the world. With respect to the old Partners, one of the first recommendations in the chapter is to "strengthen routine and crisis consultations with EAPC [Euro-Atlantic Partnership Council] partners." The report notes that the practical military ties are working quite well in PfP, but the political ties are not as robust, and "many participants complain that EAPC discussions are overly stilted and formal." The idea of strengthening consultations fits well with *NATO 2020*'s overall approach toward Allies and its new inclusive calls of partnership, but the complaint that the group of experts cite has been around since the first EAPC meetings. The previous answer was that one cannot expect real discussions to occur in a meeting with approximately 50 nations represented, occurring once a month at the PermRep/ambassador level. In a two-hour meeting, if no presentations were scheduled, each nation would have approximately two minutes to talk. Although much of the consultation process occurs in the hallways, cafes, and office spaces of NATO Headquarters, there are times when open discussions among all the Allies and Partners would be beneficial. The *NATO 2020* recommendation recognizes this, but does not offer any suggestions on how to improve the consultations.

NATO 2020 sends a mixed message on Russia, given the Georgia crisis and Russia's "conflicting signals about its openness to further cooperation with NATO." For example, "The Alliance does not consider any country to be its enemy; however, no one should doubt NATO's resolve if the security of any of its member states were to be threatened." Consequently, the recommendation that "the new Strategic Concept should endorse a policy that combines reassurance for all Alliance members and constructive reengagement with Russia," takes a firmer stance against Russia in the juxtaposition of the ideas the Allies need reassuring, while reengaging with Russia.

The actual implementation would be a continuation of NATO policy of emphasizing that NATO is open to cooperation, and trying to improve the relationship within the NATO-Russia Council. The partnership chapter also contains recommendations on Georgia and Ukraine. The gist of the message appears to be that despite the excellent channels of communication, there appears to be miscommunication within the NATO-Ukraine Commission and the NATO-Georgia Commission, and that NATO should use its "crisis management mechanisms" to supplement the information provided to it in the commissions.

The group of experts summarized their assessment on the Mediterranean Dialogue and the Istanbul Cooperation Initiative, instituted in 2004 to offer "countries in the broader Middle East bilateral security cooperation with NATO," with its recommendation that "NATO should approach its relations with countries in the Mediterranean and Middle East with strategic patience." NATO has had long-standing interests in North Africa and the Middle East, with current interest due in part to issues of nuclear proliferation, terrorism, energy security, and general threats to the peaceful international order; however, NATO has not been able to generate much with its North African and the Middle Eastern programs, although it realizes the potential benefits to be gained through increased contact and partnership with nations in the region. The practical recommendations are to aim for "an agreed statement of shared interests," and that "the Allies should be open to transparent consultations with its MD [Mediterranean Dialogue] and ICI [Istanbul Cooperation Initiative] partners on the implications of a possible nuclear breakout by Iran."

The last of the old Partners is the EU, and the group of experts recommends that NATO improve its cooperation with the EU, by both deepening the linkages as well as by increasing cooperation across more issues. Furthermore, NATO should adjust its view of the relationship away from the construct that NATO is military and the EU is civilian since the threats that both NATO and the EU face are "becoming blurred," and because the EU Treaty of Lisbon strengthened the EU's military structures and capabilities.

The partnership aspects of lessons learned from current operations are fairly straightforward. First and foremost, NATO must use a comprehensive approach to deal with contemporary threats: "Security has military, political, economic, and social dimensions." NATO must be willing and able to partner with other organizations and states as necessary to deal with specific security issues. In the future, sometimes NATO will lead, sometimes NATO will play a "complementary role." In order to achieve this balance, the group of experts recommends that NATO expand its partnership activities and agenda items, allow more differentiation between partners, and "modify procedures in order to encourage the freest possible exchange of ideas." More specifically, NATO should improve its coordination with the UN, in order to "strengthen the ability of the United Nations to fulfil [*sic*] its responsibilities." For example, NATO should provide security for UN personnel as early as possible in an operation, state its willingness to consider UN requests "in the event of genocide, other massive violations of human rights, or humanitarian emergency," and "respond positively to Security Council Resolution 1325, concerning the role of women in security and peace." NATO should also "make full use of the OSCE's toolbox" in the area of soft security to complement NATO's hard security capabilities.

The group of experts also included what to some would appear to be a Cold War relic: "The Alliance should actively pursue, under the framework of the OSCE, the negotiation of conventional arms control and confidence-building measures." One might think of the crowning achievement in this category, the Conventional Armed Forces in Europe (CFE) Treaty, and wonder who NATO would be negotiating with since it no longer has any potential adversaries. The issue here is that Russia declared a unilateral suspension of the CFE Treaty in 2007 because the NATO states had not ratified the Adapted CFE Treaty. Although there are several issues involved, the big ones are that Russian troops are still in Georgia and Moldova without the Georgian and Moldovan governments' consent, which is a violation of the CFE Treaty. The NATO Allies were hoping to use the issue of their ratification of the Adapted CFE Treaty to pressure the Russians to work out the issues with Georgia and Moldova; however, Russia's unilateral suspension of the CFE Treaty was an unexpected step beyond the boundaries that NATO had conceptually placed around the issue. The NATO nations want to bring Russia back into the CFE Treaty process and appear willing to move on to the Adapted Treaty because the limits and the inspection process are comforting and do build confidence between all states involved. With the treaties in force, each country knows the restrictions placed on its neighbors' military forces and has the capability to inspect certain parts of them. Over the long term, this core part of the treaty may be more important to European security than placing the entire treaty at risk to in an attempt to quickly solve the Georgia and Moldova issues, which might be better handled separately. Russia's unilateral suspension of the treaty also suspends the inspections and information sharing, and leaves it unclear as to whether Russia would eventually want to completely break out of the treaty limits.

In addition to the need to work better with international organizations, a clear lesson learned is that NATO has been working with "partners across the globe," also known as "operational partners." These are the countries located beyond Europe that are not enrolled in any formal partner programs, but still participate or cooperate with NATO in operations or other activities. "Australia, in fact, contributes more troops to Afghanistan than half the NATO Allies, New Zealand is also a significant contributor, the Republic of

Korea has pledged to deploy a sizable contingent, and Japan has committed billions of dollars to the reconstruction efforts there." And of course, it would not make sense for NATO to lead ISAF without Afghan and Pakistan cooperation. However, none of these countries has "a formal framework for dialogue" with NATO. The obvious recommendation is to expand and deepen partnerships with countries beyond the Euro-Atlantic region, to provide these partners access to NATO information and planning, and to "give NATO's operational partners a regular and meaningful voice in shaping strategy and decisions on missions to which they contribute." Although the recommendations are obvious, NATO's other Partners and the non-NATO, non-Partner troop-contributing nations to NATO's Balkans operations have brought up the same issues from the beginning. There are countries that are more willing to provide troops and other support to NATO-led operations than some Allies, and they would like more say in how their people and materiel are used.

The last area addressed in the partnership chapter is reminiscent of an older Cold War construct in which the non-Communist world would be marked by interlinked regional collective security organizations. MC 14/1, supporting NATO's second Strategic Concept, mentioned establishing relations with a then predicted Middle Eastern NATO-like organization. The *NATO 2020* group of experts calls for NATO to explore the possibilities of creating new regional subgroups, or "to forge more formal ties to such bodies as the African Union, the Organization of American States, the Gulf Cooperation Council, the Shanghai Cooperation Organization, or the Collective Security Treaty Organization. Any such relationship should be based on the principles of equality, mutual trust, and mutual benefit." This vision of partnering with the world for mutual benefit certainly implies NATO ties and potential commitments of some form across the globe.

The fourth chapter, "Political and Organizational Issues," contains a hodgepodge of issues and recommendations, and as the title indicates, most would traditionally be more likely to appear in NAC communiqués of political decisions reached than in a Strategic Concept. The first section deals with lessons learned from ISAF to be included in the new Strategic Concept. The list of lessons is short; most are normative in nature, some are general ideas and some are prescriptive. For example, the group of experts state that "to the maximum feasible extent, NATO's military forces should operate under a unified chain of command." In addition, "Allies should minimize the national caveats," and those that are necessary "should be clearly and explicitly stated and their impact carefully evaluated during force generation and operational planning." The structuring of the chain of command and the national caveats are political issues and processes that are likely to remain. All Allies would agree with the lessons in the abstract, but still want to be able to make accommodations when necessary for their particular national circumstances. One would hope that the reminder of the need to minimize civilian casualties, the statement that "prisoners and detainees should be treated in accordance with the principles of international law," and the conclusion that the war is not to be won by military forces alone, so NATO must partner with organizations and with Afghan government forces, are so obvious that they would not need restating in a strategic concept.

The section on establishing guidelines for determining whether NATO should take on specific missions beyond the Alliance's borders captures the tension between the vision of NATO as the expeditionary spine of democracy and the reality of an organization in which many members do not live up to their commitments. The group of experts casts this as tension between over-extension and lethargy, indicating its preference for extending. The group further implies that if NATO better managed its message, this might not be as big of an issue: "Through Transparency and effective public communications, the Alliance must strive to attract and maintain public and legislative backing for its operations." The report also recommends supporting reforms to cut the number of committees, staff, and routine/administrative costs as well as reaffirming NATO's "open door policy."

The issue of whether NATO should continue to rely on its consensus decision making model is also contained in chapter 4. The group of experts argues that there is a tension between trying to achieve consensus among 28 or potentially more Allies, and the need "to prepare for situations where rapid (indeed almost instantaneous) decision-making may be required." Apparently, the new unconventional threats create conditions under which NATO must be able to react more rapidly than ever before; however, these rapid decisions do not appear to affect Article 5 decisions since the recommendation is that the secretary general develop "further proposals for streamlining the decision-making process" in areas where consensus may not be required, while keeping the consensus rule for Article 5 decisions. Furthermore, the group of experts recommends eliminating the need for consensus decision making in some Article 5 scenarios: "The Alliance should consider giving the Secretary General or NATO military leaders certain pre-delegated authorities, based on agreed rules-of-engagement, to respond in an emergency situation such as a missile or cyber attack."

This recommendation stands in contrast to the NAC's approval of MC 48 in 1954, whereby the NAC noted that it was only approving the military's planning for the immediate use of nuclear weapons upon an attack, but not the actual use, since that was a NAC prerogative. The Washington Treaty does not specify the use of consensus, but Article 5 was specifically written to meet U.S. concerns that a treaty that bound the United States to act automatically would not be ratified by the Senate. Consequently, it is difficult to see how the United States would now agree to something less than consensus, unless it had a veto, or to give the secretary general pre-delegated authority to make decisions that would affect the United States and its personnel.

The fifth chapter, "Alliance Forces and Capabilities," which, by its title, would be expected to be most applicable as strategic guidance for military planning, includes several political issues that include the long-standing capabilities gap between the United States and the rest of NATO and NATO's nuclear policies. The group of experts found that the capabilities gap between the United States and the rest of NATO has not decreased despite several NATO initiatives since 1999. For example, *NATO 2020* delves into the details of the Comprehensive Political Guidance, which was adopted by the Alliance at the 2006 NATO Riga Summit and, among other things, set the requirement "that NATO members develop national land forces that were at least 40 percent deployable and 8 percent deployable on a sustainable basis. (These targets were later raised to 50 percent and 10 percent.)" However, in the spring of 2010, "only about a dozen" Allies have met these goals, only six of 26 European Allies spend 2 percent or more of their GDP on defense spending, and less than half the Allies meet the "Alliance benchmark of 20 percent of military spending allocated to investment." The report notes that Europeans spend too much on personnel and operations, and therefore, "generally do not have nearly enough transformed forces." However, the recommendations are relatively weak: NATO should stress the importance of transformation and prioritize the desired capabilities and military reforms since money is short.

The report attempts to deal with calls for the elimination of NATO's tactical, or sub-strategic, nuclear weapons by articulating current NATO policies. For example, "As long as nuclear weapons exist, NATO should continue to maintain secure and reliable nuclear forces, with widely shared responsibility for deployment and operational support, at the minimum level required by the prevailing security environment." Consequently, NATO needs to shore up Allied understanding of the importance of the nuclear weapons mix for deterrence. It also appears that the group of experts is concerned that some Allies might be tempted to make unilateral decisions and eliminate nuclear storage sites on their territory, since the group felt it necessary to stress that "any change in this policy, including in the geographic distribution of NATO nuclear deployments in Europe, should be made, as with other major decisions, by the Alliance as a whole." The group of experts also calls for a dialogue with Russia to "help set the stage for further reduction and possible eventual elimination of the entire class of sub-strategic nuclear weapons." Given the evolution of NATO's tactical nuclear weapons from a military necessity to a political symbol of burden-sharing, perhaps negotiations with the Russians would be the easiest way out of the quandary. In addition, the group of experts advocates that "NATO should endorse a policy of not using or threatening to use nuclear weapons against non-nuclear states that are party to the Nuclear Non-Proliferation Treaty and in compliance with their nuclear non-proliferation obligations." Such a policy would be a dramatic change for NATO since its nuclear weapons were never seen as a tit-for-tat, or second-strike weapon. NATO has consistently kept the option open to use nuclear weapons first and as a response to conventional attacks as part of its military plans and deterrence threat.

On the more military side, the section "NATO's Military Missions" articulates four NATO military missions that complement the core tasks in chapter 2. The first military mission is Article 5 with its roles to "deter, prevent, defend against any threat of aggression." The second is to "cooperate with partners and civilian institutions to protect the treaty area against a full range of unconventional security challenges." The third is to "deploy and sustain expeditionary capabilities for military operations beyond the treaty area when required to prevent an attack on the treaty area or to protect the legal rights and other vital interests of Alliance members." This articulation could be interpreted as advocating for NATO to wage preemptive or preventative warfare, and opens a wide door for NATO expeditionary operations since the new justification is not tied to Article 5 or Euro-Atlantic security, but to protecting amorphous legal rights and vital interests of individual Allies. The fourth military mission is to shape the international security environment through partner training, military assistance, and cooperation.

The section "Conventional Defence Capabilities" deals with encouraging the Allies to spend more on defense and implementing reforms, while simultaneously encouraging NATO to prioritize the capabilities requirements. More specifically, the group of experts calls for increasing Article 5 planning and exercises, although the report calls that threat unlikely and states that NATO has no enemies so there is no specified threat to plan against. Perhaps training and exercises for Article 5 scenarios may be more politically palatable than expeditionary exercises. Along the same lines, the group also proposes using the NATO Response Force in Article 5 scenarios as well as crisis management, while at the same time capitalizing "on commonality between Article 5 and expeditionary missions." In addition, the group of experts recommends improving command, control, communications, computers, intelligence, surveillance, and reconnaissance (C4ISR) commonality; strengthening special operations forces; increasing Allied Command Transformation's mission, authorities, and resources; transforming education and training within NATO; and improving NATO's maritime situational awareness capabilities.

Chapter 5 also calls for the secretary general to create "a balanced package of reform and efficiency proposals" for the upcoming NATO summit. Among other things, the package would foster more cooperation between Allies with proposals for multinational formations; pooling of transportation capabilities;

common logistics approaches; coordinated national specializations and niche capabilities; multinational procurements; and the creation of an EU-NATO "defense capabilities agency." The package would also contain proposals for more NATO common funding of C4ISR, specific deployments, and an annual NATO Response Force exercise. Finally, proposals would address reducing NATO's command structure to generate cost savings while increasing flexibility and deployability.

The report also stresses the comprehensive approach and concludes that NATO needs to work better with civilian organizations, and recommends establishing a unit within NATO to serve as its interface with civilian organizations. NATO should also integrate civilian capabilities and personnel into the defense planning process so they can be deployed with the initial combat forces. Finally, NATO should cooperate with potential partners to train, provide assistance, and exercise/evaluate their crisis management abilities. With respect to ballistic missile defense, "NATO should recognize territorial missile defense as an essential mission of the Alliance."

And in the final section of chapter 5, "Responding to Unconventional Dangers," the group of experts brings it back around to the threats discussed in chapter 1, except that only two of the unconventional threats are the same. First, NATO should broaden its efforts to fight terrorism. Second, NATO must increase its, and Allies', cyber defenses. Missile defense, however, is no longer an issue. The third issue is now to protect and mitigate the effects of a disruption of NATO's energy supplies. Finally, NATO should start to develop plans dealing with consequences of climate change, such as melting polar ice or natural disasters.

The final chapter of *NATO 2020*, "Conclusion," provides a list of the good that NATO has brought to the world. This may be incorporated into the informational parts of the new Strategic Concept, which brings us back to *NATO 2020*'s part 1, "Summary of Findings," which is marked by its reminders for NATO to pay attention to the informational aspects as it drafts the final version of the new Strategic Concept. It must appeal to Allied publics and politicians for support and funding, but NATO should also be crafting a positive message abroad to areas where it is currently engaged, as well as to areas where it would like to develop deeper partnerships. As part of this process the summary of findings boldly asserts that NATO has always been global in orientation: "The fact that NATO troops are now deployed in distant locations is not a departure from NATO's fundamental purpose." The group of experts referred back to the Harmel Report to ground this assertion, but its references to the Harmel Report allude to the Alliance's ability to adapt, the importance of Alliance cohesion, and the Alliance's interest in stability in the international environment—not to Article 5, which many would consider NATO's true fundamental purpose. Nevertheless, the summary of findings reinforces the idea that this broader, more expeditionary approach is not new at all: "NATO's fundamental identity, as the organisation that lends muscle and spine to democratic ideals, is constant." The report continues to advocate this new interpretation. In its vision and purpose, the group of experts tries to make NATO's 1960s duality of defense and détente into a parallel precedent for today. "For NATO 2020, the twin imperative is assured security for all its members and dynamic engagement beyond the treaty area to minimize threats." A further, supporting message is that there is no free ride at NATO. "To succeed, NATO must have the sustained commitment and united effort of its members. A seat at NATO's table is not an entitlement but an ongoing responsibility that each Ally must meet."

Questions for Consideration

- Should NATO's governance, consensus making by consensus, be part of the discussion on a new Strategic Concept?

  - Yes or no, and why?

- What are the pros and cons of preemptive strikes or preventative war?
- What are the potential effects of changing NATO's focus from a relatively literal interpretation of providing collective security for the North Atlantic Area to becoming an expeditionary organization?
- How often, or when, should the Strategic Concept be updated?
- Is it possible for NATO to keep its Strategic Concept up-to-date?

  - What are the implications of not keeping it current?
  - Is there a trade-off between specificity and abstractness in trying to stay current?

- Does it matter to the outside world what NATO's strategic concept is?
- Does NATO need a threat to justify its existence?
- Does NATO need a threat to induce cooperation?
- Can you envision NATO ever disbanding? If so, under what conditions?

  - What would be the implications of NATO disbanding (e.g., how would NATO infrastructure and investments be divided up)?

NATO 2020 has certainly allowed the public more insight into the development of NATO's Strategic Concept than ever before. The group of experts discussed many issues, and all will not survive the discussions within NATO's staffs and decision making bodies. NATO's concept of the role of partners is ripe for an adjustment. The reconceptualization of Article 5 to include cyber attacks, and possibly the protection of energy supplies, as well as preemptive strikes and expeditionary operations would seem to be a bit too much change for most Allies, given the actual basis for NATO's actions is still the Washington Treaty. The same holds true for any changes away from consensus decision making or pre-delegating responsibilities to the secretary general.

CHAPTER 8

Where and Who Is NATO?

It may seem strange to end the book with the deceptively simple questions of *where* NATO is and *who* NATO is, but it forms the other bookend that complements the first chapter's question of *what* NATO is. One is tempted to answer this chapter's two questions with a list the current members of the Alliance. That would be a start, but the answers to both questions, and their implications, are a bit more complex. This chapter starts with the potentially easier question of *where* NATO is before moving to the question of *who* NATO is, which begins with a short review of the different rounds of NATO's enlargement from the original 12 members to today's 28. The issue of NATO enlargement is capped with a look at some of its potential limitations, while showing that NATO's influence may continue to enlarge even if the membership ceases to expand at some point. The chapter closes with an examination of some of the peculiarities of various Allies' membership over the years, including a brief look at NATO–European Union (EU) relations.

Questions for Consideration

- Are geographic limitations still useful in determining NATO's missions?
    - If yes, how and where would you draw the lines?
    - If no, does NATO need some sort of limits, and if you think limits are needed, what kind would you propose?
- What are the linkages between NATO's geographic area of interest and Partnership for Peace (PfP) and the Mediterranean Dialogue?
- Basing NATO operations on Article 4 would suggest a broader use of coalitions of the willing within NATO. Would this strengthen or weaken NATO, and why?

Where Is NATO?

At its inception, NATO was not conceived of as a worldwide organization. Article 6 of the Washington Treaty placed geographic limits on the applicability of Article 5's commitment. In the original version of the treaty, in order to be considered a potential Article 5 case, the armed attack had to occur "on the territory of any of the Parties in Europe or North America, on the Algerian Departments of France, on the territory of or on the Islands under the jurisdiction of any of the Parties in the North Atlantic area north of the Tropic of Cancer." France notified NATO in January 1963 that the clause pertaining to the former Algerian Departments of France had ceased to be applicable in July 1962. In addition, the armed attack could be "on the forces, vessels, or aircraft of any of the Parties, when in or over these territories or any other area in Europe in which occupation forces of any of the Parties were stationed on the date when the Treaty entered into force or the Mediterranean Sea or the North Atlantic area north of the Tropic of Cancer." An armed attack against an Ally that did not meet one of these two conditions would not invoke Article 5.

The definition provided in the territorial caveat clearly delineated the area of applicability for the treaty. If territory of a signatory lying outside of these boundaries would be attacked, NATO members would not be compelled to act in any way. Colonies—the European nations still possessed many in 1949—were largely excluded on the basis of this geography. NATO members did not want to be drawn into other members' colonial conflicts. Specific Allies might create or participate in regional common defense pacts in other parts of the world, but NATO's focus would be Europe. In addition, the limiting of the treaty to North America, Europe, and the northern Atlantic would seem to leave the status of Hawaii somewhat ambiguous since it is located in the central Pacific Ocean astride the Tropic of Cancer and was a U.S. territory but not a state at the time of the Washington Treaty signing. However, given the European focus of NATO, the status of Hawaii has never been an issue. In addition, Article 6's emphasis on Europe, coupled with Article 10's restriction on invitations for accession to the NATO Treaty to *any other European State*, bounded NATO's future expansion.

The second caveat, dealing with an attack on forces, vessels or aircraft, greatly expanded the treaty's geographic area of applicability because it included those forces anywhere on, over, or below the surface in not only the northern Atlantic, but also the Mediterranean Sea. This effectively expanded the treaty area to the coast of North Africa, the Middle East, Turkey, Greece, Yugoslavia, Italy, and Spain. The inclusion of Allies' forces in parts of Europe under occupation at the Treaty's entry into force was a rather long-winded way to say that an attack on signatories' forces stationed in western

Germany, Berlin, and allied occupation zones in Austria would invoke the NATO Treaty. Although it naturally made sense, especially in light of the ongoing Berlin Blockade to include signatories' occupation troops, this essentially extended NATO's collective security arrangement to western Germany through the time of its actual accession to the NATO Treaty, to Austria until its occupation ended and the Victory Powers' forces departed in 1955, and to West Berlin through the fall of the Wall and the signing of the Two Plus Four Treaty in September 1990 ending the division of postwar Germany.

Article 6 clearly delineated the applicability of the Article 5 commitment, but it did not preclude NATO from observing events beyond the pale. In fact, the practical aspects of creating an effective collective defense demanded the sharing of intelligence on threats beyond Allied territory as well as the drafting of plans and the deployment of military forces to meet them. The NATO Treaty also did not preclude NATO from attacking targets beyond the Article 6 boundaries as part of its Article 5 defense. Article 5 limited NATO's wartime objectives "to restore and maintain the security of the North Atlantic Area" and that, on its face, from the perspective of 60 years of intervening history, seems to indicate the relatively low-level objectives of repulsing enemy forces and restoring the *status quo antebellum* but not destroying the Soviet Union and its capacity to wage war if the Soviet Army were to cross the inner-German border. However, the norm established in World War II was that carpet and atomic bombing of cities and demands for unconditional surrender were acceptable parts of a military strategy to restore and maintain security in a region.

This reasoning, however, led to the question of how far beyond its borders should NATO observe and draft plans for. If the armed attack occurred, some Allies would be involved fighting the Soviet Union and its allies in other distant, non-European theaters. Closer to home, NATO nations were concerned about the security of the Middle East because of its geographic proximity as well as the importance of the Middle Eastern oil to Europe. The early strategic concepts and guidance indicated that NATO was forecasting a world war and that NATO should coordinate at some level with certain potential neutral nations and other potential regional collective security organizations. Although subsequent strategic concepts and guidance waffled a bit on observing versus planning for military contingencies, it was clear that the Soviet Union and its Warsaw Pact allies were the primary focus of NATO's intelligence efforts and military plans during the Cold War.

The question of what NATO should do, if anything, to shape or intervene in events occurring in its periphery has proven even more complex. During the Cold War, NATO watched and condemned Soviet actions to put down protests and revolutions in Berlin in 1953, Hungary in 1956, and Prague in 1968, but NATO did not send troops in. On the other hand, cases like NATO's dual-track decision in 1979 (to deploy new intermediate-range ballistic missiles [IRBMs] while simultaneously offering to negotiate limits on IRBMs) demonstrated that the Allies were willing to use the threat of deploying new, advanced military forces as a tool to force negotiations and changes in the Warsaw Pact's stationing of medium-range nuclear missiles. However, it was not until the end of the Cold War that NATO began to deploy and use military forces beyond the North Atlantic Area as defined in Article 6 geographic caveats. (See the Timeline of Major NATO Military Operations in Appendix I.) However, these operations were not Article 5 situations, at least prior to 9/11. NATO eventually grounded its Balkan operations on Article 7 of the Washington Treaty (rights and obligations under the UN Charter) since Article 5 was not invoked, but then invoked Article 5 after 9/11. In addition, some operations were performed under UN mandates, and some were not, so different NATO operations have slightly different legal bases. Nevertheless, since 1949, NATO has greatly expanded Alliance territory by admitting new members, and NATO military forces have established relations through the PfP as far east as Russia and as far south as the Caucasus and Central Asia, and through the Mediterranean Dialogue, with select Middle Eastern and North African states. Operationally, NATO military forces have been or are in the Balkans, Afghanistan, Pakistan (earthquake relief), Iraq (training), sub-Saharan Africa, the Gulf of Aden, and the Horn of Africa.

A further point complementing the expansion of NATO's sense of *where*, is that it is no longer to be explained simply in terms of geography. It has also changed conceptually. Until 9/11, the basic assumption was that the United States would be helping Europe defend itself. Four of NATO's initial five regional planning groups evolved through NATO's major (combat) commands under SACEUR (Supreme Allied Commander Europe), SACLANT (Supreme Allied Commander Atlantic), and CINCHAN (Commander-in-Chief Channel [1952–1994]) to today's SACEUR and SACT (Supreme Allied Commander Transformation). The fifth, the Canada-United States Regional Planning Group, remained a planning group and never became a command or a NATO theater of operations, which is ironic, given that NATO's first invocation of Article 5 was in response to an attack there. The European Allies' immediate offer of assistance to the United States after 9/11 came as a surprise to the United States. There were no parallels during the Vietnam War, for example, to the provision of the NATO AWACS (airborne warning and control system) aircraft for U.S. air defense, NATO's support of International Security Assistance Force (ISAF) in Afghanistan, or NATO's Iraq training mission. Finally, NATO's inclusion of cyber threats and international terrorism and crime in strategic concepts indicates a potentially global area of operations for the modern NATO.

Questions for Consideration

- Are there limits to NATO enlargement?
  - What are some of the factors that create potential limits?
  - What are the implications of these limits?
  - What would NATO need to do to overcome these limitations?
- What about Russia—could it join?
  - What would be the impact of Russian membership?
- What are the practical differences for an Ally that is in NATO's integrated military command structure and one that is not?
  - Does it matter who, or how big the Ally is?
- What are the benefits or implications of an invitation to join the Membership Action Plan?
- What are the implications of NATO stating that Georgia and Ukraine will become members?

Enlargement Rounds

Article 10 of the Washington Treaty lays out the process for expanding NATO. The first step is that the Allies, by "unanimous agreement," extend an invitation. However, that invitation is limited to "any other European State in a position to further the principles of this Treaty and to contribute to the security of the North Atlantic area." The Treaty does not provide a definition of *Europe*, so there is some flexibility with respect to what this means. In the case of Turkey, for example, the Allies amended Article 6 of the Washington Treaty to specifically include the territory of Turkey, implying that Turkey was not part of Europe since Article 6 already covered the "territory of any of the Parties in Europe or North America." As part of the protocol of accession of Greece and Turkey, NATO modified one Article 6 clause to read: "on the territory of any of the Parties in Europe or North America, on the Algerian Departments of France, on the territory of *Turkey* or on the Islands under the jurisdiction of any of the Parties in the North Atlantic area north of the Tropic of Cancer [emphasis added]."

The apparent need to make an exception for Turkey illustrated a cultural sense of Europe in competition with a geographic sense of Europe. The Ottoman Empire was the major power in southeastern Europe for centuries, and if one uses the traditional Bosporus and Dardanelles straits as the dividing line between Europe and Asia, part of Turkey, including its largest city, Istanbul, is clearly in Europe. The perspective that required Turkey to be listed as separate from Europe has had consequences for post–Cold War definitions and concep-tualizations of what *Europe* is. Furthermore, the Russian empire was considered another 19th-century European power, but it is not clear whether the Allies would unanimously agree that all of the former Soviet republics that were previously the Russian Empire's colonies are part of Europe.

As to the principles of the treaty, the treaty itself refers back to the "prin-ciples of the Charter of the United Nations." The treaty does provide a brief listing of other principles, such as "the common heritage and civilization of their peoples, founded on the principles of democracy, individual liberty and the rule of law." The common heritage and civilization pieces emphasize the European and North American nature of the organization, yet there was no apparent need to amend the preamble when Turkey joined. The other prin-ciples would indicate that perspective members should be democratic, guar-antee individual liberty, and govern through the rule of law, and this has been overseen by the Membership Action Plan instituted in 1999. When NATO has decided that a specific aspirant for membership is far enough along to be considered for membership, NATO requests the country to submit a Mem-bership Action Plan. The reviews in the Membership Action Plan process allow NATO to ensure that the aspirant does indeed meet all NATO re-quirements before being extended a membership invitation. There is also a great deal of flexibility with respect to being able to make contributions to the security of the North Atlantic area. For example, Luxembourg's military force has historically been quite small, but Luxembourg is still considered a valuable contributor. Consequently, NATO does not have a requirement for aspirants or members to maintain a minimum number of troops. NATO does, however, have desired levels of defense spending as a percentage of the aspirant's total budget, though not all NATO members meet the level. The invited state becomes a member upon depositing its instrument of accession with the U.S. government, the treaty's depository.

There have been seven tranches of NATO's enlargement. (See the Time-line of NATO Enlargement in Appendix I.) The Washington Treaty was signed on April 4, 1949, and entered into force in August 1949. Greece and Turkey acceded in 1952, followed by the Federal Republic of Germany in 1955. Post-Franco Spain acceded in 1982. The fall of the Berlin Wall and the Two Plus Four Treaty led to German unification within NATO, and the incorporation of former East German territory and Berlin in 1990. The Czech Republic, Hungary, and Poland were the first independent post–Cold War additions in 1999, followed by the accession of Bulgaria, Estonia, Latvia, Lithuania, Romania, Slovakia, and Slovenia in 2004. Estonia, Latvia, and Lithuania were former Soviet republics that had been independent states be-tween the World War I and World War II, and Slovenia was the first former Yugoslav Republic to join NATO. Albania and Croatia joined in 2009.

With respect to future rounds of enlargement, NATO extended Membership Action Plan status to Macedonia in 1999, theoretically putting Macedonia on the path to NATO membership. However, Greece has objected to Macedonia's official name since Macedonia's independence from Yugoslavia. Greece maintains that *Macedonia* refers to an ancient Greek area, and Slavic Macedonia cannot simply take the name *Republic of Macedonia* and use it today. Consequently, NATO has cleared the Former Yugoslav Republic of Macedonia (Turkey recognizes the Republic of Macedonia with its constitutional name) for membership, pending resolution of its name issue with Greece. Montenegro entered the Membership Action Plan in 2009, and NATO extended the Membership Action Plan to Bosnia-Herzegovina in 2010, with the caveat that Bosnia-Herzegovina must resolve outstanding issues dealing with the ownership of defense properties on its territory.

In addition, at the Bucharest Summit in April 2008, NATO declared that Georgia and Ukraine "will become members of NATO," but placed them in a purgatory of sorts since they were told to apply for the Membership Action Plan, but also told that they were not going to be accepted into the Membership Action Plan until a variety of issues were resolved in both countries. Many of these issues are linked to Russia. The Russian invasion of Georgia in August 2008 to support the independence of Abkhazia and South Ossetia certainly complicated matters. The election of a more Russia-leaning president of Ukraine in February 2010, as well as long-standing postindependence disputes such as over the Black Sea Fleet and its basing, the status of the Crimea, as well as oil and gas prices and transit fees continue to keep the relationships between NATO, Ukraine, and Russia in flux.

Limits to NATO Enlargement?

There are several potentially limiting factors on NATO expansion. On the theoretical side, NATO's post–Cold War conceptions are that new members should fit into the Washington Treaty construct and be both European and democratic, with governance by rule of law. NATO has not set firm definitions for these concepts, preferring to look at specific cases under the nations' Membership Action Plan data. This allows NATO to firmly decline requests from South America or Southeast Asia to join, while leaving possibilities open for others. The Allies could modify the Washington Treaty to clearly alter the geographic limitation, but they have not shown any interest in doing this other than in the case of Turkey's admission. Changing a clause in the treaty runs the risk of opening up the entire treaty for discussion, and consensus would be required. A less realistic possibility would be to renegotiate the entire treaty and establish new membership criteria that may or may not include geographic factors.

The issue of Russian membership remains thorny. Some Allies have called for eventual Russian membership in NATO, so at face value the geographic question does not appear to be an issue. However, since Russia frequently displays concern over NATO expansion and has drawn a red line of sorts with respect to NATO's admission of more former Soviet republics, some argue that NATO should seek to alleviate Russian espoused security concerns and reduce or halt, at least temporarily, its further expansion. The counterargument is that this lets Russia, a nonmember, have a say or even determine NATO's membership. In addition, the argument runs, if Russia could eventually become a member, why should it see NATO expansion as a bad thing, since it means that Russia's neighbors have become democratic and governed by the rule of law, which makes them less-threatening neighbors. It is also not clear how NATO would function with Russia as a member. Even if there was no concern about its governance and nuclear weapons, it is not clear that Russia, the EU members, the other European states, Canada, and the United States would have compelling and overlapping security interests. Russian membership could bring NATO's border to China, and it is not clear how Article 6 would be interpreted. For example, is all of Russia European, or just part of it? Another concern of many Allies is that Russian membership in NATO would bring NATO's membership much closer to overlapping with the Organization for Security and Cooperation in Europe (OSCE), and that NATO's decision making via consensus procedure would allow Russia to limit NATO's ability to make decisions, turning it into a talk-shop.

Governance becomes a practical issue as NATO expands. The Washington Treaty does not specifically address NATO's governance other than to say in Article 9 that each member will be represented on the council that will work out the details of implementing the treaty. However, decision making through consensus has been the norm, and most observers agree that consensus is more difficult to achieve as the number of Allies increases. In addition, the expectation is that the security interests of the members become more diffuse and are less likely to converge as the new members are further dislocated from NATO's original core. Demark, for example, would not appear to have a tangible interest in protecting Kazakhstan, which is approximately 2,000 miles away, from its potential security threats and geostrategic pressures.

The UN offers an alternative model, wherein the five permanent members of the Security Council have more power than the rest of the members. However, it would be difficult to forge a consensus on who would form the inner core of NATO, and it would not be in any current member's interest to essentially give up its veto power in the consensus model. In addition, a majority of less powerful nations cannot force the strongest to expend their resources in an endeavor that they do not support. Furthermore, NATO's emphasis on security limits the opportunities for compromises in other areas, such as political or economic issues, that could offset a military decision that disadvantages a member.

Another extreme alternative would be to change NATO's governance structure to a supra government as in the case of the United States' federal government atop what were once independent sovereign states; however, this system would be hard to justify since NATO is primarily focused on security, and hard to implement, given the evolution in the EU's governance and the United States' predisposition towards independence in foreign affairs. As the EU has enlarged and deepened, the EU has opted to move to qualified majority voting in the council, although some areas still require unanimous consent among the nations. Since defense issues remain as one of the few categories requiring unanimity in decision making within the EU Council of Ministers, it is unlikely that EU members in NATO would want to change NATO's decision making by consensus procedure. Retaining consensus places a premium on deciding what countries to invite for membership since NATO has no precedent for expelling or suspending members, and it would presumably be difficult to get a country to agree to expel or suspend itself. A counterargument is that the process of membership gradually indoctrinates new states to the NATO culture; consequently, the presumed benefits of increased membership outweigh the risks of complicating NATO's decision making, even in a case like Russia. Others argue that the Euro-Atlantic Partnership Council, and the NATO-Russia and NATO-Ukraine forums are where the acculturation should take place, prior to any membership invitations.

In any event, NATO membership will not become global unless the Allies make changes to the Treaty of Washington. Consequently, wherever NATO draws a line demarking *Europe*, some nations will be left out. However, some nations that are inside the current apparent line are democratic, but not in NATO by their own choice. NATO can point to the examples of traditional neutrals like Sweden and Ireland, and Switzerland in particular because it is not in the EU or NATO, as amelioration to those nations outside of NATO. Successful, democratic, European countries exist without NATO membership, yet even these countries participate in NATO's PfP program. Every country does not need to be a member, and PfP can provide connections to NATO and to other Partners, promote cooperation, and further the spread of NATO's ideals while indirectly expanding NATO's reach and interest. The Mediterranean Dialogue and the Istanbul Cooperation Initiative, established in 2004 for countries in the broader Middle East, fulfill a similar purpose. Inside the more robust PfP, NATO and individual Allies cooperate across a range of functions with the Partners, and the Partners can request consultations with NATO when they feel threatened. In addition, the Partners, as well as non-Partner troop contributing nations, have placed military forces and civilian personnel under NATO command in NATO's Balkan operations, in

ISAF, and in the NATO Training Mission in Iraq. NATO membership probably has finite limits, but these auxiliaries extend NATO's impact far beyond the Alliance.

As a particular case, under PfP's voluntary Partnership Planning and Review Process (PARP), Partners voluntarily provide information on military capabilities that they would be willing to make available for NATO training, exercises, and operations. The operations were originally limited to peacekeeping, search and rescue, and humanitarian operations, but were expanded to include peace support operations as NATO and Partners conducted Operation Allied Force in Kosovo. PARP parallels the Alliance's defense planning process with a biennial process and Partners essentially answering an adapted defense planning questionnaire. In the PARP case, the survey asks for information on the Partner's civilian control of the military and democratic process development in addition to defense plans, policies, and budgeting information as well as detailed information on the forces that they are making available for cooperation with NATO. NATO reviews the Partner data, and in conjunction with each Partner, develops goals/objectives, and outlines measures to improve the Partner's forces' interoperability with NATO forces. The final details on each Partner's surveys are provided to Partners and Allies in a consolidated report. PARP socializes Partners in the NATO defense planning process, encourages inter-Partner as well as Partner-Alliance consultations and discussions, provides some Partner influence on NATO decision making and planning for specific training, exercises, and operations, and assists Partners so desiring to better prepare for NATO membership. It also gives NATO better insights into Partner capabilities for planning purposes, and over time, has dramatically improved Partner abilities to integrate into NATO military structures conducting exercises and operations.

Although NATO has a robust set of programs in addition to PfP to promote cooperation with other nations, including: the Mediterranean Dialogue; the Istanbul Cooperation Initiative; the special relationships with Russia, Ukraine, and Georgia; and the Standardization Agreements (STANAGs), NATO and its members still find themselves cooperating with nations that do not fit into the existing categories. Australia and New Zealand are but two examples of countries that do not have any formal partnership-type agreements with NATO, but are troop contributing nations to the NATO-led ISAF. Many other such countries have provided troops and civilians to NATO's Balkan operations as well as ISAF. NATO also provides international forums for defense-related issues. For example, the NATO-led Submarine Escape and Rescue Working Group (SERWG) includes most submarine owning nations of the world, including Australia, Brazil, People's Republic of China, India, Japan, Republic of Korea, Russia, Singapore, Sweden, and various NATO Allies.

NATO also funds, and mans the International Submarine Escape and Rescue Liaison Office (ISMERLO) at Norfolk, Virginia, under direction of the SERWG. The ISMERLO was established as a result of the tragic sinking of the Russian submarine *Kursk*. The SERWG precedes the *Kursk* sinking, and Russia was already participating at the time, but the ISMERLO is designed to be more responsive and maintain information on the location and status of the various nations' submarine rescue equipment for potential use in rescuing crews of civilian research submarines as well as military submarines. Consequently, although NATO membership is limited, NATO's connections are global. This idea resonates with *NATO 2020: Assured Security; Dynamic Engagement.*

Peculiarities of Membership

Although all members are equal with respect to NATO's decision making through consensus at the North Atlantic Council (NAC), each Ally's national economy, armed forces, and geopolitical location are different. Some contribute more in certain aspects than others. Iceland is perhaps the most unique in this respect since this founding member does not have military forces. Its representative to the Military Committee is a civilian. Iceland's location as an unsinkable aircraft carrier in the North Atlantic was an important asset for NATO's control of its sea lines of communication between North America and Europe as well as for antisubmarine operations against the Soviet Union during the Cold War. Iceland also contributed financially to NATO, the United States stationed air defense and antisubmarine forces in Iceland through a bilateral defense agreement, and NATO Security Investment Program funded some of the facilities and their maintenance; however, the United States withdrew its military forces from Iceland in 2006, so the government of Iceland assumed control of the Iceland Air Defence System. In 2008, Iceland created the Icelandic Defence Agency within the Icelandic Ministry of Foreign Affairs to oversee projects pertaining to defense and security. That includes, among other things, the operation of the air defense system and coordination with other NATO air defense systems, continued participation in NATO committees and agencies, and the provision of civilian personnel to support NATO missions. Consequently, Iceland has transitioned from providing its location and financial contributions to providing for some aspects of its own defense as well as being a "troop" contributor to NATO operations.

France and Greece are noteworthy because each nation has withdrawn, and later returned, its military forces from NATO's integrated military command structure. Both, however, remained in NATO and in the NAC. When de Gaulle removed the French armed forces from NATO's integrated military command structure in 1966, he also asked the NATO Allies to remove their troops and the pieces of the NATO military command structure from France. France's withdrawal from NATO's integrated military command structure meant that its armed forces were no longer subordinated to SACEUR and Allied Command Europe, that it no longer provided a military representative to the Military Committee (although it established a military mission to the Military Committee) or personnel to the International Military Staff or any other NATO military staffs, that it did not participate in the Defense Planning Committee or the Nuclear Planning Group, and that it no longer participated in NATO's defense planning activities. However, France continued to support the rest of NATO activities. In addition, General Lemnitzer, SACEUR, and French General Aillert established preliminary agreements in 1967 on how to reintegrate French forces into the NATO integrated military command structure if France chose to. Furthermore, although French military forces were not in NATO's integrated military command structure, they have participated under NATO command in NATO's post–Cold War operations in the Balkans and in Afghanistan, prior to French President Sarkozy's announcement in the spring of 2009 that France military forces would rejoin NATO's integrated command structure. Greece withdrew its military forces from NATO's integrated military command structure as a reaction to the handling of the Turkish invasion of Cyprus in 1974, and reintegrated its military forces in 1980.

Germany is a unique case within NATO because it assumed obligations in the Treaty on the Final Settlement with Respect to Germany, also known as the Two Plus Four Treaty, in September 1990 that restricted future Germany and NATO activities on the territory of the former German Democratic Republic (East Germany). In return for Soviet agreement that united Germany could remain in NATO and that Soviet troops stationed in East Germany and East Berlin would be withdrawn by the end of 1994, Germany, the United States, United Kingdom, and France agreed to several restrictions. Germany agreed to a permanent ceiling for its military forces of 370,000 personnel, with a further stipulation that no more than 345,000 could serve in the ground and air forces. Germany also reaffirmed its renunciation of the manufacture and possession of and control over weapons of mass destruction (WMD), as well as the continued applicability of the 1968 Nuclear Non-Proliferation Treaty. However, this did not alter German participation in NATO's nuclear sharing agreements since German armed forces assigned to former East Germany could be integrated into the NATO military command structures, "but without nuclear weapon carriers," except in the case of dual-use systems that Germany operates only in a conventional mode. NATO could still rely on German aircraft to train for and potentially fly wartime missions to deliver U.S. nuclear weapons, but these aircraft could not be stationed in the former

East Germany. Finally, Germany and the United States, United Kingdom, and France agreed that no foreign armed forces, that is, NATO Allied armed forces, and no nuclear weapons or nuclear weapons carriers would be stationed in former East Germany or deployed there. As NATO has expanded eastwards, this provision has created the effect that Allied forces in former West Germany find themselves deeper and deeper in NATO's interior instead of providing the previously favored forward defense at its borders.

Questions for Consideration

- How do you see the continued evolution of NATO-EU relations?
  - Will they remain separate, but linked organizations?
  - Could the EU absorb all of NATO's European Allies and NATO's security/military capabilities and tasks?
- What are the pros and cons of each of the following scenarios: one nation like the United States leading a coalition of the willing containing many NATO nations; NATO officially running an operation; the EU running an operation?

The development of the European Pillar within NATO, complemented by the deepening of EU governance, particularly with the Common Foreign and Security Policy, has introduced another variable into the post–Cold War European security environment. The Maastricht Treaty of 1992, which transformed the European Economic Community into the European Union, established the Common Foreign and Defense Policy and requested the Western European Union (WEU) "to elaborate and implement decisions and actions of the Union which have defence implications." (See the Timeline of European Integration in Appendix I.) Many European NATO Allies were members of the WEU, but the organizations established institutional cooperation with respect to the WEU's new EU role. Shortly thereafter, NATO agreed to use the WEU as a vehicle for strengthening the European pillar within NATO, and in June 1992 the WEU Council met in the Hotel Petersberg near Bonn, Germany, and decided that it would take on humanitarian and rescue tasks, peacekeeping tasks, and crisis management tasks, which included peacemaking and would consequently require combat forces, for the EU. The 1997 EU Amsterdam Treaty incorporated the Petersberg Tasks into the EU Treaty, and laid groundwork for the eventual integration of the WEU into the EU. In December 1999 at Helsinki, the EU established civilian and military structures as part of its developing European Security and Defense Policy (ESDP), including its own Military Committee and Military Staff, and assumed the crisis responsibility tasks of the WEU. Henceforth NATO and the EU would work directly together. At Helsinki, the EU also announced its Headline Goal, that is, the intent to be able "to deploy within 60 days and sustain for at least 1 year military forces of up to 50,000–60,000 persons capable of the full range of Petersberg tasks."

NATO and the EU agreed on a framework for cooperation in March 2003 that included the Berlin-Plus agreement. Under Berlin-Plus, NATO has the right of first refusal to lead a crisis management response. If NATO chooses not to engage in a particular crisis, but the EU wants to lead a crisis management operation, NATO, provided it reaches consensus, would give the EU access to NATO's collective assets and capabilities, including operational planning as well as command and control assets. The end effect was that NATO was no longer the sole organization with large military forces available for crisis management operations in Europe and its periphery. The EU can also lead an operation, without needing to duplicate NATO capabilities, which the NATO Allies in the EU have already contributed to. Since the capabilities require trained personnel to operate, say with NATO AWACS for example, Berlin-Plus created conditions where personnel from non-EU, NATO countries, such as the United States, would be placed under EU command. On the other hand, the expectation is that the vast majority of the troops are European, from states that are members of both NATO and the EU. Consequently, NATO and the EU are generally drawing from the same pool of forces. A German battalion serving in a NATO mission in Afghanistan is not available for an EU mission in Bosnia-Herzegovina.

> The Eurocorps provides an example of this new NATO-EU duality. The Eurocorps began as a French-German initiative in 1992, and has since grown to include Belgium, Luxembourg, and Spain as framework nations, with many other nations now also participating in the headquarters staff. Although Eurocorps is not integrated into the NATO integrated command structure (because France was not in it), it was designed to serve under NATO or EU command, and it has provided the NATO headquarters cadre for rotations in Stabilization Force (SFOR), Kosovo Force (KFOR), and ISAF.

In March 2003, the EU-led Operation Concordia replaced the NATO-led Operation Allied Harmony in Macedonia. It was the first Berlin-Plus operation, and NATO gave the EU access to its assets. Similarly, in December 2004, the EU-led Operation Althea replaced the NATO-led SFOR in Bosnia-Herzegovina. Most troops simply remained in place and changed their patches from SFOR to the EU Force. The EU Force once again used NATO assets and capabilities, and was commanded by the NATO Deputy SACEUR. The EU also coordinates several civilian operations in Kosovo and Afghanistan with NATO, and NATO and EU military forces have cooperated in airlift support to the African Union in Darfur and antipiracy operations off the Horn of Africa.

In the Lisbon Treaty, signed in 2007 and implemented in December 2009, the EU modified the name of ESDP to the Common Security and Defense Policy (CSDP). Furthermore, since the Lisbon Treaty also incorporated an article into the EU Treaty similar to the original WEU Brussels Treaty obligation for other members to render assistance if one member is attacked, and that this obligation will be consistent with NATO members' commitments, and that NATO remains the foundation of its members' collective defense even if they are in the EU too, the WEU members terminated the Modified Brussels Treaty in the spring of 2010, setting the closure of the WEU into motion.

In the spring of 2010, NATO consisted of 28 members, the EU of 27. Twenty-one nations were members of both. In NATO, Albania, Canada, Croatia, Iceland, Norway, Turkey, and the United States are not members of the EU, although Croatia and Turkey are EU candidates. As the EU has worked to develop its own military command structures to support the CSDP, these common members have worked under the premises that NATO still has an important role to play in Europe and its environs, that developing improved European military capabilities strengthens both NATO and the EU, and that they should not be paying for the same thing twice, that is, there should not be any unnecessary duplication between the EU and NATO military structures and capabilities.

The United States has been a longtime supporter of increasing European military capabilities, defense spending, and burden sharing in general. The idea that the United States would help those who help themselves, and that the Europeans should organize and take responsibility for as much of their own defense as possible reaches back to Truman and the Marshall Plan, and it is logical that NATO's EU members should not have to duplicate structures that they have already paid for and support within NATO. Furthermore, the concept that European Allies could make the same military forces available to both NATO and the EU, parallels the United States' practice of using troops assigned to NATO for national purposes when necessary. Other Allies with worldwide commitments have done the same.

The EU Treaty acknowledges the primacy of NATO for the territorial defense of its members, and the EU and NATO have developed several mechanisms for consultation, coordination, and transparency above and beyond the factor that 21 European nations have decision making responsibility and clear visibility into both organizations. Over the long term, it is conceivable that if the EU were to continue to gain more supra sovereignty, especially in the areas of foreign policy, security, and defense, the EU might not want the

NATO ties because they give the United States, a potential economic competitor, a say in European defense planning and spending. For the foreseeable future, however, it appears that the EU embraces NATO and the U.S. ties as a foundation to its own security. Perhaps the security community concept will prevail. In this case, the creation and strengthening of an EU block within NATO could make achieving consensus more difficult since only one non-EU member would be required to stalemate an issue. In addition, a change to two big pillars, the United States and EU, would certainly change the position of the remaining non-pillared NATO members of Albania, Canada, Croatia, Iceland, Norway, and Turkey. They, and their counterparts in the EU that are not members of NATO, could in some situations exert political influence over the other organization's ability to implement decisions. If NATO did not want to intervene in a crisis management capacity, but the EU did, Turkey could deny the EU access to NATO assets and capabilities. This puts Turkey, with its EU candidacy status in apparent limbo, in an interesting position.

Finally, the U.S. membership in NATO is also peculiar. The United States has been and still is a critical member of NATO. It provides the nuclear deterrent and many strategic capabilities. The United States is one of the few Allies that can militarily operate independently from NATO, and perhaps the only Ally that NATO cannot operate without. Nevertheless, the transatlantic link that NATO provides for consultations on a wide-ranging list of issues has benefited all the Allies.

The issues of *where* NATO is and *who* NATO is are important because the answers shape NATO's identity and what it is. The Washington Treaty is clear that new membership is limited to European states, so membership hangs on how *Europe* is defined. It is conceivable that the Allies could agree to a rather expansive view of what Europe is. For example, one might be able to argue successfully that a former Soviet republic like Kazakhstan could be considered for membership through its historic connection to Europe through the Soviet Union, NATO's former adversary. On the other hand, requests for membership from say Singapore, Morocco, or Argentina, based on their colonial heritage would seem much more dubious. In any event, the question of *where* NATO is affects more than the question of *who* can become members. The answer to the question *where* also determines how far afield NATO should be looking for threats. However, as NATO's concept of threats to its security has expanded from the Soviet Army to instability on its periphery to organized crime and cyberspace, it is not clear that the traditional static geospatial view of the world is adequate to address NATO's contemporary view of security. Furthermore, the peculiarities of NATO membership for some Allies, the tiered levels of association status (Partners, Mediterranean Dialogue/ Istanbul Cooperation Initiative, and nonassociated troop contributing nations), and the varying levels of interest and participation within those tiers have created conditions where, for example, some nonaffiliated nations contribute more to ISAF than many Allies and Partners do. NATO is having a global impact through these associations even though its membership is limited. Finally, the interplay between the EU and NATO will affect the continued evolution of NATO's identity.

Afterword

Readers of early drafts of this book, to whom I am indebted, pointed out that I never explicitly defined NATO in the text and that I did not explicitly weave threads of continuity through the chapters, although they also admitted that the reader reached an intuitive understanding of both by the end of the manuscript. Initially, I was leery of being too explicit in the text—following the pedagogic perspective that students learn more by wrestling with material and developing their own definitions—students would most benefit from developing their own analysis of NATO. However, in deference to my first readers' counterarguments, I will hereby try to succinctly describe NATO, highlight some short- and long-term issues that NATO faces, and highlight some areas of tension that appear frequently in the narratives told throughout the text.

NATO is an evolving collective security organization, whose identity is shaped by its members and through their interactions. The members use a rather unique process of decision making through consensus. The Cold War quip that NATO was put together to keep the Russians out, the Germans down, and the Americans in, did not reflect the actual NATO Treaty text, which, written more abstractly, has allowed the NATO Allies to adapt their understanding of NATO, its security environment, its definition of security, and its missions.

In the short term, NATO faces several issues, many of which are manifestations of long-term strategic issues. Rather than list or attempt to briefly describe the issues in detail, I simply offer the following questions in no particular order:

- Who or what would a NATO missile defense provide protection from, and what exactly would it seek to protect?
- What exactly is *cyber security*?

- Is it a NATO task, a national responsibility, or both?
- Is there an offensive aspect of cyber security?
- Do cyber security and cyber counterattacks have to occur in the cyber medium?
- What would have to be changed in order for NATO nations to consider a cyber attack to be an act of war or to qualify for Article 5 assistance?

- Who is NATO using its strategic and tactical nuclear weapons capabilities against, how is NATO using these capabilities, and what do these capabilities deter?
- What exactly is a terrorist attack, and under what conditions does it become an Article 5 type attack?
- What is the long-term vision for the NATO–Ukraine relationship, and what is the strategy for getting there?
  - Does Ukraine share the vision and agree to the strategy?
- What is the long-term vision for the NATO–Georgia relationship, and what is the strategy for getting there?
  - Does Georgia share the vision and agree to the strategy?
- Under what conditions will NATO withdraw from Kosovo?
- Are there limits to how long NATO can lead, and at what level NATO can re-source ISAF?

In the long term, NATO faces several strategic issues, the resolutions of which could dramatically alter NATO. In no particular order, I offer the following questions, which are by no means meant to be exhaustive:

- Does NATO have a long-term vision for its relationship with Russia?
  - What is the vision, and does NATO have a strategy for achieving this vision?
  - Do the Russians share this vision?
  - Are there requirements that Russia must meet to comply with NATO's vision?
  - What would it take to get Russia to agree to these requirements?
  - Are there decision points and indicators as to whether the strategy is working or needs modification?
  - Does NATO's vision entertain Russian membership in NATO?
- Does NATO have a long-term vision for its relationship with the EU?
  - What is the vision, and does NATO have a strategy for achieving this vision?
  - Does the EU share this vision?
  - Are there requirements that the EU must meet to comply with NATO's vision?
  - What would it take to get the EU to agree to these requirements?
  - Are there decision points and indicators as to whether the strategy is working or needs modification?
  - Does the vision entertain a need to retain NATO?

- Does NATO need a threat?
- How should an organization of 28 or more equal participants make decisions without injuring the spirit of Article 5 and the Washington Treaty in general?
- Are there any bounds to NATO's evolving concept of security and the missions that flow from it?
  - What criteria should NATO use to determine whether it should become involved in a crisis?
    - Security of NATO and its members?
    - Capability to act?
    - Potential to be effective?
    - Geography?
    - Potential impact on NATO and/or its members?
    - Potential result of doing nothing?
    - Human suffering?
    - Justice?
    - Impact on environment or climate?
    - Other criteria?
  - Under what conditions will NATO depart from Afghanistan?
- Does the United States get more out of NATO than it puts into it?
  - Is this a valid way to frame the question of whether the United States should stay in NATO?
- Should NATO continue forever, or what conditions might bring about its dissolution?

In addition to the issues and questions, there are several threads or themes that are better described as tensions in NATO, as evident through the narratives of various chapters of this book. I will briefly mention a few of them. One point of tension is whether NATO should be focused on the North Atlantic area, as was the case in the Cold War and its more immediate aftermath, or more globally, as in the earlier Strategic Concepts and the post–9/11 world. Another significant and long-standing area of tension exists between NATO's strategic concepts and defense plans on the one hand, and the Allies limited resourcing of these plans on the other. In the beginning of NATO, part of this disconnect could possibly be attributed to a military-civilian relationship marked by senior Allied military officers, who were regarded as true military experts who played key roles in the victories of World War II, and civilian leaders, who were not the top national leaders during World War II. The military officers used worst-case planning to try to ensure they would not be under-resourced if it came to war, which was their responsibility to win. The civilian leaders did not deny the senior military officers' requirements but did not completely fund them either. However, the gap between military requirements and military spending remained even as new generations of military officers rose through the ranks and civilian politicians took a more active role in crafting the strategic concepts. Perhaps it was the continued reliance on worst-case planning, or perhaps the United States's special role as the superpower providing the most modern and expansive military capabilities, including the nuclear deterrent, that creates part of the tension since those capabilities reduce the significance of all but the largest of the other Allies' contributions. The extension of more equitable burden sharing to tactical nuclear weapons was partially intended to ameliorate the effects of this capabilities gap by spreading the capabilities and risks among the Allies. This, however, created a political justification for the weapons that appears to have separated from and outlived their initial military justifications. A final explicit theme that I will mention is the rather remarkable degree of prescience in NATO's Strategic Concepts that resulted from the confrontation and discussion of the conflicting Allies' views of their world, their security environment, and likely future scenarios.

Timelines

The German Question

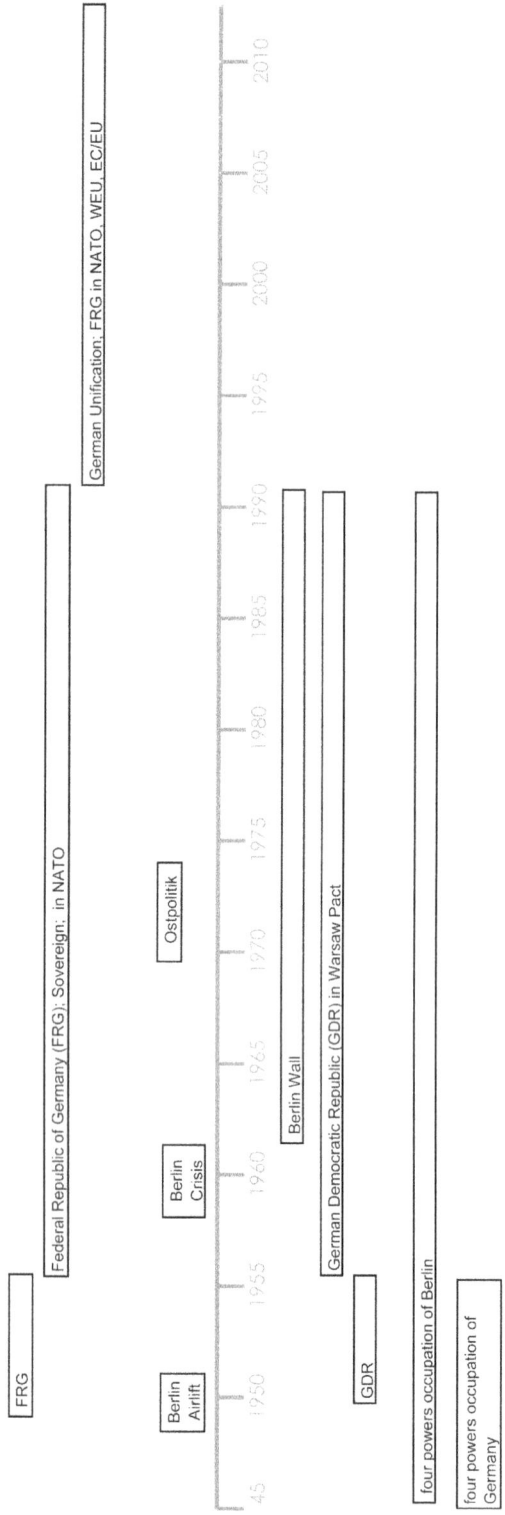

Timeline: The German Question

- German Unification; FRG in NATO, WEU, EC/EU
- Federal Republic of Germany (FRG): Sovereign; in NATO
- FRG
- Ostpolitik
- Berlin Crisis
- Berlin Wall
- German Democratic Republic (GDR) in Warsaw Pact
- Berlin Airlift
- GDR
- four powers occupation of Berlin
- four powers occupation of Germany

Years: 45 | 1950 | 1955 | 1960 | 1965 | 1970 | 1975 | 1980 | 1985 | 1990 | 1995 | 2000 | 2005 | 2010

European Security Cooperation

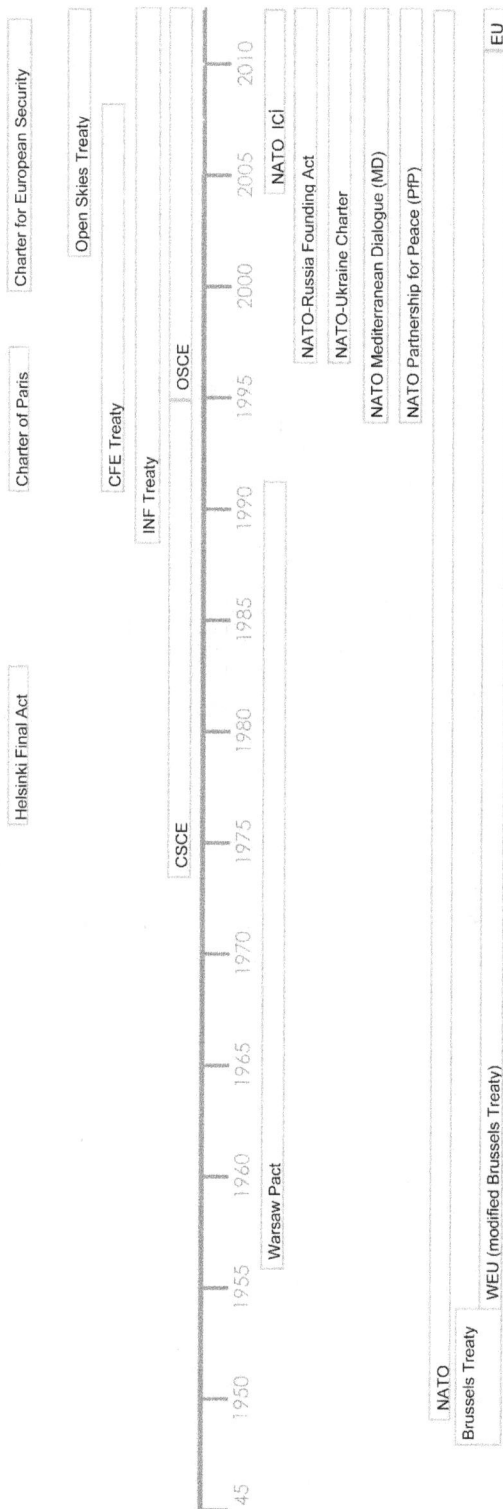

	45	1950	1955	1960	1965	1970	1975	1980	1985	1990	1995	2000	2005	2010

Helsinki Final Act

Charter of Paris

Charter for European Security

Open Skies Treaty

CFE Treaty

INF Treaty

CSCE

OSCE

NATO ICI

NATO-Russia Founding Act

NATO-Ukraine Charter

NATO Mediterranean Dialogue (MD)

NATO Partnership for Peace (PfP)

Warsaw Pact

NATO

Brussels Treaty

WEU (modified Brussels Treaty)

EU

Illustrative Non-NATO Events

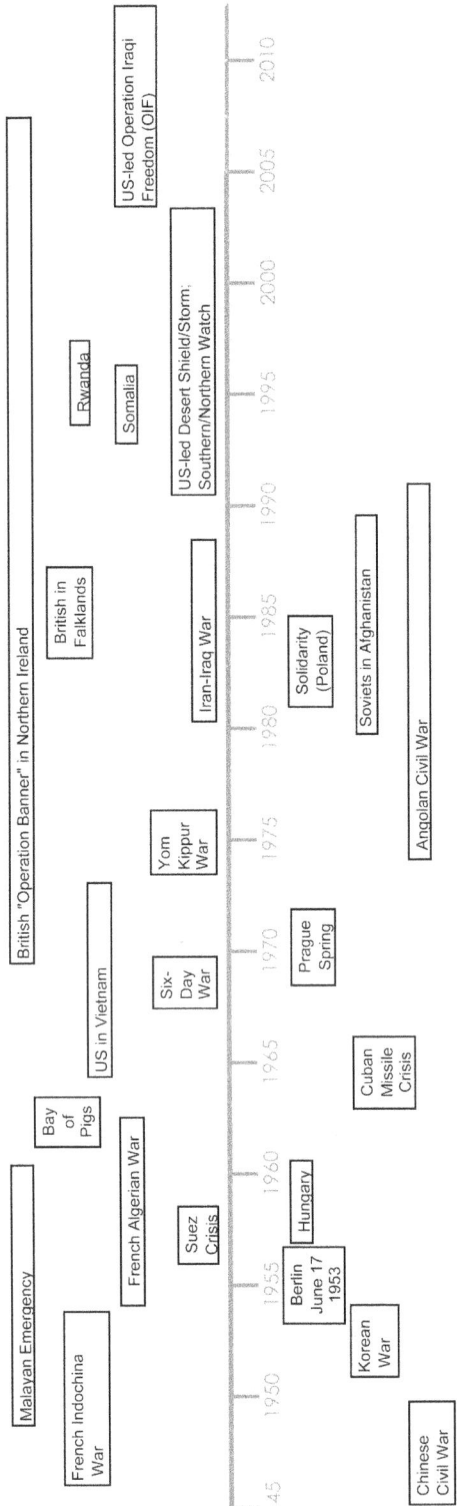

Chinese Civil War

French Indochina War

Malayan Emergency

Korean War

Berlin June 17 1953

Suez Crisis

Hungary

French Algerian War

Bay of Pigs

US in Vietnam

British "Operation Banner" in Northern Ireland

Six-Day War

Yom Kippur War

Cuban Missile Crisis

Prague Spring

Angolan Civil War

Iran-Iraq War

Solidarity (Poland)

Soviets in Afghanistan

British in Falklands

US-led Desert Shield/Storm; Southern/Northern Watch

Somalia

Rwanda

US-led Operation Iraqi Freedom (OIF)

45 1950 1955 1960 1965 1970 1975 1980 1985 1990 1995 2000 2005 2010

NATO Strategic Concepts

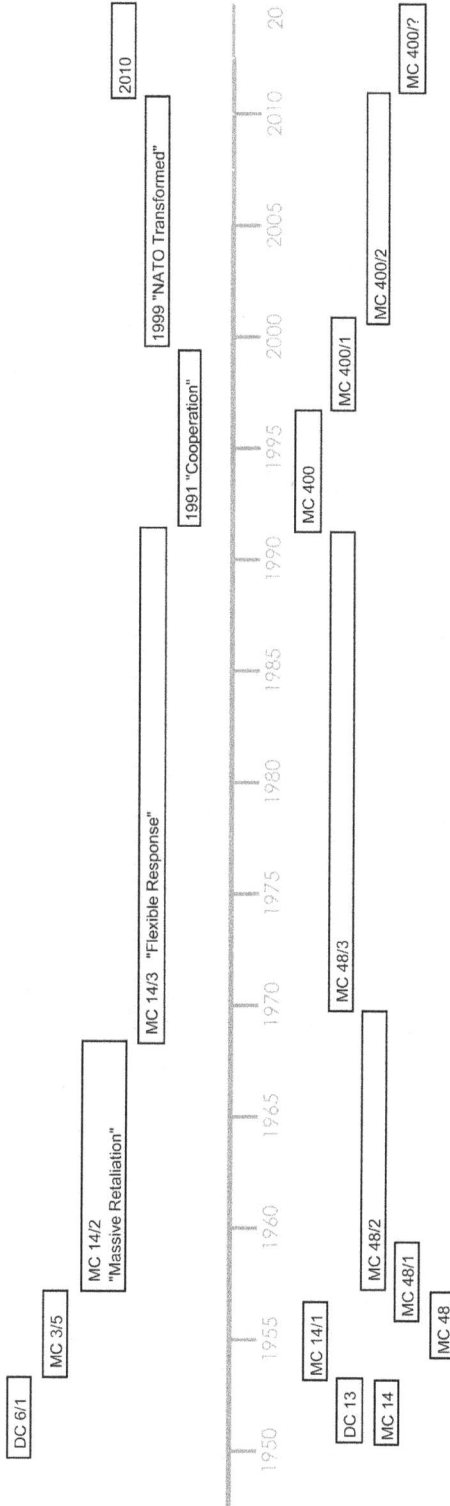

DC 6/1

MC 3/5

MC 14/2 "Massive Retaliation"

MC 14/3 "Flexible Response"

1991 "Cooperation"

1999 "NATO Transformed"

2010

Military Committee Supporting Guidance

1950   1955   1960   1965   1970   1975   1980   1985   1990   1995   2000   2005   2010   20

DC 13

MC 14

MC 14/1

MC 48

MC 48/1

MC 48/2

MC 48/3

MC 400

MC 400/1

MC 400/2

MC 400/?

NATO Enlargement

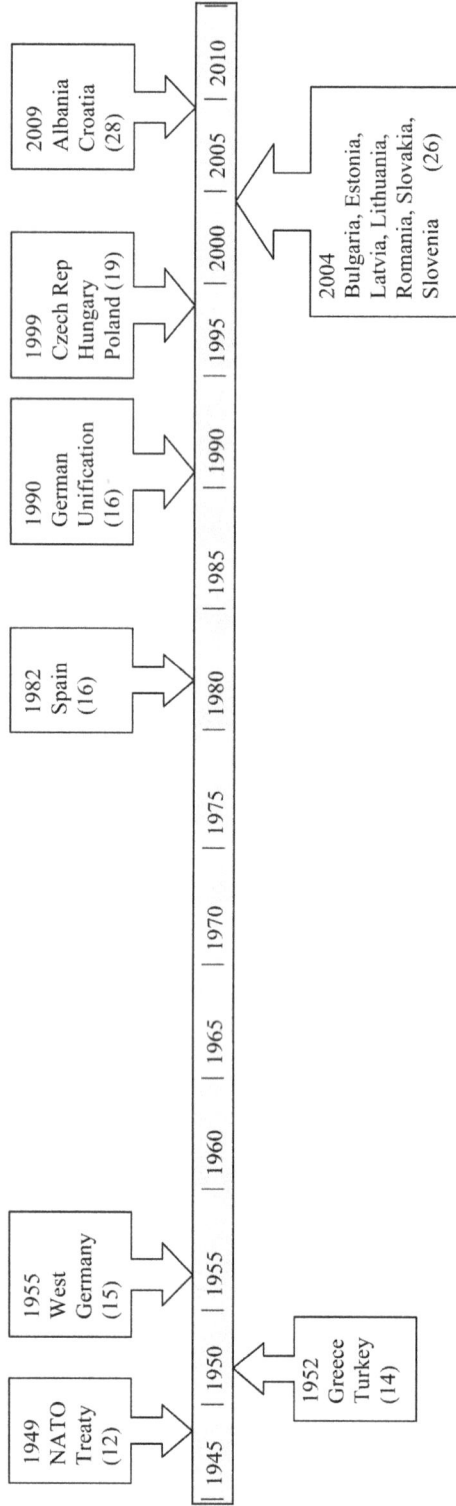

| 1949 NATO Treaty (12) |
| 1952 Greece Turkey (14) |
| 1955 West Germany (15) |
| 1982 Spain (16) |
| 1990 German Unification (16) |
| 1999 Czech Rep Hungary Poland (19) |
| 2004 Bulgaria, Estonia, Latvia, Lithuania, Romania, Slovakia, Slovenia (26) |
| 2009 Albania Croatia (28) |

| 1945 | 1950 | 1955 | 1960 | 1965 | 1970 | 1975 | 1980 | 1985 | 1990 | 1995 | 2000 | 2005 | 2010 |

Major NATO Military Operations

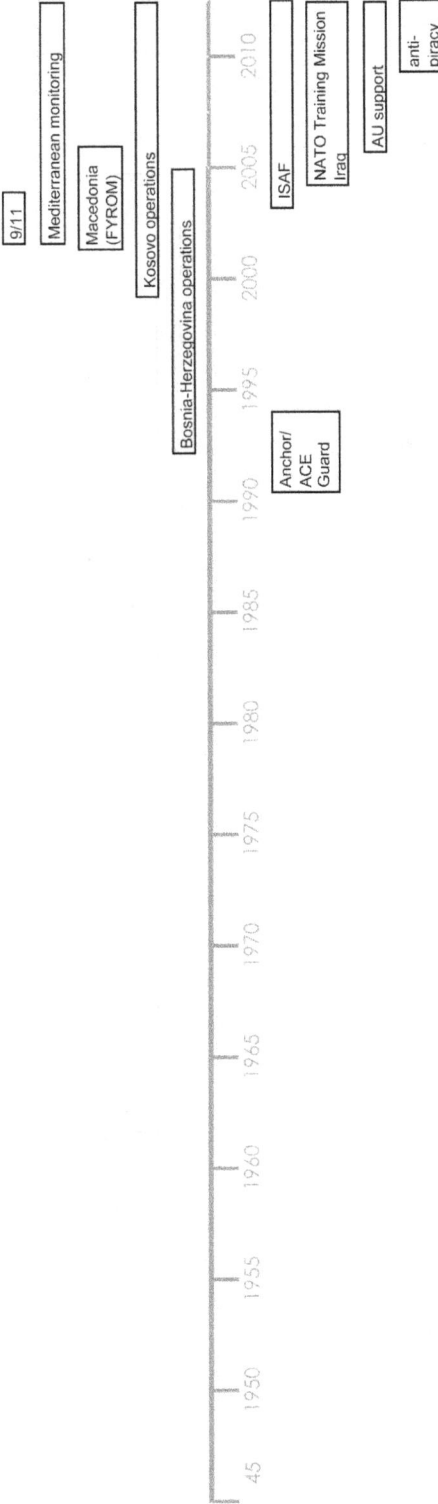

45	1950	1955	1960	1965	1970	1975	1980	1985	1990	1995	2000	2005	2010	

9/11

Mediterranean monitoring

Macedonia (FYROM)

Kosovo operations

Bosnia-Herzegovina operations

Anchor/ ACE Guard

ISAF

NATO Training Mission Iraq

AU support

anti-piracy

European Integration

Treaties of Rome

Maastricht Treaty

Amsterdam Treaty

Treaty of Nice

Lisbon Treaty

European Union (EU)

EC

European Coal and Steel Community

European Economic Community

European Community (EC)

Common Foreign and Security Policy

EU

Brussels Treaty

WEU (modified Brussels Treaty)

1950 1955 1960 1965 1970 1975 1980 1985 1990 1995 2000 2005 2010 20

Tips for Further Exploration

The first place to look for anything concerning NATO is the official NATO homepage, http://www.nato.int/. You can search the site for anything that NATO makes publicly available, including both primary and secondary source documents. For an analysis of NATO's strategy documents and copies of the documents from 1949 through 1969, you can go directly to http://www.nato.int/archives/strategy.htm. NATO also provides documents, including declassified documents, and multimedia material directly at http://www.natobookshop.org/.

The NATO Web site also contains links to the Web sites of NATO member and Partner governments, militaries, and delegations. For example, because Russia is a Partner, there are links to the official Russian Web sites.

In addition, the NATO Web site contains links to the various NATO staffs, agencies, and commands, including current operational commands such as the International Security Force (ISAF).

For information on the European Union (EU), its history, and evolving responsibilities in the fields of security/defense and foreign policy, the official EU Web site is one of the best places to start: http://europa.eu/. From there you can navigate to various EU treaty texts, official documents, statistics, an introduction to the EU, the history of the EU, and some analyses of the EU.

The U.S. Department of State is another good source: http://www.state.gov/. The State Department is a depository for many treaties, including the Washington Treaty. However, State Department has limited electronic files of treaties. Access to historical documents is available through the Office of the Historian at: http://history.state.gov/historicaldocuments/. Current treaties are the responsibility of the Office of the Assistant Legal Advisor for Treaty Affairs at: http://www.state.gov/s/l/treaty/index.htm.

Treaty texts are also available at the Library of Congress at: http://www.loc.gov/. However, the Library's electronic treaty files are also limited.

The Avalon Project at Yale Law School also provides electronic files of many documents and treaties: http://avalon.law.yale.edu/.

The U.S. Department of Defense (DoD) is useful for current news, reports, and links to other agencies: http://www.defense.gov/.

The Organization for Security and Cooperation in Europe (OSCE) home page is: http://www.osce.org/.

The Western European Union (WEU) still maintains a Web site (http://www.weu.int/), although the WEU is in the process of closing as the EU is taking over its remaining tasks.

The National Defense University Library is a good source for national security materials and links to similar institutions: http://www.ndu.edu/library/index.cfm.

The National Defense University's Institute for National Strategic Studies (INSS), through its research centers, produces numerous publications written by subject matter experts for decision makers at all levels of the Department of Defense, the government, and the community at large: http://www.ndu.edu/inss/index.cfm.

Bibliography

"Agreement among the States Parties to the North Atlantic Treaty and the Other States Participating in the Partnership for Peace regarding the Status of Their Forces, June 19, 1995," *NATO Official Texts*. August 25, 2010. http://www.nato.int/cps/en/natolive/official_texts_24742.htm.

"Agreement on Adaptation of the Treaty on Conventional Armed Forces in Europe, CFE.DOC/1/99, 19 November 1999," Organization for Security and Cooperation in Europe. August 25, 2010. http://www.osce.org/documents/doclib/1999/11/13760_en.pdf.

Ailleret, General. "Flexible Response: A French View," *Survival* (1964) 6: 6, 258–265.

"The Alliance's New Strategic Concept (1991), 07-Nov.-1991," *NATO Official Texts*. February 2, 2010. http://www.nato.int/cps/en/SID-2DD66805-AFCC6644/natolive/official_texts_23847.htm.

"The Alliance's New Strategic Concept agreed by the Heads of State and Government participating in the Meeting of the North Atlantic Council, 07 Nov. 1991—08 Nov. 1991," *NATO Official Texts*. February 2, 2010. http://www.nato.int/cps/en/natolive/official_texts_23847.htm.

"The Alliance's Strategic Concept Approved by the Heads of State and Government participating in the meeting of the North Atlantic Council in Washington D.C., 24 Apr. 1999," *NATO Official Texts*. February 2, 2010. http://www.nato.int/cps/en/natolive/official_texts_27433.htm.

"AWACS-Flugzeuge nach Afghanistan: NATO einig/REgierung will rasch Bundestagsmandat/Mehr Taliban-Angriffe denn je," *Frankfurter Allgemeine Zeitung fuer Deutschland*, Nr. 134/24D1. June 13, 2009.

"AWACS Takes Off into the 21st Century," *NATO's Sixteen Nations & Partners for Peace*, Special Edition. Uithoorn, Netherlands: Jules Perel's Publishing, 1998.

"B. Standing Group (SG): Organization of the Standing Group, 1949–1952," *NATO Archives*. January 29, 2010. http://www.nato.int/archives/tools/98-XIB.pdf.

"Background—EU-NATO: The Framework for Permanent Relations and Berlin Plus," *EU CSDP References*. August 25, 2010. http://www.consilium.europa.eu/uedocs/cmsUpload/03-11-11%20Berlin%20Plus%20press%20note%20BL.pdf.

"Chapter 3: The Opening Up of the Alliance: Partnership for Peace: The Partnership for Peace Planning and Review Process (PARP)," *NATO Publications: NATO Handbook, updated 08-Oct-2002.* March 16, 2010. http://www.nato.int/docu/handbook/2001/hb030208.htm.

"Charter of Paris for a New Europe," *Conference on Security and Cooperation in Europe*, Paris 1990. February 2, 2010. http://www.osce.org/documents/mcs/1990/11/4045_en.pdf.

"Charter on a Distinctive Partnership between the North Atlantic Treaty Organization and Ukraine, 09 Jul. 1997," *NATO Official Texts.* August 25, 2010. http://www.nato.int/cps/en/natolive/official_texts_25457.htm.

"C-M(56)138(Final), Directive to the NATO Military Authorities from the North Atlantic Council, 13 December 1956," *NATO Strategy Documents 1949–1969.* September 3, 2009. http://www.nato.int/docu/stratdoc/eng/a561213a.pdf.

"Committee of Three," *NATO Archives.* September 3, 2009. http://www.nato.int/archives/committee_of_three/index.htm.

"Committee of Three, Document CT-D/10(Revised), Committee of Three: Draft Formal Record of Proceedings (to be Annexed to the Report), 2nd November, 1956," *NATO ebookshop.* April 22, 2010. http://www.nato.int/ebookshop/video/declassified/doc_files/CT-D_10-REV1.PDF.

"Committee of Three: Index, Terms of Reference, Documents, Notes, Records, Working Papers, Meetings, and Report," *NATO Archives.* September 3, 2009. http://www.nato.int/archives/committee_of_three/CT.pdf.

"Common Foreign and Security Policy for the European Union," *EU: The European Commission: External Relations.* August 25, 2010. http://ec.europa.eu/external_relations/cfsp/index_en.htm.

"Comprehensive Political Guidance," *NATO Topics.* February 2, 2010. http://www.nato.int/cps/en/natolive/topics_49176.htm?selectedLocale=en.

"Comprehensive Political Guidance: Endorsed by NATO Heads of State and Government on 29 November 2006," *NATO Official Texts* February 2, 2010. http://www.nato.int/cps/en/natolive/official_texts_56425.htm?selectedLocale=en.

"Conseil de L'Atlantique Nord, Document. C6-D/9, Or. Angl., Resolution Approuvant La Nomination d'un Commandant Supreme, Note du Secrétaire, 19 décembre 1950," *NATO ebookshop.* April 22, 2010. http://www.nato.int/ebookshop/video/declassified/doc_files/C_6-D_9.PDF.

"Conseil de L'Atlantique Nord, Document C9-D/4(Final), Reorganization of the North Atlantic Treaty Organization: Note by the Executive Secretary, 17th March, 1952," *NATO ebookshop.* April 22, 2010. http://www.nato.int/ebookshop/video/declassified/doc_files/C_9-D_4-FINAL.PDF.

"Conseil de L'Atlantique Nord, Document C-M(52)20, NATO-EDC Relations: Report by the Committee to Examine the EDC Treaty, May 26, 1952," *NATO ebookshop.* April 23, 2010. http://www.nato.int/ebookshop/video/declassified/doc_files/C-M(52)20.PDF.

"Conseil de L'Atlantique Nord, Document C-M(52)135 (Original: French), Progress of Work by the Interim Commission: Report by the French Permanent Representative, Chairman of the Interim Commission of the Conference for setting up a European Defence Community, 15th December, 1952," *NATO ebookshop.*

April 23, 2010. http://www.nato.int/ebookshop/video/declassified/doc_files/ C-M(52)135.PDF.

"Conseil de L'Atlantique Nord, Document C-M(54)38, Resolution on Political Consultation Adopted by the North Atlantic Council on 23rd April, 1954, 26th April, 1954," *NATO ebookshop*. April 22, 2010. http://www.nato.int/ ebookshop/video/declassified/doc_files/C-M(54)38.PDF.

"Conseil de L'Atlantique Nord, Document C-M(54)71 (Original: French), Statement by Mr. Mendes-France, Chairman of the North Atlantic Council, at the Meeting of the North Atlantic Council held on 9th September, 1954, 10th September, 1954," *NATO ebookshop*. April 23, 2010. http://www.nato.int/ ebookshop/video/declassified/doc_files/C-M(54)71.PDF.

"Conseil de L'Atlantique Nord, Document C-M(54)83 (Final), Protocol to the North Atlantic Treaty on the Accession of the Federal Republic of Germany: Note by the Secretary General and Vice-Chairman of the Council, 25th October, 1954," *NATO ebookshop*. April 23, 2010. http://www.nato.int/ebookshop/ video/declassified/doc_files/C-M(54)83-FINAL.PDF.

"Conseil de L'Atlantique Nord, Document C-M(54)84 (Revised), Protocols to the Brussels Treaty: Note by the Secretary General and Vice-Chairman of the Council, 22nd October, 1954," *NATO ebookshop*. April 23, 2010. http://www. nato.int/ebookshop/video/declassified/doc_files/C-M(54)84-REV1.PDF.

"Conseil de L'Atlantique Nord, Document C-M(54)91, Results of the Four-Power Meeting: Note by the Secretary General and Vice-Chairman of the Council, 21st October, 1954," *NATO ebookshop*. April 23, 2010. http://www.nato.int/ ebookshop/video/declassified/doc_files/C-M(54)91.PDF.

"Conseil de L'Atlantique Nord, Document C-M(54)93 (Final), Resolution on the Results of the Four and Nine Power Meetings (Adopted by the North Atlantic Council on 22nd October 1954), 22nd October, 1954," *NATO ebookshop*. April 23, 2010. http://www.nato.int/ebookshop/video/declassified/doc_files/ C-M(54)93-FINAL.PDF.

"Conseil de L'Atlantique Nord, Document C-M(56)25, Public Relations Aspects of Political Consultations in NATO: Note by the Secretary General and Vice Chairman of the Council, 8th March, 1956," *NATO ebookshop*. April 22, 2010. http://www.nato.int/ebookshop/video/declassified/doc_files/C-M(56)25.PDF.

"Conseil de L'Atlantique Nord, Document C-M(56)126, Letter or Transmittal of the Report of the Committee of Three, 17th November, 1956," *NATO ebookshop*. April 23, 2010. http://www.nato.int/ebookshop/video/declassified/doc_files/ C-M(56)1262.PDF.

"Conseil de L'Atlantique Nord, Document C-M(56)127(Revised), Report of the Committee of Three on Non-Military Co-Operation in NATO: Note by the Deputy Secretary General, 10th January, 1957," *NATO ebookshop*. April 23, 2010. http://www.nato.int/ebookshop/video/declassified/doc_files/ C-M(56)127-REV1.PDF.

"Conseil de L'Atlantique Nord, Document C-M(56)131, Comparison of Economic Growth in the Sino-Soviet Bloc and in NATO Countries: Note by the Chairman of the Committee on Soviet Economic Policy, 30th November, 1956,"

NATO ebookshop. April 22, 2010. http://www.nato.int/ebookshop/video/
     declassified/doc_files/C-M(56)131.PDF.

"Conseil de L'Atlantique Nord, Document C-M(57)102, Measures to Reduce Western
     Dependence on the Suez Canal: Note by the Secretary General and Chairman
     of the Council, 27th June, 1957," *NATO ebookshop*. April 23, 2010. http://
     www.nato.int/ebookshop/video/declassified/doc_files/C-M(57)102.PDF.

"Conseil de L'Atlantique Nord, Document C-M(58)138 (Original: French), Interim
     Report of the Secretary General on Political Co-Operation, 17th November,
     1958," *NATO ebookshop*. April 23, 2010. http://www.nato.int/ebookshop/
     video/declassified/doc_files/C-M(58)138.PDF.

"Conseil de L'Atlantique Nord, Document C-M(58)175, Wartime Oil Reserves in
     the European NATO Area: Report by the Petroleum Planning Committee to
     the Council, 22nd December 1958," *NATO ebookshop*. April 23, 2010. http://
     www.nato.int/ebookshop/video/declassified/doc_files/C-M(58)175.PDF.

"Conseil de L'Atlantique Nord, Document CT-D/1 (Revised), Committee of Three
     [Questionnaire], 28th June, 1956," *NATO ebookshop*. April 22, 2010. http://
     www.nato.int/ebookshop/video/declassified/doc_files/CT-D_1-REV1.PDF.

"Conseil de L'Atlantique Nord, Document CT-D/6 (Original: French), The attached
     note on procedures for the pacific settlement of disputes within various interna-
     tional organizations, has been prepared by the International Staff in response to
     the Committee's request, 17th August, 1956," *NATO ebookshop*. April 22, 2010.
     http://www.nato.int/ebookshop/video/declassified/doc_files/CT-D_6.PDF.

"Conseil de L'Atlantique Nord, Document CT-D/7, The attached outline of what
     NATO has done so far in the non-military fields has been prepared by the
     International Staff in response to the Committee's request, 28th August, 1956,"
     NATO ebookshop. April 22, 2010. http://www.nato.int/ebookshop/video/
     declassified/doc_files/CT-D_7.PDF.

"Conseil de L'Atlantique Nord, Quatrieme Reunion, Londres, Council Record No. 7,
     R.4/7, Summary Record of Decisions 15th—18th May, 1950, 20th May, 1950,"
     NATO ebookshop. April 22, 2010. http://www.nato.int/ebookshop/video/
     declassified/doc_files/C_4-R-4_7.PDF.

"Conseil de L'Atlantique Nord, Summary Record C-R(54)18, Summary Record of
     a meeting of the Council held at the Palais de Chaillot, Paris, on Friday 23rd
     April, 1954 at 3.30 p.m., 23rd April, 1954," *NATO ebookshop*. April 22, 2010.
     http://www.nato.int/ebookshop/video/declassified/doc_files/C-R(54)18.PDF.

"Conseil de L'Atlantique Nord, Summary Record C-R(56)23, Summary Record of a
     meeting of the Council held at the Palais de Chaillot, Paris, XVIe., on Saturday,
     5th May, 1956, at 3 p.m., 5th May, 1956," *NATO ebookshop*. April 22, 2010.
     http://www.nato.int/ebookshop/video/declassified/doc_files/C-R(56)23.PDF.

"Conseil de L'Atlantique Nord, Summary Record C-R(56)44, Summary Record of a
     Restricted meeting of the Council held at the Palais de Chaillot, Paris, XVIe,
     on 3rd August, 1956," *NATO ebookshop*. April 23, 2010. http://www.nato.int/
     ebookshop/video/declassified/doc_files/C-R(56)44.PDF.

"Conseil de L'Atlantique Nord, Summary Record C-R(56)45, Summary Record
     of a Restricted meeting of the Council held at the Palais de Chaillot, Paris,

XVIe., on Monday, 6th August, 1956, at 4.30 p.m., 8th August, 1956," *NATO ebookshop*. April 23, 2010. http://www.nato.int/ebookshop/video/declassified/doc_files/C-R(56)45.PDF.

"Conseil de L'Atlantique Nord, Summary Record C-R(56)46, Summary Record of a restricted meeting of the Council held at the Palais de Chaillot, Paris, on Tuesday, 14th August, 1956, at 10.15 a.m., 17th August, 1956," *NATO ebookshop*. April 23, 2010. http://www.nato.int/ebookshop/video/declassified/doc_files/C-R(56)46.PDF.

"Conseil de L'Atlantique Nord, Summary Record C-R(56)48, Summary Record of a meeting of the Council held at the Palais de Chaillot, Paris, XVIe, on Wednesday, 5th September at 3.30 p.m., 8th September, 1956," *NATO ebookshop*. April 23, 2010. http://www.nato.int/ebookshop/video/declassified/doc_files/C-R(56)48.PDF.

"Conseil de L'Atlantique Nord, Summary Record C-R(56)69 (Part II), Summary Record of a meeting of the Council held at the Palais de Chaillot, Paris, XVIe., on Tuesday, 11th December, 1956 at 11 a.m., 11th December, 1956," *NATO ebookshop*. April 23, 2010. http://www.nato.int/ebookshop/video/declassified/doc_files/C-R(56)69-PART2.PDF.

"Conseil de L'Atlantique Nord, Summary Record C-R(56)70. Summary Record of a meeting of the Council held at the Palais de Chaillot, Paris, XVIe., on Tuesday, 11th December, 1956 at 3.30 p.m., 11th December, 1956," *NATO ebookshop*. April 22, 2010. http://www.nato.int/ebookshop/video/declassified/doc_files/C-R(56)70.PDF.

"Conseil de L'Atlantique Nord, Summary Record C-R(63)2, Summary record of a meeting of the Council, held at the Permanent Headquarters, Paris, XVIe, on Wednesday, 16th January, 1963 at 10.15 a.m., 22nd January, 1963," *NATO ebookshop*. April 23, 2010. http://www.nato.int/ebookshop/video/declassified/doc_files/C-R(63)2.PDF.

"Conseil de L'Atlantique Nord, Summary Record CT-R/1, Committee of Three: Decisions Reached during Meetings Held on 20th-22nd June, 1956, at the Palais de Chaillot, Paris, 28 June, 1956," *NATO ebookshop*. April 22, 2010. http://www.nato.int/ebookshop/video/declassified/doc_files/CT-R_1.PDF.

"Conseil de L'Antique Nord, Verbatim Record C-VR(53)22, Verbatim Record of the Twenty Second Meeting of the Council held on Friday, 24th April, 1953 at 11 a.m. at the Palais de Chaillot, Paris XVIe, 24th April, 1953," *NATO ebookshop*. April 23, 2010. http://www.nato.int/ebookshop/video/declassified/doc_files/C-VR(53)22.PDF.

"Conseil de L'Antique Nord, Verbatim Record C-VR(56)69(Final), Verbatim Record of the Sixty Ninth Meeting of the Council held on Tuesday, 11th December, 1956 at 10.30 a.m. at the Palais de Chaillot, Paris XVIe, 11th December, 1956," *NATO ebookshop*. April 22, 2010. http://www.nato.int/ebookshop/video/declassified/doc_files/C-VR(56)69-FINAL.PDF.

"Conseil de L'Antique Nord, Verbatim Record C-VR(56)70, Verbatim Record of the Seventieth Meeting of the Council held on Tuesday, 11th December, 1956 at 3.30 p.m. at the Palais de Chaillot, Paris XVIe, 11th December, 1956," *NATO ebookshop.* April 22, 2010. http://www.nato.int/ebookshop/video/declassified/doc_files/C-VR(56)70.PDF.

"Consultative Council of Western Powers," *International Organization, 3*, no. 1. (1949), 166–169. February 6, 2008. http://links.jstor.org/sici?sici=0020–8183%281949 02%293%3A1%3C166%3ACCOWP%3E2.0.CO%3B2–8.

"D.C. 6, Note by the Secretary to the North Atlantic Defense Committee on the Strategic Concept for the Defence of the North Atlantic Area, 29th November 1949," *NATO Strategy Documents 1949–1969.* November 20, 2009. http://www.nato.int/docu/stratdoc/eng/a491129a.pdf.

"D.C. 6/1, Note by the Secretary to the North Atlantic Defense Committee on the Strategic Concept for the Defence of the North Atlantic Area,' 1 December 1949," *NATO Strategy Documents 1949–1969.* November 19, 2009. http://www.nato.int/docu/stratdoc/eng/a491201a.pdf.

"D.C. 6/1, Note by the Secretary to the North Atlantic Defense Committee on the Strategic Concept for the Defense of the North Atlantic Area,' 1 December 1949," *NATO ebookshop* (photocopy of actual document). August 13, 2010. http://www.nato.int/ebookshop/video/declassified/doc_files/DC_006_1_ENG_PDP.pdf.

"D.C. 13, North Atlantic Defense Committee Decision on D.C. 13: A Report by the Military Committee on North Atlantic Treaty Organization Medium Term Plan, Note by the Secretary, 28 March 1950," *NATO Strategy Documents 1949–1969.* September 3, 2009. http://www.nato.int/docu/stratdoc/eng/a500328d.pdf.

"D.C. 13, Report From the Military Committee to the North Atlantic Defense Committee on North Atlantic Treaty Organization Medium Term Plan, 28 March 1950," *NATO ebookshop* (Photocopy of actual document) August 13, 2010. http://www.nato.int/ebookshop/video/declassified/doc_files/DC_013_ENG_PDP.pdf.

"Declaration by NATO Defence Ministers following their meetings in Brussels on 10 and 11 June 2010, Press Release: (2010) 079, 11 Jun. 2010," *NATO Press Releases.* August 26, 2010. http://www.nato.int/cps/en/natolive/news_64321.htm?mode=pressrelease.

"Declaration of the Heads of State and Government participating in the Meeting of the North Atlantic Council, Brussels, 2–3 March 1988," *NATO Ministerial Communiqus* (sic). August 26, 2010. http://www.nato.int/docu/comm/49–95/c880303a.htm.

"Declaration of the Heads of State and Government participating in the Meeting of the North Atlantic Council, Brussels, 29–30 May 1989," *NATO Ministerial Communiqus* (sic). August 26, 2010. http://www.nato.int/docu/comm/49–95/c890530a.htm.

"Declaration on Alliance Security: Issued by the Heads of State and Government participating in the meeting of the North Atlantic Council in Strasbourg/Kehl on 4 April 2009," *NATO Official Texts.* February 2, 2010. http://www.nato.int/cps/en/natolive/news_52838.htm.

"Declaration to Complement the Charter on a Distinctive Partnership between the North Atlantic Treaty Organization and Ukraine, as signed on 9 July 1997, 21 Aug. 2009," *NATO Official Texts.* August 25, 2010. http://www.nato.int/cps/en/natolive/official_texts_57045.htm.

"DPC/D(67)23, Defence Planning Committee: Decisions of the Defence Planning Committee in Ministerial Session, Note by the Chairman, 11 May 1967," in Gregory W. Pedlow, ed. *NATO Strategy Documents 1949–1969*, SHAPE, 1997. pp. 333–344. 8 Jan 2010 http://www.nato.int/docu/stratdoc/eng/a670511a.pdf.

"Enhancing NATO-Ukraine Cooperation: Short-Term Actions, 21 Apr. 2005," *NATO Official Texts*. August 25, 2010. http://www.nato.int/cps/en/natolive/official_texts_21741.htm.

"The Euro-Atlantic Partnership—Refocusing and Renewal, 23 Jun. 2004," *NATO Official Texts*. August 25, 2010. http://www.nato.int/cps/en/natolive/official_texts_21015.htm?selectedLocale=en.

"Europa: Gateway to the European Union," *European Union Official Web site*. August 25, 2010. http://europa.eu/index_en.htm.

"EU Common Security and Defence Policy," *Council of the European Union: Security and Defence*. August 25, 2010. http://www.consilium.europa.eu/showPage. aspx?id=261&lang=EN.

Fadok, David S. *Juggling the Bear: Assessing NATO Enlargement in Light of Europe's Past and Asia's Future*, INSS Occasional Paper 24, USAF Academy: USAF Institute for National Security Studies, 1999.

"Final Communiqué: Chairman: Mr. J. Luns: Bonn Programme for Peace in Freedom—Re-building international trust—Respect for Polands fundamental rights—Call for a political solution in Afghanistan—Unremitting Soviet military build-up—Alliance maintenance of effective deterrent, 09 Dec. 1982—10 Dec. 1982," *NATO Official Texts*. June 10, 2010. http://www.otan.nato.int/cps/en/SID-358CD1E5–3BB839D2/natolive/official_texts_23149.htm.

"Final Communiqué: Chairman: Mr. P. H. Spaak, Secretary General of NATO, 16 Dec. 1957—19 Dec. 1957," *NATO Official Texts*. June 10, 2010. http://www.nato.int/cps/en/SID-87DBAC14–2238E312/natolive/official_texts_17551.htm.

"Final Communiqué: Chairman : Mr. D. U. Stikker: Disarmament—Berlin—Procedures relating to the role of nuclear weapons ("Athens guidelines")—U.S. commitment to NATO of Polaris submarines—Triennial review—Political, Scientific and Economic questions—Economic development of Greece and Turkey, 04 May. 1962—06 May. 1962," *NATO Official Texts*. June 10, 2010. http://www.nato.int/cps/en/SID-14F0683A-491DFDB6/natolive/official_texts_26582.htm.

"Final Communiqué issued at the Ministerial Meeting of the North Atlantic Council at NATO Headquarters, Brussels, 01 Dec. 1994," *NATO Official Texts*. August 25, 2010. http://www.nato.int/cps/en/natolive/official_texts_24430.htm.

"Final Communiqué of the first Session of the North Atlantic Council—(Terms of Reference and Organisation), 17 Sep. 1949," *NATO Official Texts*. August 12, 2010. http://www.nato.int/cps/en/natolive/official_texts_17117.htm.

"Final Communiqué, Defence Planning Committee, Brussels 11th-12th December, 1979, Chairman: Mr. J. Luns. *NATO Ministerial Communiqus* (sic). June 10, 2010. http://www.nato.int/docu/comm/49–95/c791211a.htm.

"Final Communiqué: Press Communiqué M-NAC-1 (95)48 Issued by the North Atlantic Council in Ministerial Session at Noordwijk, The Netherlands, 30 May 1995," *NATO Ministerial Communiqus* (sic). June 10, 2010. http://www.nato.int/docu/comm/49–95/c950530b.htm.

"Final Communiqué, 13 Dec. 1962—15 Dec. 1962, Chairman : Mr. D. U. Stikker: Cuban missile crisis—Berlin—Political Consultation to be intensified disarmament—Triennial Review—Nuclear problems—Defence Ministers meeting on 15th December," *NATO Official Texts*. June 10, 2010. http://www.nato.int/cps/en/SID-5AAB5598-C9ABDC7F/natolive/official_texts_26579.htm.

"Final Statement: Meeting of the North Atlantic Council at the level of Foreign Ministers held at NATO Headquarters, Brussels, Press Release: (2009) 190, 04 Dec. 2009," *NATO Press Releases*. August 26, 2010. http://www.nato.int/cps/en/natolive/news_59699.htm?mode=pressrelease.

"Forward by Lord Carrington," *NATO Letter: 1956–1986 Special Anniversary Issue* (reprint of *NATO Letter: Non-Military Co-Operation in NATO: Text of the Report of the Committee of Three*, 1957), *NATO ebookshop*. April 22, 2010. http://www.nato.int/ebookshop/video/declassified/doc_files/NATO%20LETTER%20Version%20anglaise.pdf.

"Founding Act on Mutual Relations, Cooperation and Security between NATO and the Russian Federation Signed in Paris, France, 27 May 1997," *NATO Official Texts*. August 25, 2010. http://www.nato.int/cps/en/natolive/official_texts_25468.htm.

Gallis, Paul, "NATO in Afghanistan: A Test of the Transatlantic Alliance," *CRS Report for Congress Order Code RL33627*. January 28, 2008. http://opencrs.com/document/RL33627/2008–01–07/.

"The Harmel Report: Full Reports by the Rapporteurs on the Future Tasks of the Alliance," 1967. *Nato Archives*. September 2, 2009. http://www.nato.int/archives/harmel/harmel.htm.

"The Harmel Report: The Future Tasks of the Alliance: Report of the Council (North Atlantic Council Ministerial Communiqué, Brussels, 13th-14th December 1967)," *NATO on-line library Ministerial Communiqus* (sic).August 2, 2009, http://www.nato.int/docu/comm/49–95/c671213b.htm.

"The Harmel Report: Les relations interalliées, Rapport du Rapporteur du Sous-Groupe 2, M. P. H. SPAAK, Le 4 octobre 1967," *NATO Archives*. September 3, 2009. http://www.nato.int/archives/harmel/harmel02.htm.

"The Harmel Report: Report of Sub-Group I: East-West Relations," *NATO Archives*. September 3, 2009. http://www.nato.int/archives/harmel/harmel01.htm.

"The Harmel Report: Report of Sub-Group III: General Defence Policy: The future security policy of the Alliance," *NATO Archives*. September 3, 2009. http://www.nato.int/archives/harmel/harmel03.htm.

"The Harmel Report: Report of Sub-Group IV: Relations with Other Countries: Developments in regions outisde (sic) the NATO area," *NATO Archives*. September 3, 2009. http://www.nato.int/archives/harmel/harmel04.htm.

Headquarters, International Security Assistance Force, Kabul Afghanistan, "ISAF Commander's Counterinsurgency Guidance: Protecting the people is the mission. The conflict will be won by persuading the population, not by destroying the enemy. ISAF will succeed when GIRoA earns the support of the people." *NATO Offical Texts*. August 27, 2009. http://www.nato.int/isaf/docu/official_texts/counterinsurgency_guidance.pdf.

International Security Assistance Force Afghanistan, "ISAF Chronology Table," *NATO*. August 24, 2010. http://www.isaf.nato.int/en/chrono.html.

Ischinger, Wolfgang, and Ulrich Weisser, "NATO and the Nuclear Umbrella," *New York Times*, February 17, 2010. http://www.nytimes.com/2010/02/16/opinion/16iht-edischinger.html.

"Istanbul Cooperation Initiative," *NATO Policy Document*. August 25, 2010. http://www.nato.int/docu/comm/2004/06-istanbul/docu-cooperation.htm.

"Istanbul Cooperation Initiative (ICI)," *NATO Topics*. August 25, 2010. http://www.nato.int/issues/ici/index.html.

"Joint Declaration Issued at the British-French Summit, Saint-Malo, France, 3–4 December 1998," *EU Institute for Security Studies (ISS-EU)*. August 25, 2010. http://www.consilium.europa.eu/uedocs/cmsUpload/French-British%20Summit%20Declaration,%20Saint-Malo,%201998%20-%20EN.pdf.

Klein, Jean, "France, NATO, and European Security," *International Security*, 1, no. 3 (1977), 21–41 Published by: The MIT Press, 15 Jun 2010 http://www.jstor.org/stable/2626653.

"Kosovo Force," *NATO Kosovo Force (KFOR)*. August 26, 2010. http://www.nato.int/kfor/.

Kristensen, Hans M., *U.S. Nuclear Weapons in Europe: A Review of Post-Cold War Policy, Force Levels, and War Planning*, Natural Resources Defense Council, 2005. June 2, 2010. http://www.nrdc.org/nuclear/euro/euro.pdf.

Kugler, Richard L., and Hans Binnendijk, "Should NATO Write a New Strategic Concept?", in *Transforming NATO: An NDU Anthology*, edited by Hand Binnendijk and Gina Cordero, 275–301. Washington, DC: Center for Technology and National Security Policy at National Defense University, 2008. August 18, 2010. http://www.ndu.edu/CTNSP/docUploaded/Transforming_NATO.pdf.

"London Declaration On A Transformed North Atlantic Alliance: Issued by the Heads of State and Government participating in the meeting of the North Atlantic Council, London 5–6 July 1990," *NATO Ministerial Communiqus* (sic). August 26, 2010. http://www.nato.int/docu/comm/49–95/c900706a.htm.

"M.C. 3, Memorandum by the Standing Group to the North Atlantic Military Committee transmitting The Strategic Concept for the Defense of the North Atlantic Area, 19 October 1949," *NATO Strategy Documents 1949–1969*. September 3, 2009. http://www.nato.int/docu/stratdoc/eng/a491019a.pdf.

"M.C. 3/2, Note by the Secretary to the North Atlantic Military Committee on the Strategic Concept for the Defense of the North Atlantic Area, 28 November 1949," *NATO ebookshop* (photocopy of actual document). April 22, 2010. http://www.nato.int/ebookshop/video/declassified/doc_files/MC_003_2_ENG_PDP.pdf.

"M.C.3/5 (Final), Note by the Secretary to the North Atlantic Military Committee on The Strategic Concept for the Defense of the North Atlantic Area, 3 December 1952," *NATO Strategy Documents 1949–1969*. September 3, 2009. http://www.nato.int/docu/stratdoc/eng/a521203a.pdf.

M.C. 14, North Atlantic Military Committee Decision on M.C. 14, Strategic Guidance for North Atlantic Regional Planning, Note by the Secretary, 28 March

1950," *NATO Strategy Documents 1949–1969*. November 20, 2009. http://www.nato.int/docu/stratdoc/eng/a500328c.pdf.

M.C. 14/1 (FINAL), North Atlantic Military Committee Decision on M.C. 14/1, A Report by the Standing Group on Strategic Guidance, Note by Secretary, 9 December 1952," *NATO Strategy Documents 1949–1969*. January 8, 2010. http://www.nato.int/docu/stratdoc/eng/a521209a.pdf.

"MC 14/2(Revised)(Final Decision), Final Decision on MC 14/2(Revised), A Report by the Military Committee on Overall Strategic Concept for the Defense of the North Atlantic Treaty Organization Area, 23 May 1957," *NATO Strategy Documents 1949–1969*. September 3, 2009. http://www.nato.int/docu/stratdoc/eng/a570523a.pdf.

"MC 14/3(Final), Final Decision on MC 14/3, A Report by the Military Committee to the Defence Planning Committee on Overall Strategic Concept for the Defense of the North Atlantic Treaty Organization Area, 16 January 1968," *NATO Strategy Documents 1949–1969*. September 3, 2009. http://www.nato.int/docu/stratdoc/eng/a680116a.pdf.

"M.C. 48 (FINAL), North Atlantic Military Committee Decision on M.C. 48, A Report by the Military Committee on the Most Effective Pattern of NATO Military Strength for the Next Few Years, Note by the Secretary, 22 November 1954," *NATO Strategy Documents 1949–1969*. January 8, 2010. http://www.nato.int/docu/stratdoc/eng/a541122a.pdf.

"M.C. 48/1 (FINAL), North Atlantic Military Committee Decision on M.C. 48/1, A Report by the Military Committee on The Most Effective Pattern of NATO Military Strength for the Next Few Years—Report No. 2 (Note by the Secretary), 9 December 1955," *NATO Strategy Documents 1949–1969*. January 8, 2010. http://www.nato.int/docu/stratdoc/eng/a551209a.pdf.

"MC 48/2 (Final Decision), Final Decision on MC 48/2, A Report by the Military Committee on Measures to Implement the Strategic Concept, 23 May 1957," *NATO Strategy Documents 1949–1969*. January 8, 2010. http://www.nato.int/docu/stratdoc/eng/a570523b.pdf.

"MC 48/3(Final), Final Decision on MC 48/3, Measures to Implement the Strategic Concept for the Defence of the NATO Area, 8 December 1969," *NATO Strategy Documents 1949–1969*. January 8, 2010. http://www.nato.int/docu/stratdoc/eng/a691208a.pdf.

"Meeting of the North Atlantic Council, Declaration of the Heads of State and Government, Bonn, 10 June 1982," *NATO Ministerial Communiqus* (sic). August 26, 2010. http://www.nato.int/docu/comm/49–95/c820610a.htm.

"Membership Action Plan (MAP)," *NATO Topics*. August 25, 2010. http://www.nato.int/cps/en/natolive/topics_37356.htm.

"Military Series/Series Militaires (List of Committees and Working Groups)," *NATO Archives*. June 1, 2010. http://www.nato.int/archives/committees_ims_v3.pdf.

"Ministerial Communiqués 1970–1979," *NATO Ministerial Communiqus* (sic), August 12, 2010. http://www.nato.int/docu/comm/comm7079.htm.

"Ministerial Communiqués 1997," *NATO Ministerial Communiqus* (sic), August 12, 2010. http://www.nato.int/docu/comm/comm97.htm.

"Ministerial Communiqués 1998," *NATO Ministerial Communiqués '98*, August 12, 2010. http://www.nato.int/docu/comm/1998/comm98.htm.

"Ministerial Communiqués 1999," *NATO Ministerial Communiqus* (sic), August 12, 2010. http://www.nato.int/docu/comm/1999/comm99.htm.

"Ministerial Communiqués 2000," *NATO Ministerial Communiqus* (sic), August 12, 2010. http://www.nato.int/docu/comm/2000/comm2000.htm.

"Ministerial Communiqués 2001," *NATO Ministerial Communiqus* (sic), August 12, 2010. http://www.nato.int/docu/comm/2001/comm2001.htm.

"Ministerial Communiqués 2002," *NATO Ministerial Communiqus* (sic), August 12, 2010. http://www.nato.int/docu/comm/2002/comm2002.htm.

"Ministerial Communiqués 2003," *NATO Ministerial Communiqus* (sic), August 12, 2010. http://www.nato.int/docu/comm/2003/comm2003.htm.

"Ministerial Communiqués 2004," *NATO Ministerial Communiqués*, August 12, 2010. http://www.nato.int/docu/comm/2004/comm2004.htm.

"Ministerial Communiqués 2005," *NATO Ministerial Communiqués*, August 12, 2010. http://www.nato.int/docu/comm/2005/comm2005.htm.

"Ministerial Communiqués 2006," *NATO Ministerial Communiqués*, August 12, 2010. http://www.nato.int/docu/comm/2006/comm2006.htm.

"Ministerial Communiqués 2007," *NATO e-Library*, August 12, 2010. http://www.nato.int/docu/comm/2007/comm2007.html.

"Ministerial Communiqués 2008," *NATO e-Library*, August 12, 2010. http://www.nato.int/docu/comm/2008/comm2008.html.

"A More Ambitious and Expanded Framework for the Mediterranean Dialogue, 28 Jun. 2004," *NATO Official Texts*. August 25, 2010. http://www.nato.int/cps/en/natolive/official_texts_59357.htm.

NATO Handbook, Brussels: NATO Information Service, 1989

NATO Handbook, Brussels: NATO Office of Information and Press, 2001.

NATO Handbook, Brussels: NATO Public Diplomacy Division, 2006. August 24, 2010. http://www.nato.int/docu/handbook/2006/hb-en-2006.pdf.

The NATO Handbook: 50th Anniversary Edition, Brussels: NATO Office of Information and Press, 1998.

NATO—April 1952—April 1957: Text of Lord Ismay's report to the Ministerial Meeting of the North Atlantic Council in Bonn, May 1957, NATO, 1957. September 3, 2009. http://www.nato.int/archives/ismayrep/index.htm.

NATO 2020: Assured Security; Dynamic Engagement, Analysis and Recommendations of the Group of Experts on a New Strategic Concept for NATO, Brussels: NATO, 2010. May 17, 2010. http://www.nato.int/nato_static/assets/pdf/pdf_2010_05/20100517_100517_expertsreport.pdf.

"NATO Declassified 1949–1959," *NATO ebookshop*. April 22, 2010. http://www.nato.int/ebookshop/video/declassified/#/en/home/.

"NATO's Assistance to Iraq," NATO Topics. August 26, 2010. http://www.nato.int/cps/en/natolive/topics_51978.htm.

"NATO's Mediterranean Dialogue," *NATO Topics*. August 25, 2010. http://www.nato.int/cps/en/natolive/topics_52927.htm.

"NATO's Operations: 1949—Present," *NATO.int*. February 24, 2010. http://www.aco.nato.int/resources/21/NATO%20Operations,%201949-Present.pdf.

"NATO's Role in Afghanistan," *NATO Topics*. August 26, 2010. http://www.nato.int/cps/en/natolive/topics_8189.htm.

"NATO-Russia Relations," *NATO Topics*. August 25, 2010. http://www.nato.int/cps/en/natolive/topics_51105.htm.

"NATO-Russia Relations: A New Quality Declaration by Heads of State and Government of NATO Member States and the Russian Federation, 28 May. 2002," *NATO Official Texts*. August 25, 2010. http://www.nato.int/cps/en/natolive/official_texts_19572.htm.

"NATO-Ukraine Relations," *NATO Topics*. August 25, 2010. http://www.nato.int/cps/en/natolive/topics_37768.htm.

"North Atlantic Council, Alliance Defence for the Seventies (Annex to the Communiqué), 3rd-4th Dec. 1970," *NATO Ministerial Communiqus* (sic). August 23, 2010. http://www.nato.int/docu/comm/49–95/c701203b.htm.

"North Atlantic Council, No.720, North Atlantic Council Communique (sic) I, For the Press, September 17, 1949," *NATO ebookshop*,. April 22, 2010. http://www.nato.int/ebookshop/video/declassified/doc_files/C_1_COMMUNIQUE1.PDF.

"North Atlantic Council, Council D-1/4, North Atlantic Council (Second Session) Directive to the Defense Financial and Economic Committee, November 18, 1949," *NATO ebookshop*. April 22, 2010. http://www.nato.int/ebookshop/video/declassified/doc_files/COUNCIL_D-1_4.PDF.

"North Atlantic Council, Document AC/24-D/28, NATO Information Conference, February 1953: Report by the Director of Information on the Work and Functions of the NATO Information Service,3rd February, 1953," *NATO ebookshop*. April 22, 2010. http://www.nato.int/ebookshop/video/declassified/doc_files/AC_024-D_028.pdf.

"North Atlantic Council, Document: C6-D/7, Resolution on the Creation of an Integrated Force, 19th December, 1950," *NATO ebookshop*. April 22, 2010. http://www.nato.int/ebookshop/video/declassified/doc_files/C_6-D_7.PDF.

"North Atlantic Council, Fifth Session, New York, Document No. 5/2, C5-D/2, Report of the North Atlantic Council Deputies, 14th September 1950," *NATO ebookshop*. April 22, 2010. http://www.nato.int/ebookshop/video/declassified/doc_files/C_5-D_2.PDF.

"North Atlantic Council, Fifth Session, New York, Document No. 10 (Final), C5-D/10, Press Communique (sic), 26th September 1950, New York," *NATO ebookshop*. April 22, 2010. http://www.nato.int/ebookshop/video/declassified/doc_files/C_5-D_10-FINAL.PDF.

"North Atlantic Council, Fifth Session, New York, Document No. 11 (Final), C5-D/11, Resolution on the Defence of Western Europe, 26th September, 1950, New York," *NATO ebookshop*. April 22, 2010. http://www.nato.int/ebookshop/video/declassified/doc_files/C_5-D_11-FINAL.PDF.

"North Atlantic Council, Fifth Session, New York, Summary Record No. 5/1, C5-R/1, Summary Record of the First Meeting held in New York on 15th September, 1950, at 10:30a.m., 15th September, 1950, (including Corrigendum 15.9.52)," *NATO ebookshop*. April 22, 2010. http://www.nato.int/ebookshop/video/declassified/doc_files/C_5-R_1.PDF.

"North Atlantic Council, Fifth Session, New York, Summary of Record No. 5/2, C5-R/2, Summary Record of the Second Meeting, held in New York on 15 September 1950 at 3 p.m., 16 September 1950," *NATO ebookshop*. April 22, 2010. http://www.nato.int/ebookshop/video/declassified/doc_files/C_5-R_2.PDF.

"North Atlantic Council, Fifth Session, New York, Summary Record No. 3, C5—R/3, Summary Record of the Third Meeting, September 16, 1950, 10:30 a.m., 17th September 1950," *NATO ebookshop*. April 22, 2010. http://www.nato.int/ebookshop/video/declassified/doc_files/C_5-R_3.PDF.

"North Atlantic Council, Fifth Session, New York, Summary Record No. 5, C5-R/5, Summary Record of the Fifth Meeting held in New York, 18 September 1950 at 10:30 a.m., 19 September 1950," *NATO ebookshop*. April 22, 2010. http://www.nato.int/ebookshop/video/declassified/doc_files/C_5-R_51.PDF.

"North Atlantic Council, Fifth Session, New York, Verbatim Record No. 1, G5-VR/1, Verbatim Record of the First Meeting Held in New York on 15th September 1950, at 10:30 a.m., 15th September 1950," *NATO ebookshop*. April 22, 2010. http://www.nato.int/ebookshop/video/declassified/doc_files/C_5-VR_11.PDF.

"North Atlantic Council, Fifth Session, New York, Verbatim Record No. 2, C5-VR/2 (Part), Statement by the Chairman of the Council, 15 September 1950," *NATO ebookshop*. April 22, 2010. http://www.nato.int/ebookshop/video/declassified/doc_files/C_5-VR_2-PART.PDF.

"North Atlantic Council, Fifth Session, New York, Verbatim Record No. 6, C5—VR-6, 18 September 1950," *NATO ebookshop*. April 22, 2010. http://www.nato.int/ebookshop/video/declassified/doc_files/C_5-VR_6.PDF.

"North Atlantic Council, Final Communiqué: Chairman: Mr. M. Brosio, Synopsis: Commemoration of XXth Anniversary—Peace-keeping and peace-making—Aims of Alliance recalled—Disarmament and Arms Control Defence and deterrence—Berlin—European settlement problems Challenges to modern society, Washington, 10th–11th Apr. 1969," *NATO Ministerial Communiqus* (sic). August 23, 2010. http://www.nato.int/docu/comm/49–95/c690410a.htm.

"North Atlantic Council, Fourth Session, London, May 1950, Council Document No.1. (D-4/1), Report of the International Working Group on Review of Progress in Implementing the North Atlantic Treaty in the Year Since Its Signature, 15th May, 1950," *NATO ebookshop*. April 22, 2010. http://www.nato.int/ebookshop/video/declassified/doc_files/C_4-D-4_1.PDF.

"North Atlantic Council, Fourth Session, London, May 1950, Council Document No. 12 (Final), D-4/12, (Final), Council Resolutions, 18th May, 1950," *NATO ebookshop*. April 22, 2010. http://www.nato.int/ebookshop/video/declassified/doc_files/C_4-D-4_12-FINAL.PDF.

"North Atlantic Council, Ninth Session, Document C9-D/19, Resolution on German Participation in Western Defence (Adopted by the North Atlantic Council on 22nd February 1952 at the Third Meeting of its Ninth Session), 22nd February 1952," *NATO ebookshop*. April 23, 2010. http://www.nato.int/ebookshop/video/declassified/doc_files/C_9-D_19.PDF.

"North Atlantic Council, Ninth Session, Document D-D(52)35(Final), Report by the Council Deputies on Relations Between the EDC and NATO, 20th

February, 1952," *NATO ebookshop*. April 23, 2010. http://www.nato.int/ ebookshop/video/declassified/doc_files/D-D(52)35-FINAL.PDF.

"North Atlantic Council, Sixth Session, Brussels, December, 1950, Document: C6-D/1(Also DC.29/1), Joint Report on the German Contribution to the Defence of Western Europe by the North Atlantic Council Deputies and the Military Committee to the North Atlantic Council and the Defence Committee, 13th December, 1950 (Including corrigendem dated 18.12.50," *NATO ebookshop*. April 23, 2010. http://www.nato.int/ebookshop/video/declassified/doc_files/ C_6-D_1.PDF.

"North Atlantic Council, Seventh Session, Document C7-D/19 (final), Resolution for Coordinated Analysis of NATO Defence Plans (Approved by the Council at the meeting held on 19th September, 1951 at 5.15 p.m., September 19, 1951," *NATO ebookshop*. August 13, 2010. http://www.nato.int/ebookshop/ video/declassified/doc_files/C_7-D_19-FINAL.PDF.

"North Atlantic Council, Summary Record C-R(52)1, Summary record of a meeting of the Council held at Palais de Chaillot, Paris, on Monday 28th April at 10.a.m, 29th April, 1952," *NATO ebookshop*. April 22, 2010. http://www.nato. int/ebookshop/video/declassified/doc_files/C-R(52)1.PDF.

"North Atlantic Council Deputies, Document No. 17 (Revised), D—D/17 (Revised), Information Service, 11th August, 1950," *NATO ebookshop*. April 22, 2010. http://www.nato.int/ebookshop/video/declassified/doc_files/D-D_17-REV1. PDF.

"North Atlantic Council Deputies, Document No. 18 (Revised), D-D/18, A Proposal for Action by Council Deputies, 4th August, 1950," *NATO ebookshop*. April 22, 2010. http://www.nato.int/ebookshop/video/declassified/doc_files/D-D_18-REV1.PDF.

"North Atlantic Council Deputies, Document C7-D/23(Final), Resolution on the Accession of Greece and Turkey to the North Atlantic Treaty (Approved by the Council at the meeting oat 2.15 p.m. on 20th September, 1951 (C7-R11, Item I)), 17th October, 1951," *NATO ebookshop*. April 23, 2010. http://www. nato.int/ebookshop/video/declassified/doc_files/C_7-D_23-FINAL.PDF.

"North Atlantic Council Deputies, Document: D-D(51)44, Establishment of an International Staff for NATO: Draft Resolution submitted by the Chairman, 13th February, 1951," *NATO ebookshop*. April 22, 2010. http://www.nato.int/ ebookshop/video/declassified/doc_files/D-D(51)44.PDF.

"North Atlantic Council Deputies, Document: D-D(51)45, Composition and Terms of Reference of the Working Group on the Establishment of an International Budget for NATO, 13th February, 1951," *NATO ebookshop*. August 13, 2010. http://www.nato.int/ebookshop/video/declassified/doc_files/D-D(51)45.PDF.

"North Atlantic Council Deputies, Document: D-D(51)62, Importance of Information Activities: Draft Resolution by the Ad Hoc Working Group on the Conflict of Ideas, 2nd March, 1951," *NATO ebookshop*. April 22, 2010. http://www. nato.int/ebookshop/video/declassified/doc_files/D-D(51)62.PDF.

"North Atlantic Council Deputies, Document: D-D(51)88, Appointment of Supreme Allied Commander Atlantic, Note by the Secretary, 3rd April, 1951," *NATO*

ebookshop. April 22, 2010. http://www.nato.int/ebookshop/video/declassified/
doc_files/D-D(51)88.PDF.

"North Atlantic Council Deputies, Document: D-D(51)123 (Final), NATO Reor-
ganisation: Press Communiqué, Note by the Secretary, 4th May, 1951," *NATO
ebookshop*. April 22, 2010. http://www.nato.int/ebookshop/video/declassified/
doc_files/D-D(51)123-FINAL.PDF.

"North Atlantic Council Deputies, Document D-D(51)280, Protocol to the North
Atlantic Treaty on the Accession of Greece and Turkey: Note by the Executive
Secretary, 9th November, 1951," *NATO ebookshop*. April 23, 2010. http://www.
nato.int/ebookshop/video/declassified/doc_files/D-D(51)280.PDF.

"North Atlantic Council Deputies, Document D-D(52)67, Resolution on the Ap-
pointment of Lord Ismay as Vice-Chairman of the North Atlantic Council and
Secretary-General of the North Atlantic Treaty Organization (Approve by the
Council Deputies at their meeting on 12th March, 1952), 13th March, 1952,"
NATO ebookshop. April 22, 2010. http://www.nato.int/ebookshop/video/
declassified/doc_files/D-D(52)67.PDF.

"North Atlantic Council Deputies, Document No. D-D/163, Berlin Security: Note by
the Secretary, 23rd October, 1950," *NATO ebookshop*. April 23, 2010. http://
www.nato.int/ebookshop/video/declassified/doc_files/D-D_163.PDF.

"North Atlantic Council Deputies, Document: D-D/174 (Or. FR), Contribution of
Germany to the Defence of Western Europe: Statement made by the French
Deputy at the 28th Meeting of the Council Deputies held on the 13th November, 1950, 14th November, 1950," *NATO ebookshop*. April 23, 2010. http://
www.nato.int/ebookshop/video/declassified/doc_files/D-D_174.PDF.

"North Atlantic Council Deputies, Document. D-D/190, Provisional Arrangements for
the Participation of Germany in the Defence of Western Europe: Memorandum
by the United States Deputy, 22nd November, 1950," *NATO ebookshop*. April 23,
2010. http://www.nato.int/ebookshop/video/declassified/doc_files/D-D_190.PDF.

"North Atlantic Council Deputies, Summary Record D-R/33, Summary Record of
the Thirty Third Meeting of the Council Deputies held at 19 Belgrave Square,
London, S.W.1. on Friday, 24th November, at 3 p.m., 25th November, 1950,"
NATO ebookshop. April 23, 2010. http://www.nato.int/ebookshop/video/
declassified/doc_files/D-R_33.PDF.

"North Atlantic Council Deputies, Summary Record: D-R(51)9, Summary Record of
a meeting of the Council Deputies held in the Council Chamber, 13, Belgrave
Square, London, S.W.1. on Monday, 12th February, 1951, at 3 p.m., 14th February,
1951," *NATO ebookshop*. April 23, 2010. http://www.nato.int/ebookshop/video/
declassified/doc_files/D-R(51)9.PDF.

"North Atlantic Council Deputies, Summary Record: D-R(51)10, Summary Record
of a Meeting of the Council Deputies held at 13, Belgrave Square, London,
S.W.11. on Wednesday, 14th February, 1951 at 3.0 p.m., 16th February, 1951,"
NATO ebookshop. April 22, 2010. http://www.nato.int/ebookshop/video/
declassified/doc_files/D-R(51)10.PDF.

"North Atlantic Military Committee, Standing Group SGM-1136–51, Memorandum for the Standing Group, Subject: Association of Greece and Turkey with

NATO, 18 July 1951," *NATO ebookshop.* April 23, 2010. http://www.nato.int/
    ebookshop/video/declassified/doc_files/SGM-1136-51_ENG_PDP1.PDF.

"The North Atlantic Treaty, Washington D.C.—4 April 1949," *NATO Official Text.*
    February 15, 2008. http://www.nato.int/docu/basictxt/treaty.htm.

"NSC 20/4, Report to the President by the National Security Council, Note by the
    Executive Secretary on U.S. Objectives with Respect to the USSR to Counter
    Soviet Threats to U.S. Security, Washington, November 23, 1948," *NSC-68:
    Forging the Strategy of Containment with Analyses by Paul H. Nitze,* edited by
    S. Nelson Drew, 24–32, Washington, DC: National Defense University (GPO),
    1996. February 6, 2008. https://digitalndulibrary.ndu.edu/cdm4/document.
    php?CISOROOT=/ndupress&CISOPTR=29659.

"Operation Joint Endeavour (IFOR—20 Dec. 1995–20 Dec. 1996)," *NATO Archives.*
    August 26, 2010. http://www.nato.int/ifor/ifor.htm.

"Organisation du Traité de L'Atlantique Nord, NHO/63/1, From ASG for Political
    Affairs, Subject: Monograph on « the evolution of NATO political consulta-
    tion 1949–1962, 2nd May, 1963," *NATO ebookshop.* April 22, 2010. http://
    www.nato.int/ebookshop/video/declassified/doc_files/NHO(63)1.PDF.

"Organisation du Traité de L'Atlantique Nord, PO/58/990, The Situation in the Mid-
    dle East, Conditions, Dangers and Prospects, Analyses, Facts and Figures: Note
    by the Secretary General, 21st August, 1958," *NATO ebookshop.* April 23,
    2010. http://www.nato.int/ebookshop/video/declassified/doc_files/PO(58)990.
    PDF.

"Organisation du Traité de L'Atlantique Nord, PO/59/394, Discussions of the Coun-
    cil on the Middle East, 11th March, 1959," *NATO ebookshop.* April 23, 2010.
    http://www.nato.int/ebookshop/video/declassified/doc_files/PO(59)394.PDF.

"Organisation du Traité de L'Atlantique Nord, RDC/510/56, Canadian Contribu-
    tion to the United Nations Emergency Force, 27th November, 1956," *NATO
    ebookshop.* April 23, 2010. http://www.nato.int/ebookshop/video/declassified/
    doc_files/RDC(56)510.PDF.

"Organisation du Traité de L'Atlantique Nord, RDC/524/56, Memorandum: The Im-
    pact of the Present Crisis on the Economies of NATO Countries, 7th Decem-
    ber, 1956," *NATO ebookshop.* April 23, 2010. http://www.nato.int/ebookshop/
    video/declassified/doc_files/RDC(56)524.PDF.

"Organisation du Traité de L'Atlantique Nord, RDC/526/56, Memorandum: Norwe-
    gian Participation in the United Nations Emergency Force in Middle East,
    7th December 1956," *NATO ebookshop.* April 23, 2010. http://www.nato.int/
    ebookshop/video/declassified/doc_files/RDC(56)526.PDF.

"The Organization for Security and Co-operation in Europe," *Organization for Security
    and Cooperation in Europe.* August 25, 2010. http://www.osce.org/.

"The Partnership for Peace," *NATO Topics.* August 25, 2010. http://www.nato.int/
    cps/en/natolive/topics_50349.htm.

"Partnership for Peace: Framework Document Issued by the Heads of State and Gov-
    ernment participating in the Meeting of the North Atlantic Council, 10 Jan.
    1994—11 Jan. 1994," *NATO Press Releases.* August 25, 2010. http://www.nato.
    int/cps/en/natolive/official_texts_24469.htm.

"Partnership for Peace: Invitation Document issued by the Heads of State and Government participating in the Meeting of the North Atlantic Council, 10 Jan. 1994—11 Jan. 1994," *NATO Press Releases*. August 25, 2010. http://www.nato.int/cps/en/natolive/official_texts_24468.htm.

"Partnerships with non-NATO countries," *NATO Topics*. August 25, 2010. http://www.nato.int/cps/en/natolive/topics_51103.htm.

Pedlow, Gregory. "The Evolution of NATO Strategy, 1949–1969," *NATO Strategy Documents 1949–1969*. September 3, 2009. http://www.nato.int/docu/stratdoc/eng/intro.pdf.

"Potsdam Conference: The Berlin (Potsdam) Conference, July 17-August 2, 1945, (a) Protocol of the Proceedings, August 1, 1945," *The Avalon Project at Yale Law School*, February 18, 2008. http://avalon.law.yale.edu/20th_century/decade17.asp.

"Presidency Conclusions: Nice European Council Meeting, 7, 8 and 9 December 2000," *EU CFSP References*. August 25, 2010. http://www.consilium.europa.eu/uedocs/cmsUpload/Nice%20European%20Council-Presidency%20conclusions.pdf.

"Press Conference with NATO Secretary General, Lord Robertson and Russian Minister of Foreign Affairs, Igor Ivanov, 23 Nov. 2001," *NATO Speeches*. August 25, 2010. http://www.nato.int/docu/speech/2001/s011123a.htm.

"Press Statement: Meeting in Extraordinary Session of the NATO-Russia Permanent Joint Council at Ambassadorial Level, 13 September 2001," *NATO Press Releases*. August 25, 2010. http://www.nato.int/docu/pr/2001/p010913e.htm.

"Proclamation 2914: Proclaiming the Existence of an National Emergency, December 16, 1950," *NSC-68: Forging the Strategy of Containment with Analyses by Paul H. Nitze*, edited by S. Nelson Drew, 129–130, Washington, DC: National Defense University (GPO), 1996. February 6, 2008. https://digitalndulibrary.ndu.edu/cdm4/document.php?CISOROOT=/ndupress&CISOPTR=29659.

"Remarks by the Secretary General of NATO, Lord Robertson, at the Joint Press Conference with the Foreign Minister of Russia, Mr. Igor Ivanov, the Foreign Minister of Belgium, Mr. Louis Michel, 7 Dec. 2001," *NATO Speeches*. August 25, 2010. http://www.nato.int/docu/speech/2001/s011207b.htm.

"Remarks of Secretary of State George C. Marshall, Harvard University, June 5, 1947," *Department of State*. February 1, 2008. http://usinfo.state.gov/products/pubs/marshallplan/marshall.htm.

"Report on the Comprehensive Review of the Euro-Atlantic Partnership Council and Partnership for Peace, 21 Nov. 2002," *NATO Official Texts*. August 25, 2010. http://www.nato.int/cps/en/natolive/official_texts_19548.htm.

"Riga Summit Declaration: Issued by the Heads of State and Government participating in the meeting of the North Atlantic Council in Riga on 29 November 2006," *NATO Press Releases*. August 25, 2010. http://www.nato.int/cps/en/natolive/official_texts_37920.htm.

"Rome Declaration on Peace and Cooperation, Press Communiqué S-1(91)86 Issued by the Heads of State and Government participating in the meeting of the North Atlantic Council in Rome 8th Nov. 1991," *NATO Ministerial Communiqus* (sic). August 26, 2010. http://www.nato.int/docu/comm/49–95/c911108a.htm.

"S.G. 80/2, Report by the International Working Team to the Standing Group on Association of Turkey and Greece with NATO Military Planning, 29 November 1950," *NATO ebookshop* 23Apr 2010 http://www.nato.int/ebookshop/video/declassified/doc_files/SG_080_2_ENG_PDP.pdf.

"SFOR Stabilization Force (in Bosnia and Herzegovina)," *NATO*. August 26, 2010. http://www.nato.int/sfor/index.htm.

SHAPE, *1250/SHGS/90, Treaty on Conventional Armed Forces in Europe, 28 Dec 1990*, SHAPE, Belgium, December 28, 1990.

"SHAPE Reading List: NATO History and Issues," *NATO SHAPE*. January 25, 2010. http://www.nato.int/shape/Library/SHAPE_Reading_List.pdf.

"Special Meeting of Foreign and Defence Ministers Brussels 12th December, 1979, Chairman: Mr. J. Luns," *NATO Ministerial Communiqués*. June 10, 2010. http://www.nato.int/docu/comm/49–95/c791212a.htm.

"Speech: Address by H. E. Paul-Henri Spaak, Secretary General of NATO, before the Overseas Press Club New York, November 1, 1957," *NATO online library: NATO Speeches* . June 10, 2010. http://www.nato.int/docu/speech/1957/s19571101.htm.

"Statement by the North Atlantic Council, 12 September 2001," *NATO Press Releases*. August 25, 2010. http://www.nato.int/docu/pr/2001/p01–124e.htm.

"Statement by the North Atlantic Council on the Treaty on Conventional Armed Forces in Europe (CFE), 28 Mar. 2008," *NATO Press Releases*. August 25, 2010. http://www.nato.int/cps/en/natolive/official_texts_8439.htm?selectedLocale=en.

"Statement by the North Atlantic Council on the Russian Recognition of South Ossetia and Abkhazia Regions of Georgia, 27 Aug. 2008," *NATO News*. August 25, 2010. http://www.nato.int/cps/en/natolive/news_43517.htm?selectedLocale=en.

"Statement of the Presidency of the Permanent Council of the WEU on behalf of the High Contracting Parties to the Modified Brussels Treaty—Belgium, France, Germany, Greece, Italy, Luxembourg, The Netherlands, Portugal, Spain and the United Kingdom, Brussels, 31 March 2010," *Western European Union*. June 17, 2010. http://www.weu.int/.

"Statement on Afghanistan by Ministers of Foreign Affairs of Nations participating in the International Security Assistance Force (ISAF), Press Release: (2009) 191, 04 Dec. 2009," *NATO Press Releases*. August 26, 2010. http://www.nato.int/cps/en/natolive/news_59701.htm?mode=pressrelease.

"Strasbourg / Kehl Summit Declaration Issued by the Heads of State and Government participating in the meeting of the North Atlantic Council in Strasbourg / Kehl, Press Release: (2009) 044, 04 Apr. 2009," *NATO Press Releases*. August 25, 2010. http://www.nato.int/cps/en/natolive/news_52837.htm?mode=pressrelease.

"Summit Declaration on Afghanistan Issued by the Heads of State and Government Participating in the Meeting of the North Atlantic Council in Strasbourg / Kehl on 4 April 2009, Press Release: (2009) 045, 04 Apr. 2009," *NATO Press Releases*. August 26, 2010. http://www.nato.int/cps/en/natolive/news_52836.htm?mode=pressrelease.

"Summits & Ministerial Meetings," *NATO On-line Library*. August 12, 2010. http://www.nato.int/docu/comm.htm.

"Text of the Report of the Committee of Three on Non-Military Cooperation in NATO, Approved by the North Atlantic Council Dec. 13, 1956," *NATO*. September 3, 2009. http://www.nato.int/docu/basictxt/Bt-a3.htm#FN1.

Texts of Statements and Communiqués Issued during 1999, Brussels: NATO Office of Information and Press, 2000. August 12, 2010. http://www.nato.int/docu/comm/1999/comm99en.pdf.

"Towards a Partnership for the 21st Century: The Enhanced and more Operational Partnership—Report by the Political Military Steering Committee on Partnership for Peace, 25 Apr. 1999," *NATO Official Texts*. August 25, 2010. http://www.nato.int/cps/en/natolive/official_texts_27434.htm.

"Treaty of Economic, Social, and Cultural Collaboration and Collective Self-defense (Brussels Treaty), March 17, 1948," *The Avalon Project at Yale Law School*, February 1, 2008. http://www.yale.edu/lawweb/avalon/intdip/westeu/we001.htm.

"Treaty on Conventional Armed Forces in Europe," and "ADDENDUM to Treaty on Conventional Armed Forces in Europe and Related Documents (Vienna, 15–31 May 1996)," *State Department*. August 25, 2010. http://www.state.gov/www/global/arms/treaties/cfe.html.

"Treaty on European Union, Official Journal C 191, 29 July 1992," *European Union*. June 17, 2010. http://eur-lex.europa.eu/en/treaties/dat/11992M/htm/11992M.html.

"Treaty on the Final Settlement with Respect to Germany, September 12, 1990," *U.S. Diplomatic Mission to Germany*. April 21, 2010. http://usa.embassy.de/etexts/2plusfour8994e.htm.

"Truman Doctrine: President Harry S. Truman's Address Before a Joint Session of Congress, March 12, 1947," *The Avalon Project at Yale Law School*, February 6, 2008. http://www.yale.edu/lawweb/avalon/trudoc.htm.

"United States: Mutual Defense and Assistance Act of 1949, Approved October 6, 1949," *The American Journal of International Law*, 44, no. 1, Supplement: Official Documents (1950), 30. February 18, 2008. http://links.jstor.org/sici?sici=0002-9300%28195001%2944%3A1%3C29%3AUSMDAA%3E2.0.CO%3B2-Q.

"Vandenberg Resolution (S. Res. 239, 90th Cong., 2d sess., June 11, 1948)," *The Avalon Project at Yale Law School*, February 6, 2008. http://www.yale.edu/lawweb/avalon/decade/decad040.htm.

X. (1947). "The Sources of Soviet Conduct." *Foreign Affairs* (pre-1986), 25(000004), 566. Retrieved October 19, 2010, from ABI/INFORM Global. (Document ID: 66751275).

Index

About the Author

BRIAN J. COLLINS is an actively serving Air Force officer, currently teaching National Security Studies at the Industrial College of the Armed Forces at the National Defense University. He has served staff tours on the Joint Staff, where he worked NATO issues in J-5, and at SHAPE, in Mons, Belgium, where he worked the initial NATO military contacts with former Warsaw Pact members that eventually blossomed into NATO's Partnership for Peace program. He has served flying tours in USAF and NATO AWACS units, and participated in NATO's Balkan operations. While with the NATO AWACS Component, he was also responsible for flight testing and aircraft modernization programs. He was an Olmsted Scholar at the Freie Universität Berlin, and earned his PhD in international relations at Georgetown University. He is also a graduate of the German Armed Forces Staff College (Führungsakademie der Bundeswehr) and the Kennedy School at Harvard. He has published numerous articles, and one book: *Behind the Cyberspace Veil: The Hidden Evolution of the Air Force Officer Corps.*